W9-BCG-798

The Forgotten Leaders of the Revolution

BOOKS BY HOWARD SWIGGETT

NON-FICTION

The Forgotten Leaders of the Revolution

The Great Man: George Washington as a Human Being

The Extraordinary Mr. Morris: A Life of Gouverneur Morris

War out of Niagara: Walter Butler and the Tory Rangers

The Rebel Raider: A Life of John Hunt Morgan

Diary of a Rebel War Clerk, J. B. Jones, edited with notes

March or Die: A History of the French Foreign Legion

The Pinkerton Story (with James D. Horan)

NOVELS

The Strong Box

The Power and the Prize

ADVENTURE

The Stairs Lead Nowhere

Most Secret, Most Immediate

The Hidden and the Hunted

The Forgotten Leaders of the Revolution

BY HOWARD SWIGGETT

Doubleday & Company, Inc., Garden City, New York, 1955

At the Country Life Press, Garden City, N.Y.
First Edition

LIBRARY OF CONGRESS CATALOG CARD NUMBER 55-5568

To My Aunt

JULIA COURTNEY BROOKSHIRE

With Deep Affection and Recollection

Preface

THE *Lives* of the leaders of our Revolution and young Republic portray a group of grave patriots, soldiers or statesmen, selflessly dedicated solely to the service of their country.

In his memoir of Abigail Adams, her grandson, Charles Francis Adams, pointed out that "something like a void in our annals appears to exist. . . . Our history is for the most part wrapped up in the forms of office. . . . Statesmen and generals . . . are made to assume a uniform of grave hue. . . . We look for the workings of the heart, when those of the head alone are presented to us." Adams was thinking in part of biographers like James McHenry's, who found his *Letters* to his wife "disappointing in that they give no information except as to personal and family matters."

In the chapters which follow I have tried, largely from unpublished letters, to fill some of the void of which Adams wrote. It was of course at once apparent that the patriot leaders, even as Shylock, had hands, organs, dimensions, senses, affections, passions. The great anxiety which hung over them was not that independence could be lost or gravely affected by foreign intervention, but that through some mischance personal bankruptcy and a debtors' prison might engulf them. The need to make or marry money obsessed them, the best of them included.

Feeling reasonably sure of the prosperity of their country, they wanted "a modest independency" and "a seat in the country" for themselves. Men often disclaim a liking for political office and power. These men really meant it. It was always difficult adequately to fill the great administrative and diplomatic posts, not for lack of men of attainments, but because those men did not want to leave their homes. This resulted in a curious benefit to the country. The few who were willing to serve were constantly rotated in office and gained an experience, a facility in administration, which we have not seen since.

As one reads of the fierce party strife and the bitter personal calumnies of the 1790s it is easy to see the country as divided against itself beyond repair. Yet two men as unlike as Gouverneur Morris and Senator Maclay each spoke of the "sunshine."

No one in his later private letters displays those qualities more than John Adams, who to many is a dour Puritan. Writing his wife from Leyden in Holland in 1780 when his two small boys were with him, he told her: "I should not wish to have children educated in the common schools of this country where a littleness of soul is notorious. . . . Frugality and industry are virtues everywhere but avarice and stinginess are not frugality." No one can read the letters of these two happy lovers without realizing theirs was indeed the love that changeth not. Adams signs this letter from parent to parent:

I am, as I ever was and ever shall be

Yours, yours, yours.

And back comes her answer:

Your letters are always valuable to me but more particularly so when they close with an affectionate assurance of regard which, though I do not doubt, is never repeated without exciting the tenderest sentiments and never omitted without pain to the affectionate bosom of

Your Portia.

Except where debt darkened their lives, the majority of the leaders were sunny and sensible. The unhappy were rare. Hamilton seemed incapable of easy happiness as did Monroe and in both cases financial worries had something to do with it but far from all. Hamilton seems to have had those limitless cravings for power which destroy charity and reason, those temperers of humanity. How significant it is that, when equally brave and more vigorous men scorned to fight a duel, Hamilton, second to none in mentality, should have seconded John Laurens's duel with Lee, all but fought Monroe, and finally, like his son, been killed on what the best men no longer regarded as "the field of honor." To a challenge from Colonel Udny Hay, Timothy Pickering had replied, "I was neither afraid nor ashamed to say I should not fight." He spoke not only for himself but for all "sensible" men of the time.

On President Adams's inauguration Hamilton sent him a letter by Senator Tracy of Connecticut, "a long, elaborate letter . . . Containing a whole system of instructions for the conduct of the President, the Senate and the House of Representatives." Adams said, "I read it very deliberately and really thought the man was in a delirium."

The truly great, however, made no effort to be wise for all time. Franklin, in urging the signing of the Constitution, wonderfully said, "I confess there are several parts of this Constitution which I do not at present approve but I am not sure I shall never approve them." John Jay, writing his erstwhile friend Robert R. Livingston as to the political issues which divided them, did not assert he was right and Livingston wrong but said, "Time here or hereafter will correct errors." No one indulged in that present-day commonplace of Congress, "Never again shall. . . ." They wisely knew that never again might be tomorrow in a changing world.

Even the wildest Republican had his favorite Federalist and John Adams wrote sunnily to Benjamin Rush in 1811: "In point of Republicanism, all the differences I ever knew or could discover between you and me, or between Jefferson and me consist of

"1. I was a monarchist because I thought a speech more manly, more respectful to Congress and the nation. Jefferson and Rush preferred messages.

"2. I held levees once a week. . . . Jefferson's whole eight years was a levee. . . .

"4. Jefferson and Rush were for liberty and straight hair. I thought curled hair was as Republican as straight."

Research for a book such as this consists in large measure of that otherwise forbidden pleasure, reading other people's letters. Frequently those of relatively minor characters provide fascinating side lights on human foibles and ambitions.

One is the case of William Paterson, New Jersey delegate to the Constitutional Convention, later senator, then governor, and in 1793 appointed by Washington to the Supreme Court—and of two odd characters who tried to further his career.

When William Livingston, so long governor of New Jersey, died in 1790, his fellow Elizabethan, Jonathan Dayton, was one of the first to learn of it. Dayton, born in 1760, was the youngest man to sign the Constitution, and at sixteen had been one of the youngest Continental officers. His youth seems to have been against him in many ways. However he became Speaker of the House and later a senator from New Jersey. In the former position he was discovered to have personally retained $18,000 of a federal appropriation which was with great difficulty recovered from him. And when senator he was of course indicted with his crony, Aaron Burr, for treason though not tried.

On Livingston's death he wrote at once to Paterson, hoping that he would succeed Livingston and asking if he might sponsor the idea. Paterson, fifteen years older, was willing "if my friends all agree, though a public life is liable to a thousand casualties, casualties from which a private one is entirely exempt."

The plan, however, was premature. On August 20, 1795, Edmund Randolph, as we shall see, resigned as Secretary of State. Exactly one week later another fellow, quite as queer as Dayton, came forward in the person of Tench Coxe to push Paterson for the Cabinet.

Coxe was born in Philadelphia in 1755 and at the outbreak of the Revolution was a partner in his father's trading firm. There seems to be no doubt that he joined the British in '76, and came back with Howe's army at the occupation in '77. But apologists say he merely had "speculative opinions upon the probable event of the measure of independency." He was arrested, and attainted when the British evacuated Philadelphia, but no one appeared against him. By the end of the war he was again a merchant of standing and by 1786 a delegate to the Annapolis Convention, and then to Congress, a unique record of its kind. He does not seem to have had any marked attractiveness to overcome natural prejudice against him, but he does appear to have had a grasp of economics beyond most men of the times.

In September 1789, Hamilton, on being appointed Secretary of the Treasury, first "determined on William Duer as my assistant." Duer, then secretary of the Treasury Board, was already deep in his enormous speculations and resigned in a few months. Hamilton chose Tench Coxe to replace him.

The post did not require presidential appointment, and it is hard to imagine Washington's appointing a former Loyalist and is even a little surprising that he agreed to it when done. Coxe had been begging Madison to help him to office and told him he had private means amounting to £30,000. Maclay, the diarist, said Coxe had "a writing itch" and that Hamilton needed "gladiators of the quill." In the end Coxe lost his last

Federalist post as Commissioner of the Revenue under President Adams in '97 for his allegations against the President's supposed monarchism. Fittingly in the end he was befriended by Joel Barlow.

But in August 1795, when Randolph resigned and Bradford, the Attorney General, died within a week, Coxe wrote to Paterson, then on the Supreme Bench, that he had "impressed on Pickering the expediency of the utmost care at this delicate moment in filling the two vacancies in the Federal Government." No one could deny the moment was delicate, or care expedient, or that there were two vacancies in the federal government—perhaps Coxe hoped for the lesser one. At any rate he told Paterson that he had recommended strongly to Pickering that he persuade Washington to give Paterson the State Department.

If Paterson wanted the post, as he probably did, he must have wished people like Dayton and Coxe would leave his future to himself, for Washington offered the State Department to four other men before, for lack of a better, he gave it to Pickering, until then Secretary of War. Anyone but Coxe would have known that Pickering was the last man to propose someone else for Randolph's post.

But that strange month another minor political tragedy occurred. On August 13 the *New York Daily Advertiser* carried a dispatch from Charleston, South Carolina, of July 31, reading, "The Hon. John Rutledge sailed this day for Baltimore on his way to the seat of government having accepted the proferred office of Chief Justice of the United States."

Rutledge had been serving on the Bench with Paterson and been elevated following Jay's resignation. Arriving in full confidence of prompt confirmation, Rutledge later in the fall was rejected by the Senate.

In December, Chancellor Livingston wrote his brother: "I am sorry for the mortification Rutledge will feel in being made the sport of a party. If his appointment is now so improper how has it happened that many of these Senators who now vote against him were formerly his advocate for the second place on the bench? Who is to succeed him? I suppose Paterson or Wilson. The place is too important for a native American." The last mordant sentence refers to the fact that Paterson was born in County Antrim, Ireland, and James Wilson (a Signer) near St. Andrews, Scotland.

Finally, in 1799, Oliver Ellsworth resigned as Chief Justice and the ten years since Governor Livingston's death had not dulled Dayton's plans for Paterson but on January 20, 1801, "with grief, astonishment and almost indignation I hasten to inform you that contrary to the hopes and expectations of us all, the President has this morning nominated General Marshall, the present Secretary of State, for the office of Chief Justice. The eyes of all parties had been turned on you whose pretensions were, in every respect, the best. [The Senate would reject even John Marshall if you would accept.]" On the twenty-eighth Dayton wrote again that he had tried to get President Adams to see the light and prevail on John Marshall to take a lower seat. The President alone was "inflexible," so Marshall was confirmed: "all Federalist members worked together in the most perfect understanding and concert."

Paterson died in 1806 of "overwork." He was only sixty-one—and the patriot leaders on the average lived considerably longer. If he really wanted the two great offices—which only John Jay, John Marshall, and Charles Evans Hughes have held—he ought to have sought better advocates than Coxe and Dayton.

In the Robert R. Livingston Papers there is a questionnaire on New York State which Barbé-Marbois in 1781 sent to Secretary Livingston to be completed for the use of the French military and diplomatic missions. It is almost as extensive and in some ways as sinister as the G-2 an occupying or invading power might issue today. The more one reads it the more remarkable its implications are.

It asks for the present "charter" of New York and the previous "Constitution" and an "exact description of limits and boundaries" of the state. All "memoirs" or "pamphlets" published in the state's name, whether colony or state, "relating to interior or exterior affairs" are wanted, together with a "history" and "notice of counties, cities, townships, villages, rivers, rivulets and *navigables.*" "Products, trees, plants and natural riches" to be catalogued and "population, different religions, colleges and public establishments" to be set forth. A description of "the administration of justice, of the laws . . . the customs and manners of the people, the commerce, manufacture and interior and exterior trade" is to be given with a list of "those objects which inhabitants are obliged to get from Europe." The "weights, measures and currency of hard monies" with "details relating to exchange with Europe" will be shown. The roads "now building" are to be listed and all seaport facilities shown, and all information on "marine and navigation." Public income and expense to be itemized and "measures taken with regard to estates and possessions of Tories," with "present condition and pay of regular troops and militia." "Mines and other subterranean riches . . . with some proofs of the mines and extraordinary stones" is required and "notice of all that can increase progress of human knowledge"—the reference in this last phrase is not clear. Perhaps it refers to an increase in French knowledge of New York. And then finally there is a "cultural" question: "description of Indians in the state before the European settlement—those who are still remaining . . . indication of Indian monuments discovered."

It sounds as though the French intended to be long in New York and to exercise considerable power there. While John Jay was one of those who believed the French reluctance to attack New York City arose from their conviction that in any peace treaty England would still hold onto it, there were many others sure that any postwar American government would require a French garrison, as the paramount power, to maintain itself.

I quote these two minor but perhaps not unimportant matters because throughout the book I have not tried for the set pieces or what Walter Scott called "the big Bow-wow." The letters of these men contain wonderful trifles of insight —Wadsworth's single sentence about General Greene's son; Cabot's few words about Wadsworth's powers of judgment and persuasion; Nicholson's note to Morris as to how he watched for him "going home along the canal." And who has ever told the whole story of himself in twenty-three words as Nicholson did in writing his tailor about a greatcoat for Mr. Sundcliffe?

The book has some new truths about the leaders but others must judge whether they are of interest or value. I wrote it from profound, though good-humored, impatience of long standing with the pious theme of biographies and speeches (once called orations) portraying The Founding Fathers—that dreadful expression—as a group apart to whom, unlike the rest of us, love, fun, money, indolence, and a desire for security did not mightily matter. They did not pretend to each other they were men apart. When the federal Congress convened for the first time in Philadelphia in a stormy December, a South Carolina senator hoped that "the shipwrecks and overturned carriages won't sour the whole Congress."

The men I have dealt with are not of the first rank of patriot greatness though it is a question whether anyone but Washington and Franklin was. The strength of the patriot cause lay in the fact that around Washington there was, in Brooks Adams's phrase, "a body of the most remarkable men whom America has ever produced." These men somehow were able to put their individual abilities and energies to the service of the whole body and that "body" knew how to utilize them for what they were most fitted. The talents of Elias Boudinot were not brilliant but who, through a long life, was more dependable or more valuable at what he was set to do? Even those whose lives ended in failure, like Robert Morris and William Duer, contributed in their time qualities of enterprise and optimism without which other men might have lost heart. To the whole, Elbridge Gerry perhaps gave no more than difference of opinion, yet in a democracy what is more necessary? In later life Wadsworth or Gates was merely a certain rich man, yet without him, to whom could the needy then have turned? Typical of the best of their time are the Carolinian Pinckneys, and the New Yorkers, Jay and Livingston, but the time also had its fantastics like Littlepage and Thomas Rodney, its "tragic hero," Edmund Randolph and its "nondescript of humanity," *Colonel Satan*, Aaron Burr.

Of the many luminaries of whom I have not written, I most regret the omission of Charles Thomson, secretary of all the Continental Congresses. But he, who of them all knew the greatest secrets, burned all his papers.

It is a matter of unceasing surprise to me, though not so, I am told, to those better read than I, that the patriot leaders, forgotten and unforgotten, all knew each other. The physical world in which they lived was not small. The land area of the thirteen original colonies was 337,469 square miles, sixty thousand square miles less than France and Spain combined but approximately equal to the Low Countries and Scandinavia, or to France, the Low Countries, and Switzerland, or France and the British Isles. But the lack of roads and bridges, over the wide rivers, with the forest everywhere, made travel enormously difficult. The army and the Continental Congresses of course drew men together but even before that these people were forever visiting and sightseeing as in summers today.

The houses of many of these men live after them, varied yet each faultless, at Charleston and Charlottesville, Lebanon and Litchfield, Bedford and Clermont, Braintree and Elizabeth Town, the last with the great hall of William Livingston and the smaller jewel of Elias Boudinot's. These were the places they wanted never to leave. Seeing them today, the thoughts of Christian, seeing the New Jerusalem, come to mind—*which when he had seen he wished himself among them.*

At my request the publishers have included no pictures of these men and women. The reason is simple. In the main they did not have their portraits painted until late in life when their outward beauty or brilliance had faded and to look at the paintings is not to see these leaders or these ladies.

I am particularly grateful to the Connecticut Historical Society in Hartford for the kindness shown me in making the Jeremiah Wadsworth and Oliver Wolcott Papers available; to the manuscript division of the Library of Congress for the Pinckney Family Papers and to Miss Josephine Pinckney and Mrs. Charles Cotesworth Pinckney for permission to quote them; to the Firestone Library at Princeton for the trouble taken in letting me see the original of Booth Tarkington's play, *Colonel Satan*, dealing with Aaron Burr in Paris; to the New York Historical Society for use of their Gates, Burr, and Robert R. Livingston Papers, and their newspaper files of the Federalist Period; to the Historical Society of Pennsylvania and particularly the staff, who in temperatures like that of July 1787 let me use the John Nicholson Letter Books, the Thomas McKean Papers, and others cited hereafter; and as always to my friends of the Manuscript and American History Rooms of the New York Public Library.

Mr. R. W. G. Vail, director of the New York Historical Society, Mr. Wilmer Leech of its staff, and Mr. Robert W. Hill and Mr. Ivor Avellino of the New York Public Library are aware of my special indebtedness to them.

Howard Swiggett

Hewlett, L.I., N.Y.

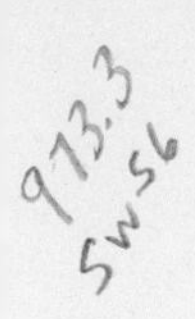

Contents

The Forgotten Leaders of the Revolution

CHAPTER I

Delicious Retirement

FEW things would have surprised the civil and military leaders of our Revolution more than the idea that there was some moral obligation on men to "go on working." They not only wished with few exceptions to retire from the strains of public or business life but, given "a competence" and a country seat, they looked on indolence as rather noble in itself—an opportunity actually to read and think and write to their friends; to oversee their fields and crops and their cattle on a thousand hills; to beautify their houses and gardens for themselves and the friends near and far they asked constantly to stay with them. In 1775, Adams spoke feelingly of Washington's coming out of his "delicious retirement" to command the army. It was to that they all wished to return—whether Washington, Adams, Jefferson, or Robert R. Livingston writing to John Jay as soon as the treaty was signed, ". . . the return of peace renders it unnecessary to make any further sacrifices of fortune, time and health to the publick and I hope . . . in some measure to repair the waste of all that the War has occasioned and to live the rest of my life for my friends, my family and myself."

Elias Boudinot wrote his wife: "My whole Plan has been to glide through this troublesome scene of things [looking forward to] domestic ease and enjoyment free from the bustle of the world." George Cabot did not even wish to be bothered by farming on his estate. When William Jackson, who had been secretary of the Constitutional Convention, wrote Jeremiah Wadsworth that "a predilection for public life had determined me to wish" to be a secretary of the Senate, Wadsworth was dumfounded. A sense of duty might drive men to public office but having "a predilection" to be anything but a country gentleman was incredible.

Except for the very few, the pleasures of indolence were constantly overshadowed by the fear of poverty or of bankruptcy. It was true to a degree hard to understand today and of course the basic cause was the fact that debtors went to prison.

Most commercial enterprise involved enormous hazards—cargoes lost or captured at sea; faulty titles to property; the general absence not only of a stable currency but often of actual media of exchange. Bills of private bankers or promoters like Robert Morris or William Duer might one day be "prime," all but equal to gold, and the next be at a heavy discount or gone to protest. There was no conservative field of investment—"safe as houses" was not yet a maxim. The "wild lands" attracted many but very few, except Jeremiah Wadsworth, Gouverneur Morris, and William Short retained an ultimate profit from them.

Debts, their own or those owed them, were constantly in men's minds as evidenced not only by their letters but by the notations on the backs of letters. On the reverse side of the invitation to be a pallbearer at the funeral of Benjamin Franklin, Thomas McKean itemized fourteen accounts he owed, to a total of £36. The inventory of the estate of Chancellor Livingston, who died in 1813, amounted to about $100,000. Stock of the Bank of the Manhattan Company was valued at $12,000. There were other prime assets besides his lands but there were also one hundred and twenty-six notes owed him, some for as little as $7.00.

While it is true that the getting, borrowing, or lending of money takes up more space in the letters of the period than would be the case in similar letters today, the writers are wonderfully free from envy of the more fortunate, from a desire for power over others or a desire to outdo the Joneses. They wanted in the main to lead untroubled homekeeping lives and to have other "gentlemen" do the same—certainly broad social sympathies were not characteristic of them, though private charities were many and apparently well run.

Their marriages were generally happy with the result that the members of families were devoted to each other. From the Pinckneys in South Carolina to the Jays and Livingstons in New York and the Wadsworths in Connecticut there is the same pattern of honor to father and mother, and of happy love between parent and child, brother and sister. From London young Pierre Jay writes his mama of "a little jaunt tomorrow which I think will be useful to Papa for tho' the Treaty is finished he still has . . . constant applications of every kind. The shoes you wrote for shall not be forgotten. Is Maria [his sister] still pleased with [her school at] Bethlehem." True, Mrs. Richard Montgomery wrote her brother, Chancellor Livingston, from Ireland where she was settling her husband's estate, "Let not my affairs be talked over in the circle . . . to you only will I speak," but that is a passing exasperation that happens in the nicest of large families. Except for the great debtors and the nondescripts, the correspondence of all these people is a happy, wholesome record.

The best of them were prepared to forgive and forget what had happened in the war. Seldom has Winston Churchill's phrase "In victory, magnanimity" had more noble amplification than in the reply John Jay sent back to Livingston's letter, already quoted:

"My opinion would be to pardon all except the faithless

and the cruel and publickly to declare that by this rule they should be judged and treated. Indiscriminate severity would be wrong as well as unbecoming, nor ought any man to be marked out for vengeance because, as King James said, he would make a Bonny Traitor . . . it is just and reasonable as to the residue who have either upon principle openly and fairly opposed us or who from timidity have fled from the storm and remained inoffensive. Let us not punish the first for behaving like men nor be extremely severe to the latter because nature has made them like women."

Although there was an amazing longevity among the leaders, life's brief span was a subject of constant mention in their letters. It was a form of deference to the Almighty, and no doubt in part the superstitious hope that He was more likely to spare a man who did not expect much more life. More than either, however, was the fact that certain diseases, like tuberculosis, were always fatal, that diphtheria was a great killer of old and young, and above all that the coastal ports were ravaged every summer by the plague which they did not know was yellow fever. It would be a mistake, however, to generalize about longevity or early death at the time. There is no pattern. A sister of Robert Livingston, Catherine, died in 1752 aged seven years, and another sister born that year was given her name. She lived ninety-seven years. Another sister, Margaret, died at thirty, while a brother, John, died at ninety-six.

Morbid fear of death seems to have been almost wholly absent. As John Armstrong, Jr., was about to leave to be Minister to France in 1804 he wrote an older man, asking him to have as many particulars of Washington's life as he could remember ready to tell him when he came to say good-by as "I believe after one meeting more we shall part forever." When George Clinton Tallmadge, beloved grandson of the wartime governor of New York and Vice-President of the United States, set out to campaign for the Senate, his spartan grandfather wrote him, "I hope you will not be shot through the body when you have not a surgeon near . . . provide your servant with a probe so he can give a temporary dressing should your wound not be instantly mortal."

Of the three Presidents next after Washington, Adams died at ninety-one, Jefferson at eighty-three, and Madison at eighty-five. The frail health of the first and third had prevented their bearing arms in the Revolution but as they lived on and on they began to take great pride in their health and survival.

Jefferson wrote Adams in 1813, "I believe we are under a half a dozen at present. I mean the Signers of the Declaration. Yourself, Gerry [sixty-nine, died the next year], Carroll [seventy-six, would live to be ninety-five] and myself are all I know to be living. I am the only one South of the Potomac. Is Robert Treat Paine [he was eighty-two and died the next year] or Floyd [he was seventy-nine and would live to be eighty-seven] living?"

Eight years later at eighty-six, John Adams wrote back, "As brother Floyd has gone, I am now the oldest of the little Congressional group that remain." Jefferson the following year wrote that "General Stark is off at the age of 93. Charles Thomson [secretary of the Continental Congresses] still lives at about the same age, cheerful, slender as a grass-hopper but with his memory impaired. [He lived two more years.]"

In 1829, Madison at seventy-eight wrote the youthful Monroe (seventy-one) that he hoped health would permit them both to attend the "Meeting of the Visitors at the University [of Virginia] in July, In haste, always yours." Two years later with not unpleasing pride he announced, "I am the only living Signer [of the Constitution] since the death of Mr. Lansing [a delegate but *not* a Signer] who disappeared so mysteriously not very long ago." In '29, Lansing, then seventy-five, was believed to have been murdered on his way to the Albany boat at the foot of Cortlandt Street in New York.

So much has been made of the "quaint" advertisements in

the journals of the period that we are likely to forget how important and interesting the news they contained was, or how widely it was quoted in readers' correspondence.

Allotments of space in the papers did not greatly differ from that of today. There is more advertising than news—store advertising, legal notices, help and situation wanted—mainly by or for young women of good character possessed of "a fine breast of milk"—and a few personals. Foreign news predominates, with dispatches ranging from Hamburg across Europe to Constantinople. If, as presumably was the case, they had reader interest in America the level of knowledge here was much higher then than now, so obscure are the policies and politicians described.

All too familiar, though, are "accounts from Poland [1786] that the scarcity of provisions is so great in many parts that the inhabitants are obliged to dig under the snow for the roots and stalks of maize to subsist upon." And even then Russia was revealing her world-shaking discoveries—this one archaeological—"a subterranean city . . . in Siberia which appears to have been populous and magnificent . . . an equestrian statue around the neck of which was a golden chain two hundred feet in length." As Jefferson asked Madison a year later: "What has become of that subterranean city discovered in Siberia?"

There was news, too, of the sensational scandal of the Queen's Necklace in France. They heard in Richmond that Madame de la Motte had been beheaded, Cardinal de Rohan given "life exclusion at his estate" and Cagliostro discharged. But a month later New York had the facts from London that the Cardinal as well as Cagliostro had been acquitted but Madame de la Motte got a life sentence, after being whipped at four corners in Paris, branded on the shoulder and having her head shaved like the women *collaboratrices* of 1944.

Domestic "human interest" stories were carried. Three teenagers at a convent school who, dreading separation at the term's end "as their parents lived far apart," wrote to the

Grand Signor, the Sultan at Constantinople, asking him to take all three of them "to wives" in his harem. A postal clerk, uncertain as to how to route the letter, gave it to a superior who opened it and blighted their hopes by informing the school authorities. And there was a gruesome story of how justice was done. A slave ship came into a Southern port shortly after one of the male slaves aboard had been killed by a ship's officer. "A public autopsy was held on deck in the harbor before the slaves, many of whom jumped in the sea." There was some feeling even among the port officials that an autopsy before these naïve, terror-struck blacks was perhaps needlessly cruel, but their qualms were allayed on finding that "all officers had mistresses among the slave women" and that these ungrateful wretches had all secured knives with which to kill their paramours. "This was fortunately found out in time and all the women were punished."

But there were happier love affairs to report in the "society news," such as the marriages in New York of Mr. James Monroe to Eliza Kortwright, youngest daughter of Lawrence Kortwright, a wealthy merchant, and of John Kean, the Treasurer of the United States, to Susan Livingston at famous Liberty Hall in Elizabeth, New Jersey, still occupied by their descendants.

And Colonel David Humphreys, of Washington's staff, arrived from France with the swords to go "under the awards of Congress" to Colonel Marinus Willett for his defense of Fort Schuyler against St. Leger in '77; to Colonel Tilghman of the staff who had died but a month before; to Colonel Meigs of the Connecticut Line for his audacious raid across Long Island to burn the British supplies and shipping in Sag Harbor; and to Captain Pierce, who had carried the news of Greene's victory at Eutaw Springs to Congress.

One is surprised to find, during the summer of 1787, no mention of the Constitutional Convention sitting in Philadelphia until one recalls the oath of secrecy the remarkable delegates took and kept—even from those closest to them. But on September 21, four days after its signing, the *New York Packet* published it in full, together with Washington's long letter to Congress urging its adoption.

A few old reliable jokes were often repeated from newspaper to newspaper. The most popular seems to have been that about the hunchback, asked by a British officer, "What have you got there under your coat?" to which the wit replied, "Bunker Hill—damn your red coat." And another by a member of a minority race, who when asked by a white man, "Whose Indian are you?" replied, "I am God Almighty's Indian. Whose Indian are you?"

An official report from the genial Thomas Hutchins, geographer to the United States, was carried by the papers in spite of its holding a racial group up to ridicule. He wrote from Pittsburgh of a council with Indian chiefs during which he made a few remarks on temperance. He said, "Brothers, Do you drink water (no grunt by any of the tribes). Then we will give you a few kegs of whiskey (a general snort)!"

Those other Indians of the Tammany Society feasted as the Constitutional Convention opened, and their tenth toast—after those to "General Washington and Lewis XVI, his Amiable Queen, etc., etc."—was "May the industry of the beaver, the frugality of the ant and the constancy of the dove be the perpetual characteristics of the Sons of St. Tammany."

The *New York Packet's* account of the commencement ceremonies at Columbia College in '89 contains the frankest report of such things ever written. It speaks for tens of thousands of listeners living and dead: "The whole was concluded by a very pathetic address by the Honorable William Samuel Johnson, President."

By and large a "pathetic address" was more characteristic of them than humor. When the Confederation Congress was oscillating between Trenton and Annapolis, it filled Boudinot with dark foreboding. "I cannot help thinking of Rome and Constantinople," he wrote Livingston, perhaps carried away by reading Gibbon. But there are flashes of comedy in many letters. James Lovell, the Adamses' apostle, was a dour man but, seeking a pass for a worried, "most sincere American, Nathaniel Balch," he wrote, "If a pass is necessary for him and his effects, your order for one cannot be more justly given than in the case of the serio-comic, good, fearful Mr. Balch."

Anecdotes of ready wit, such as that of Senator Uriah Tracy of Connecticut, are rare. He was talking to John Randolph of Virginia when a drove of mules passed and Randolph said, "There go some of your constituents, Tracy."

"Yes, sir," Tracy replied, "they are on the way to Virginia to teach school."

One of the first cases of the conflict of labor and management is humorously recounted in a letter Du Ponceau wrote Livingston late in '83 about a Mr. Meredith of Philadelphia. Meredith was married to a niece of Gouverneur Morris and by all accounts, and particularly his conduct toward Morris's wife, was one of the most pretentious and bigoted reactionaries of his time.

Du Ponceau says that a steelworker petitioned Meredith to ask the Pennsylvania Assembly "to lay duties on or totally prevent the import of foreign steel" or all American labor would be ruined. It was all but a hundred years before the steel manufacturers felt that way. Meredith said that commerce should not be restrained for the sake of a few tradesmen. "The war had enriched too great a number of them and they should return to their former way of living. 'You mechanics,' he added, 'are now the richest people in the city. You live better even than the merchants. For my part I know very well that if I go ever so early to market I can never get supplied with a good turkey—tradesmen run away with them all.' " (Wages must come down! Labor is eating the best cuts of meat!)

The outcome was politically fatal to Mr. Meredith. The story began to be repeated and embroidered "around town in a thousand different places" and at last it was reported that Mr. Meredith had moved in the House that "a law should be enacted to prevent tradesmen from eating turkeys"!

As a result Mr. Meredith's party were forced to withdraw his name and put a silversmith on the ticket in its place.

The same letter refers to the familiar question of the soldier vote. Conservatives objected to their voting on the grounds that as a result of military discipline "they had no will of their own." The soldier answer of course was, "You had no objection to our fighting and now you have some to our voting . . . we have fought for the rights of voting and we will now exercise it."

The myth-making process began its work on Washington very early. One remembers the survivor of Germantown who agreed the Commander might have uttered an execration there but certainly not a curse. There does not seem to have been a single anecdote of the time which did not ascribe to him a habitual dignity, close to caricature, and a verbal solemnity close to satire.

Consider this: "When Washington passed through Litchfield his soldiers to evince their attachment to him threw a shower of stones at the windows of the Episcopal Church. He promptly reproved them saying, 'I am a Churchman and wish not to see the church dishonored and desecrated in this manner.' "

Or the story of one Clemons "with a square bottle of rum who ran up to General Washington, saying, 'Great and glorious Washington! Will you condescend to take a dram with such a poor dog as I am?' The General with his habitual, dignified courtesy took the bottle and put it to his lips, to the immense gratification of his enraptured admirer who always believed he had drunk with General Washington."

Yet in a way neither of these anecdotes is more incredible than the train of incongruous thought actually started in that capacious and marvelously balanced mind during an afternoon in August 1787 as he listened from the chair of the presiding officer to the debate on the floor of the Constitutional Convention.

The subject there was slavery. Roger Sherman of Connecticut expressed his disapproval of the trade but thought it best to do nothing as abolition seemed to be going on and the good sense of the several states would probably by degrees complete it. George Mason of Virginia, author of the Bill of Rights, called it "an infernal traffic originating in the avarice of British Merchants" and held it essential that the new general government have the power to put a stop to it. Oliver Ellsworth of Connecticut, where no problem existed–himself to be a Chief Justice–said, "Let us not intermeddle," and Charles Pinckney of South Carolina, where it was an enormous problem, said, "Any attempt to take away the right will produce serious objections to the Constitution itself." Dickinson, Gouverneur Morris, and Edmund Randolph advised against positive action one way or the other.

When they had adjourned for the day and Washington had gone back to Robert Morris's house, he wrote a letter on a matter he had been revolving in his mind as he listened to the debate. The letter was to Clement Biddle, one of his officers during the war, now a Philadelphia merchant and Washington's agent as well.

"Since I came to this City, if I recollect rightly [which he always did], you asked me if I had had or could put up a quantity of Herrings next season for sale. Having revolved the matter in my mind I wish to be informed if there is any responsible character who would enter into a contract for a number to be delivered next season? . . ."

Sources: The Jay–Livingston letters and Barbé-Marbois questionnaire in the Preface are from Robert R. Livingston Collection, N.Y.H.S. Newspaper quotations from files of N.Y.H.S. Washington's letter on herrings from Clement Biddle Papers, Historical Society of Pennsylvania. Dayton to Paterson, Dayton Miscellaneous Mss., N.Y.P.L.

CHAPTER II

A Solid Man of Connecticut:
JEREMIAH WADSWORTH

On his way to Cambridge to take command of the army in 1775, General Washington was loaned a horse by Jeremiah Wadsworth, one of "the solid men of Connecticut."

In many ways Wadsworth was the prototype of the businessmen of the time. A consistent money-maker in trade, finance, and wild lands, yet a man to be trusted with the funds of widows and orphans; completely patriotic but with a keen eye for war profits; shrewd and a little ruthless, but a man to whom the distressed turned for help; fitted for diplomatic appointment, but never offered it, probably declining if it had been; widely acquainted with the patriot leaders from home to the Georgia border, and above all, like the best of them, interested most in his farming and his "seat" in the country.

Wadsworth was born in 1743 and at the age of twenty-four had married Mehitable Russell, nine years his senior. They had a son and two daughters. Chastellux described him as "very tall and well-made" and his portraits are of a man with a round, rather immature face, good-humored and good-looking.

His share in the Revolution was as valuable as any man's with the exception of the fighting soldiers, the veteran diplomats, the best of the state governors, like George Clinton and the elder Trumbull of his own state, or the two Morrises at the Finance Office. Nothing he did in the national interest was bungled, though it is also true little or none of it was without advantage to himself.

In 1778 when the service of supply so completely broke down and Nathanael Greene was made Quarter Master General, while retaining his field command, he appointed Wadsworth Commissary General with the assimilated rank of colonel. Wadsworth did extremely well, aided by the luck of the lucky man—his own state had the first grain surplus of the Revolution and almost immediately one of beef and pork as well. It is now generally believed that both Greene and he made considerable profits out of army purchasing, but the purchases were of prime quality and they were delivered, and such private advantages were not in grave conflict with the customs of the time. Further, there seems little doubt that Wadsworth's private-enterprise buying prevented a large rise in prices which would have followed the proclamation that all that he bought was for the government, to say nothing of the fact that his credit was better than that of Congress.

With the arrival of the French the next year, it was imperative that they have as their purchasing agent an American who knew the markets and the sources of supply—and that such a man should be able to get along easily with them. In partnership with John Church, Schuyler's son-in-law (and hence Alexander Hamilton's later brother-in-law), Wadsworth received the appointment.

Wadsworth served them well. They were well fed and satisfied, and although it was an easier job than buying for the Continentals, since he could pay in hard money, and although by 1783 Church reported their personal profit as £34,685 (a great fortune at the time) it would have been disastrous to the cause had the French been dissatisfied. And as to the hard money they supplied him with, it always lay in the power of Congress at least to propose that the French buy Continental currency with hard money and use it.

Apparently only Edmund Pendleton saw that the method was unwise. In the month before Yorktown he wrote Colonel Hendricks: "Colonel Wadsworth and Carter [Church], the French agents, have their riders all round the country buying flour and beef with specie. This will effectively prevent the [Virginia] Commissioners from procuring any. . . . I wish the executive would fall on some method to get the cash from the French Army and furnish the supplies. . . ."

The French at Yorktown were well fed, though so were the Continentals, and as for Wadsworth, as he himself noted, the mission had been very valuable in broadening his contacts south of the Potomac. And the year before it was at his house in Hartford that Washington had held the Council of War with Rochambeau.

It is interesting to note, as evidence of the way men of the time from Washington to Wadsworth thought of their own fields and crops, however great the crisis, that just before setting out for Virginia, Wadsworth wrote one of the Trumbulls at Lebanon, "I beg you will send me over the man who makes the hay scales immediately as the hay begins to be cut. Don't let him fail by any means."

The measure and value of Wadsworth is really summarized in a letter Colonel Pickering as Q.M.G. wrote him in June 1780, when Wadsworth was in the French service. It was about the Continental Army's need for salted beef and pork. A more ruthlessly efficient, single-minded officer than Pickering never lived. There was no natural friendship between them. If anything, the spartan Pickering would have been likely to suspect the Corinthian Wadsworth. But thus tersely he wrote him: "An instant exertion is indispensably necessary and the exertion of an active individual of extensive credit and influence. This of course points to you.

". . . Congress and the Commander-in-Chief have already

written Governor Trumbull but governments are too slow. . . . [Twelve to fifteen hundred barrels of meat must start to us at once.]"

In the month before Valley Forge, Colonel Jedediah Huntington of the Connecticut Line told his father, "I have wrote Colonel Wadsworth for some Connecticut made spirits from Corn Stalks for General Washington to send to his friends in Virginia." Good food, good drink, good husbandry were part of the Washington-Wadsworth friendship. Colonel John Trumbull, writing to Wadsworth from headquarters "at 6 P.M. April 9, 1783," said, "His Excellency being most engaged *at table* [his italics] with Captain Stapleton, D.A.G. of the British Army who is so *polite* [his italics] as the bearer of Peace from Sir Guy Carleton, desires me to thank you for the salmon." And when the later fame of Royal Gift, the all but ascetic, blue-blooded jackass sent Washington by the King of Spain, spread to Connecticut, Wadsworth begged to buy or to borrow him for breeding. William Edgar sent him a China sow and boar on whose bloodlines he expatiated to the envious master of Mount Vernon. In the year of the peace Wadsworth sent his wagons all the way to the Mohawk Valley for some famous beer, but Aaron Burr had to write him: "I am just returned from Claverac to find your waggons here. General Gansevoort [the defender of Stanwix] who made the beer you were so fond of could not be prevailed on to brew again."

Most of the trivia of the Wadsworth Papers has to do with such aspects of the life of a country gentleman, or with the less pleasant ones of being a rich man.

In the eyes of the run of men of the time, Washington, Wadsworth, and Robert Morris were the Great Triumvirate from whom anyone could borrow. All sorts and conditions of men, foreign and domestic, constantly appealed to them for loans large and small. In time Robert Morris began to adopt the attitude and actual words of his appellants.

While Wadsworth was in France in '83 a French officer

whom he scarcely knew, Jennings de Kilmaine, wrote to borrow that day "seven louis d'or as the Duke of Lauzun has gone to the country. P.S. J [sic] shall receive your answer at the house at which J dine."

Back home Silas Deane had needed £100 and sent intercessors to Wadsworth for it who were apparently unsuccessful. One of them, Jacob Silver, afterwards wrote Deane, "I concluded he had done it as he made no objection to advancing the money at that time, *so trifling a sum* [author's italics] could have been of little consequence to him to advance." Mr. Silver then sadly observes, "Men and manners are always changing with the times and circumstances."

So it went with this certain rich man all his life. The government was alleged to owe Thomas Fanning $16, "which I lay before your worship and I desire you to [reimburse] to me therefore."

The Signer, John Witherspoon, president of Princeton, just after his second marriage at sixty-eight wrote that he would not be "easily induced to sell flour at forty pounds to pay a note to Jeremiah Wadsworth—nor a horse either."

Henry Knox wrote out of a clear sky in his generous, sprawling hand: "I pray you to furnish my brother on my behalf with $1,500. If the money is in New York so much the better."

The following month (November 1788) Robert Morris himself, asked by Wadsworth to meet a debt arising from a trade transaction, replied that Wadsworth must realize how "acceptable remitting" would be "to a man in debt ardently struggling to free himself by paying as fast as he can," but he must defer the pleasure. It was perhaps the first of ten years of similar Morris letters to many people.

Bland indeed was the response of Richard Bland Lee when asked to pay. "I have not been unmindful of the debt I owe you but having great use for money in making improvements on my farm and supposing to a person of your wealth that the immediate payment would not be very important I have hitherto remained easy on the subject. If however it should be essential to you I will . . . in the course of 120 days . . . [consider it]." Two years later Lee wrote an airy, four-page letter on horse breeding and grape cuttings, ending casually, "Would you lend me $4,000 on a mortgage of two houses in Philadelphia, which [I bought for $700] returnable in one and two years in equal installments."

The lexicographer, Noah Webster, was better pay. On due date he sent $60, asked Senator Uriah Tracy to pay forty more on his account, and "the remainder I will find soon."

The next year Senator Tracy, leaving the Senate, was himself in difficulties. He appealed to Benjamin Tallmadge, Washington's intelligence officer, now (thanks to Wadsworth's early help in procuring goods for him to start his store on six months' credit) a prosperous merchant of Litchfield, Connecticut. He told Tallmadge he needed $3000 and pointed out that the merchants in Boston had given Timothy Pickering "a handsome sum under the name of a purchase of his wild-lands" on the occasion of Adams's forcing him out of the Cabinet. For his part he rejoiced that it had been done "for they could not have found a more deserving man and family." Pickering had spent his whole life in public service at two to five thousand dollars a year, Tracy said, but he himself had left "the best business in the country" for "short of $1,000." Then he hastily says this is not a request for a gift or loan but "to ask what [is] proper for me to do. . . ."

Tallmadge took charge of his affairs and worked out a settlement, scaling his $3000 indebtedness down to $1024.19. He then wrote Wadsworth to ask how much Wadsworth would chip in to pay the balance. "Not a petition," Tallmadge said.

All of these incidents could be duplicated almost word for word from the papers of any of the patriot leaders who were not themselves bankrupt—and would not be hard to find in similar present-day "papers. . . ."

On July 20, 1783, Wadsworth sailed for France with John

Church, to settle their final French Army accounts and with the profits import French merchandise.

Socially and financially Wadsworth was a great success in France. If the contacts he made had not naturally been with the royal government, his experience, capacity, and knowledge of the language would have made him an excellent successor to either Jefferson or Gouverneur Morris as later American Minister.

One of the first orders he received from home, with no suggestion as to how it would be paid for, came from Joel Barlow, who said he was publishing his poems in a few months and would Wadsworth send "100 reams of elegant demi-paper for duodecima pages." He had also been "advised by some friends to dedicate the poems to the King of France." What was Wadsworth's advice?

It is probable that Wadsworth's life in France was not greatly unlike that of Gouverneur Morris a few years later. Neither ever lost sight of the business they were engaged on and there are three letters indicating that Wadsworth, like Morris, was not blind to the attractions of the French beauties.

Two are from Villemaugry in the year '84. He had heard from Madame de Corny (Jefferson's friend) that Wadsworth had been ill and not able to meet Madame d'Osenais, "a charming woman or at least she was so when I first knew her but I have been told she had turned devotée which perhaps may take from her amiableness. Yet he who seems to pay her some attention is certain to get a reward . . . she is a woman one may be delighted to be acquainted with, let the thing go as it will." Two weeks later he urges Wadsworth "to pay attention to health since you have two enemies to fight, the ladies and the climate."

The other letter is from Gouverneur Morris sixteen years later and acknowledges some seeds sent for the gardens at Morrisania. It concludes: "I hope you continue to enjoy as good health as while you were sucking the bag. If you feel young, rejoice but stop there. The receipt to preserve health in advanced age contains a large mixture of abstinence not so much from food as from—fun."

There was one deliberate difference between Wadsworth's and Morris's life in France. Morris was a bachelor, Wadsworth a husband and the father of three children. There is abundant and charming evidence of his happy home life and in '83, like a good father, Wadsworth had taken his sixteen-year-old boy Daniel to France with him. We should probably not have known it if on September 30, 1784, Jacob Hiltzheimer, the livery-stable owner who was the intimate of them all, had not written in his *Diary*, "Colonel Jeremiah Wadsworth set out for Hartford with his son. They just arrived from France."

In 1786 half the original stock of the Bank of North America was owned by Wadsworth and his partner Church, Robert Morris, and William Bingham, and Wadsworth was briefly the second president of the bank, participating also in the foreign cargo ventures of William Constable and Company.

The leading venture capitalists of the time were this whole group.

On June 19 that year (1786) the country suffered an irreparable loss when Nathanael Greene died after a sunstroke at his plantation in Georgia. The *New York Packet* of July 13 carried the news. The minute guns were firing from Fort Wayne in Savannah during the funeral and immediately afterward the local Cincinnati met and elected Greene's oldest boy, aged eleven, to the Society to take his seat at eighteen.

Such were the public honors to this really remarkable man. But privately he left a widow of thirty-three, the lovely Caty of the Revolution, and four young children. His affairs were hopelessly entangled and his war accounts still unsettled with the Congress. Ten years later they still had not been fully settled.

The lives and fortunes of scores of men of the time, soldiers and diplomats, were bedeviled by their inability to get a settlement from Congress. On July 18, 1789, George Read wrote Caesar Rodney, his fellow Delaware Signer, that he had seen Michael Hillegas, the Treasurer of the United States, as to $1500 out of $3000 authorized by Congress for the Flying Camp Battalion of the Delaware Line in 1776. All he could get out of Hillegas was that he had "no recollection of any part of the business and no papers." The causes were various: the lack of hard money—Washington's secret service money was at times below $20 hard; the varied media of exchange—paper money, state and federal warrants, scrip, I.O.U.s; the absence of specific budgets and appropriations; the inability of a central accounting to keep up to date because of slow communication; more than that the fact that almost all persons, above the laboring class, lived on a system of credit—field commanders like Greene in the southern campaign could issue scrip for supplies but in many cases must pay in I.O.U.s of their own. One of Washington's most insistent proposals for the reorganization of the army at Valley Forge was the appointment of an auditor general; and to a degree not usually recognized, the fact that double-entry bookkeeping, though discovered by a monk in the fifteenth century, was not in general commercial or government use until the second half of the nineteenth century, the result being that there was almost no way of offsetting conflicting claims.

The executors of the Greene estate were Edward Rutledge of South Carolina, Jeremiah Wadsworth of Connecticut, and Mrs. Greene. The estate was apparently solvent if the arrears of pay as a major general were good assets, and his army accounts were accepted. But to live he had had to borrow from rich men like Robert Morris (rich in the Revolution), Lafayette, and Wadsworth and the first two held mortgages on his property in Georgia and Rhode Island.

In September 1786 the three executors met at Newport, Rhode Island—many of the South Carolina grandees, like the Rutledges and Pinckneys, summered there—and Wadsworth came away from the meeting very depressed about the outlook.

> I went to Westerly to look at General Greene's farm—it will want a considerable advance to save it from ruin. It has been and still is wretchedly managed.
>
> The demand Colonel Carrington [acting for the Confederation Congress] has against General Greene for monies drawn from [Carrington] of the publick in Charleston may very fairly be rendered to the Auditor General and charged to General Greene's account—and if that brings a balance against the General we can readily pay it agreeable to the Resolution of Congress.
>
> . . . I hope Colonel Carrington will see the propriety and necessity, as I do not know any other way the balance can be paid.
>
> When General Greene wrote him for the money, he promised if he failed to get it discounted to draw more than all the monies and stocks out of my hands.

Washington himself, knowing of the distress, offered at once to educate the oldest son, his namesake, George Washington Greene, in whatever way or place his mother and Wadsworth and Rutledge approved.

All this required long correspondence from Hartford to New York to Charleston, with all the mail delays of the time. In April '87, Wadsworth wrote Charles Thomson, secretary of Congress, that he felt "Mrs. Greene best claim her dower and let the creditors have the rest." Rutledge had advised him that personal creditors in Charleston were claiming they were secured by mortgages on Wadsworth. Catharine wrote from New York that her Rhode Island in-laws were "her enemies" and that she was coming to Hartford, where her youngest boy was living with the Wadsworths, who told Thomson that "in case of your death or mine before the debts are extinguished I fear the family will be ruined."

In July Catharine arrived in Hartford. Wadsworth wrote his co-executor Rutledge, ". . . so large a family and so expensive a one calls for considerable advances." And then he added the ominous news that those archetypes of public and private generosity, the Marquis de Lafayette and Mr. Robert Morris, were relying on "Greene's mortgage to me to secure the payments of their debts due from General Greene and will produce his letters to justify their claims." If such "friends" as these were insistent what could be expected of the run of creditors?

There was some excuse for Morris who, though the general public did not know it, was himself in grave difficulties. For Lafayette there was little, though much has been made of his having Greene's son sent to France to be educated in his household. And as he pressed his right to be a preferred creditor—in what contrast to his conduct in a few years about the money he owed Gouverneur Morris—he airily ordered thirty-five copies of Barlow's *Vision of Columbus* for the King, and ten for himself for twenty-five louis d'or.

The suggestion of young Greene's going to France, however, had its merits. Wadsworth wrote Rutledge that the "boys for want of regular schooling early [were] behind boys of their age." He sailed in May. Wadsworth wrote Rutledge that his "talents were by no means contemptible but his idle curiosity and disinclination to study . . ." Knox saw him in New York and wrote Wadsworth, "Washington [the boy] is the most unconcerned person in America at his departure." With characteristic generosity Knox gave Barlow, who was with him, "fifty dollars as contingent money."

Up to the time of the boy's sailing, Wadsworth had provided the money on which Mrs. Greene and the children lived but now told Rutledge he could not do so next year. "She must go on credit." To support properly an extra family of five must well have strained the ready-cash resources of even so rich a man as Wadsworth and he no doubt felt Rutledge and other friends could take a share. And all this time it must be remembered there was a Mrs. Jeremiah Wadsworth, nine years older than her husband, twenty than Catharine Greene. And there were three Wadsworth children, Daniel, Catherine, and Harriet.

Catharine Greene's first letter still extant to Wadsworth was written from New York on September 19, 1788. It reached him at a time when he may well have been gravely concerned at the death at thirty-six of Eliza Whitman, that strange and tragic spinster of Hartford.

This truly romantic tragedy was the subject of a novel, *The Coquette* by Hannah Foster Webster, published in 1797 and running through many editions for fifty years thereafter. In itself the tragedy "set in a Puritan environment was almost Hellenic or more Gallic than Greek," the most recent student of it wrote.[1]

Elizabeth Whitman was the eldest daughter of the Reverend Dr. Elnathan Whitman, pastor of the Second Church in Hartford, closely related to the Trumbulls, the Burrs, and the Edwards families, and to Wadsworth's in-laws, the Russells. Her closest friends were Eliza Stiles, daughter of the president of Yale, and Ruth Baldwin, sister of Abraham Baldwin, Signer of the Constitution and first president of what was to be the University of Georgia.

During the long betrothal and early period of the marriage of Joel Barlow and Ruth Baldwin, Barlow and Eliza corresponded in a cerebrally erotic and inexplicable style in which she was also his "wife." Two months before her death Barlow had left for France. Aside from her long "affair" with him, whatever its nature was, the rake, Pierrepont Edwards, son of the theologian, had been a suitor, and the Reverend Buckminster, a Yale divine. After her death the Hartford gossips talked about the many times Wadsworth himself had been seen leaving her house late at night. People also remembered she had frequently gone to his office to exchange French gold.

As to Wadsworth, Charles Bolton, writing *The Elizabeth Whitman Mystery* in 1912, said, "No breath of scandal has ever touched his name. Like Edwards he continued to hold high office throughout these eventful days in Elizabeth's his-

[1]Francis Parsons, *The Friendly Club and other Portraits* (Hartford, 1922).

tory." Perhaps the truth was not so simple, nor was he then in "high office."

Early in June 1788 a lady arrived alone at the Bell Tavern in Danvers, Massachusetts, where she said she was to await her husband's arrival. She kept entirely to herself but among her effects this poem was later found:

> Sweet as the sleep of innocence, the day
> By transports measured, lightly danced away
> To love, to bliss the union'd soul was given
> And each too happy, asked no brighter heaven.

No husband appeared. On July 10 she gave birth to a dead child and puerperal fever, then so terrible, followed. Even so she was able to burn her letters.

On the twenty-fifth she died. "Sundry baby clothes were found among her effects, one silver probe, one pair of silver forceps."

The identity of the father of her child remains a mystery. It was said that she believed herself secretly married. President Stiles said she had known many French officers in Newport—but that was eight years before—and that one of them was her husband, that it was remittances from him she had exchanged at Wadsworth's countinghouse.

Bolton said there was "no proof except vulgar suspicion that [she] sinned further than by marrying the man she loved at the mature age of thirty-six [and concealed it]." But who was he? Buckminster had been married since 1782, Edwards since 1769—and a year after Eliza Whitman's death Washington appointed him federal district attorney for Connecticut and the state made him Speaker of the General Assembly.

Barlow's departure for France, as the agent of the Scioto Company and escort to young Greene, is natural enough on the face of it. Yet he can hardly have been unaware that his "second wife" was many months pregnant and his extraordinarily self-engrossed life is not incompatible with a man fleeing his responsibility. Nor is what followed between Wadsworth and Caty Greene without "the breath of scandal" if her words mean what they appear to.

As Wadsworth read her first "personal" letter to him there was also before him the *Independent Chronicle* of the previous day which said: "[Elizabeth Whitman] refused two as good offers of marriage as she deserved because she aspired higher than to be a clergyman's wife; and having coquetted till past her prime fell into criminal indulgences proved pregnant."

The letter from Catharine Greene, written in a good hand and well spelled (the general had worried greatly about her spelling), began, "My dear Friend," and said he had told her that her securities would remain in his hands "subject to no demands but mine and the children's" but that now he told her he intended "to appropriate those bonds to securing Mr. Morris's and the Marquis's debt. At which time I was too much affected to ask an explanation . . . as I understand but little about business it is necessary to write in the most simple and plain manner for my comprehension.

"I consider Mr. Morris's and the Marquis's debts of honor and would starve rather than that they should not be paid but situated as I am, would it not be better to let them take the common chance with the other creditors and then for me out of the dower or what shall of my estate remain to pay them the whole amount? My friend [General Greene] sacrificed his valuable life, left me a widow and of course almost friendless. His children were deprived of a father and his country of one of its greatest ornaments to secure us that independence which he knew could only give us friends and command respect in a world as degenerate as this."

She goes on to defend Greene's borrowing for his army, done "rather than let a rude and unfeeling soldiery loose in an unprotected country, a soldiery who were irritated by the injustice they received from a country they were fighting to free—without clothes, possessions or money."

In conclusion she says that if she must go South "my two

little girls must go to Bethlehem." There is something very appealing about the last. Her reference is to the famous seminary there, the most famous girls' school in this country, and distraught and "hopeless"—as Mrs. Knox wrote she found her—she was determined on nothing but the best for her daughters.

They were accepted there, though entrance was difficult even for a Washington niece, early in November and on the eleventh she sailed for Charleston. Wadsworth's agent in Philadelphia, Phineas Miller, advanced her $200, which he hoped Wadsworth would approve, or if not "pardon the foibles of inexperience." The incident is of later and amusing interest.

Wadsworth wrote Rutledge of her sailing, saying, ". . . her situation here has been truly disagreeable, her family growing and expensive without any resources."

Looking back, we see the situation between Wadsworth and her as the familiar one of trustee and widow of a close friend, and his conduct as kindly if prudent. In May 1787—that is to say, eighteen months before her sailing to Charleston—she was in Hartford evidently for some time and thereafter largely in New York, where business with William Constable, Gouverneur Morris, and others frequently brought Wadsworth.

On January 31, 1789, Catharine wrote Wadsworth the first of a half dozen letters which imply that they talked of more than wills and testaments. They are in large measure unique in that period of American life when the extramarital affair between two people of social prominence, though doubtless not unknown, is not even hinted at in anyone's correspondence. The most fascinating thing about them is their human quality and their small sad details of dalliance. These and the fact that Wadsworth and she should inevitably have been drawn together, by their natures, the circumstances of privacy in which the estate conferences were held, her lonely dependence, affectionate nature, his resources, and his appeal for women, as evidenced by Villemaugry's letters to him in France.

Whatever happened between them, it seems evident Wadsworth was prompted not by love but by curiosity and momentary desire and kept careful check on anything more than that.

Catharine wrote: "You say in your private letter that you were nearly involved in a serious misunderstanding for not receiving my letter from New York. Is it that you burnt my letters or is it [illegible] that you have not explained. I thought my letters burnt long since—— Why should the loss of them afflict you—— They were not worth preserving besides, to comfort you I have two of them–which you desired to keep and which I will return when you please." That he wrote her "private" and "public" letters is clear. The "serious misunderstanding" may well refer to some slip to Mrs. Wadsworth. Catharine's letters were evidently "private" enough to make burning prudent except for two perhaps so "private" he could not bring himself to destroy and did not feel he could safely have among his papers.

"But why did you burn *that unfortunate letter which you never mentioned to me* [her italics]. It is true I did not call upon you for it because I was vexed that you should torture the G's [her late husband's] letter into meanings he never thought of–and which nothing but his spirit descending [sic] heaven would ever make me believe. You say an explanation of that letter would have made you happy or miserable–this is all mistery to me. I can not solve it." This sounds very much as though Wadsworth had told her, truthfully or otherwise, that he had found a letter from Greene to him written during the Revolution which he has interpreted (tortured) into meaning that she had gone beyond mere flirtation with someone at headquarters. She appears to deny it and Wadsworth with practical skill tantalizes her, perhaps to arouse her, plays on it, saying he has burned it without showing it to her, not daring to be made miserable by knowledge that there was someone else.

"You say you are unhappy–because you never expected to see me again—— I told you before I left you, that it depended on yourself alone—— I still consider myself as a kind of Ambassador liable to be recalled by my Sovereign—but tell me seriously—did you for one moment of your life think of coming to Georgia to see me—if you do—it will convince me, of what I have long doubted and I should I believe submit to be a [illegible] but I must bid you adieu."

It surely means that Wadsworth, curiosity and desire assuaged by possessing her in New York, protests conventionally the unhappiness of her fortunate departure for Georgia. She says the cure of it lies with him, that in effect she is willing always to be his though she knows he would never risk reputation and security for love.

"Tell Natty his mama will write to him as soon as he can read her letter—and tell him also that his Heifer has had three calves which are all marked for him as shall be all the increase." Her second boy was still living in the Wadsworths' household. "You have no reason for the jealousy you mention. I give you my word." Lothario has shrewdly made the point of his jealousy and distrust.

The same day Catharine wrote him a "public" letter to say that the first Georgia senators were "Colonel Few and a Captain Gunn of the Light Horse—the most notorious and infamous fellow in the whole army. He was disgraced, ran away to Georgia and married a pretty fortune."

On April 4 she wrote her next and brief private letter, after having eaten so many strawberries she could hardly write, to say, "Thank God, your Harriet has recovered. I love her in spite of her dislike for me." She is referring to his youngest child, who died a few years later of tuberculosis. With the precocious insight of the invalid, Harriet may well have understood what was going on between her father and Catharine Greene, when others did not.

Two weeks later she wrote privately again.

I have a thousand things to communicate but my little secret hope of seeing you soon makes me forego my propensity—perhaps in a month you will see me in New York. Nothing but the fear of unnecessary expense will prevent me from declaring in person how much affection I feel for you. I am, your devoted

C. Greene.

P.S. I believe I forgot to mention my noble lover to you. The Marquis of ——, I forget what, but he had very serious propositions.

It is gratifying to see the contest was not wholly Experience against Innocence. One must hope the money-maker in Hartford was disturbed by a marquis propositioning the lovely lady.

In June she started northward, writing Wadsworth: "I hope I may find you in New York when I arrive—I shall be much mortified if I do not—but I will tell you more when I see you which period I look forward to with more impatience than I can describe."

That they met there we know from Wadsworth's letter to Rutledge of August 20 from New York, saying that she was there—and adding that though Mr. Morris was "in want, [he] will take no advantage over the other creditors." It must be said that it always seemed unlikely that Morris, with all his faults, would take advantage, however fair, of beauty in distress.

On November 15, 1789, Catharine wrote to Wadsworth, back in Hartford, "I have long expected letters from you and hope my disappointment is owing to the carelessness of who has had charge of them for not one line have I received since you left this place." The money-maker, busy with new turnpikes, his ships, and his purchases of government securities from distressed holders, had evidently said to himself, "This better not go on. It has no future. Bad thing to mix business with pleasure."

In December, Catharine returned to Savannah without seeing him and it is doubtful if they ever met again. December 27 she wrote him her last private letter. It is a wise and disillusioned little letter, which sees through the pretenses and doubtless the vows of the lover gone cold. But it is sweet and "amiable," that quality in women which men of the time—as indeed of all times—valued so highly.

"You talk of going to Europe to settle your affairs. Why should I say a word upon the subject? I have long since lost my influence, if ever I had any—and it is not all fair play between you and myself—or you cannot be the man I have taken you for—some person I suspect has poisoned your mind against me. Pray tell me."

His letter to her had apparently used the familiar device of saying, "In any event I know there have been others," for she continues:

You will repent your unkind suspicions. I used to have the sweetest proofs of friendship from you . . . but by some means or other the stile is changed. God bless you and yours, you [illegible].
Adieu, the man waiteth, adieu

C. Gr. [sic]

How one would like to know the name she called him. The fictional device of telling a love story by letters alone is a difficult one and perhaps has never been successful with letters of only one of the lovers. Yet in these few actual letters of hers we see clearly the characters of both and what passed between them. And it is, so far as I know, the only account, however incomplete, of an affair, in America, such as was normal enough in England or France.

Catharine Greene lived until 1814, ten years longer than Wadsworth, both dying in their sixty-first year. Mrs. Wadsworth, the senior of both, outlived them, dying in 1817 at eighty-two. It was in 1792 that Mrs. Greene met another Connecticut man, Eli Whitney, on a ship going to Savannah. Finding himself unemployed on arrival, she asked him to stay at her house. And there he invented the cotton gin.

Cold yet designing as Wadsworth appears in his relations with Catharine Greene, he may well have broken off with her because of the coming of love and death in his own household.

Harriet, who "disliked" her, was twenty and the illness from which she had "recovered" was tuberculosis, then so inevitably mortal. While Wadsworth had been with Catharine in New York, John Trumbull, "the patriot artist," had returned from France to begin the gathering of "heads" and data for his historical pictures. He was thirty-three and Harriet had "loved" him since childhood. Her older brother Daniel would marry Trumbull's sister Faith.

What followed is a familiar story of the times. With the delicate but devoted "dear country cousin" the painter and man of the world easily fell in love himself. Or so it is called. The mawkish, self-centered morbidity of his letters to her cannot be ascribed wholly to the customs of the time. Gouverneur Morris at twenty did not write Kitty Livingston in such a vein. Harriet, doubtless aware that her health made marriage impossible, must have wondered what in the world they meant, what it was he wanted of her. How one must wish Hiltzheimer, on December 18, 1790, had done more than record—or that his heirs had let more be printed—that "Colonel Wadsworth, member of Congress from Connecticut, and his daughter, Mr. Trumbull and his daughter [Faith] and Mr. John Trumbull breakfasted with me."

A week later, on Christmas Day, Trumbull wrote her: "You must think me a strange, unaccountable creature, my dear friend. It would have been wiser perhaps not to have made the declaration I have, but disguise and suspense were becoming more tormenting to me than any certainty could be. . . . I owe to you and myself a long explanation—you will not perhaps think the better of me but I shall be more at ease when nothing that agitates me is concealed from you." (However much the revelation may overburden her.)

"My conduct since I have been in America has been governed by the sort of discordant passions—in your conversation the other evening you made use of an expression which wounded them all. I did not answer you, I could not. I came home and wrote angrily." He goes on to say that acquaintance with her virtues gave "the warmest applause of reason" to what had once been only prejudice in her favor. (Her virtues and doubtless her father's money.) "I have even dared to indulge a fond hope that after all my wanderings and follies, Heaven will at last give me, in your friendship, Rest and Happiness." How revoltingly self-centered this is. *He* is to have "Rest and Happiness" after all *his* follies. "I know I am not worthy of the Happiness which I solicit: but be you my Instructress–exert the power you possess over my mind and teach me how to merit your kindness. [Do not banish] me from that share in your general friendship with which you have hitherto honored me.

"To your candour and sincerity I commit myself, on you and on this hour it depends to render my future Life precious or tedious to me. . . ."

He wrote in all twenty-six of these letters; none was of manly love, all of masculine egotism, and none could have been anything but confusing and tormenting to the sick girl in Hartford. The last was dated November 1791.

Trumbull came back from his American travels a month or so later and stayed at his brother Jonathan's, at East Haddam down the Connecticut River from Hartford. Apparently he did not see Harriet, perhaps was not allowed to. In any event he got a servant girl of his brother's, Temperance Ray, with child and a son was born to her that year (1792).

In November Harriet was sent, in her brother's care, to Bermuda in last hope of recovery. There was the brief improvement before the end but in April she died there just before Wadsworth was to send one of his own vessels to bring her home. Deeply moving are the letters of young Daniel to his "Dear Mama," his "Beloved Friend and Sister" Catherine, and "my beloved Father" about her.

He had to pay what he thought was a great price for a chaise to drive Harriet in and wrote that "this was a case of necessity and I thought it my duty to purchase it let it cost what it would–– You will, I have no doubt, be of my opinion and believe that I would not willingly be extravagant or put my dear Father to any unreasonable expense."

To his sister Catherine he wrote on Christmas Eve: "We have just returned from sailing—we have been gone two hours and Harriet has never enjoyed one of our little excursions on the water so much. . . . This is such a Sunday as we used to admire when we were children in May when we used to sit out-doors in the shade and hear cocks crowing loud and answering each other."

In March '93, as Harriet worsened, he wrote, "I pray you, my beloved Father, to be with us as much as possible and comfort my poor Mother and Sister . . . be assured that I will conduct with all the firmness of which I am capable. . . ."

And then came the note sent in by the pilot boat "forty miles from Philadelphia" on April 26.

Possibly, my dear Father, you have not yet received letters from me informing you that our dear Harriet was no more—she expired the 10th in her perfect senses, smiling and happy. . . . I will thank you to write me in New York to the care of Mr. Watson; for I should not have the resolution to leave that place until I hear from you the situation of the Family and whether they can bear to see me—— I am tolerable well—— Adieu, my Beloved Father,—give my best love to my dear Mother, Aunts and Sister.

Your obedient and affectionate son

Daniel Wadsworth

There is another aspect of these letters worth noting. In almost all the family letters of the period—the Pinckneys', the Jays', the Wadsworths', the Livingstons', to name but few —there is evidence of wholesome, happy, devoted family life, devoid of all the "complexes" bequeathed by antique Greece to modern novelists.

One wonders what the elder Wadsworth's feelings were toward John Trumbull. Years later from London Trumbull wrote asking Church, not Wadsworth, to buy $1000 in shares in the Litchfield Turnpike for him.

In 1797, John Barker Church, Wadsworth's partner in the

French Contract of the Revolution, moved himself and his family permanently to New York from London, bringing substantial capital with him. There he and his wife, Angelica Schuyler, had been the leaders of what might now be called the "international set." In the capital and at their country house, Down Place, they had entertained all the visiting Americans of note—Gouverneur and Robert Morris, the Pinckneys and the Jays—and the royalist émigrés from France, such as Madame de Staël, Talleyrand, Beaumetz, the Duc de Liancourt, the De la Tour du Pins—she the beauty of the beautiful Dillon clan—the last four of whom they had provided with their introductions in America.

As soon as Church arrived he wrote Wadsworth: "Angelica desires me to give her love to you . . . and is very anxious to see and embrace you. Send my Account Current for our friend Hamilton [Church's brother-in-law], not being very accurate in his accounts is not clear that he has not made some mistakes respecting the monies you have paid him on my account." (The last is an amusing side light on the great Secretary of the Treasury. "Others he saved, himself he could not save.")

Wadsworth replied that he would come to New York and Church wrote, "You must not think of going anywhere else [than our house] and Catherine [the Churches' teen-age daughter] wants a Beau very much and means to attach you to her."

Letters and visits back and forth followed. An invitation for Catherine Church to visit in Hartford had to be declined because she could not leave her mother, who "grows very big [with child]. . . . She is a good deal inconvenienced by her burden but I hope in three or four weeks she will be rid of it."

Wadsworth's young kinsman, James, had a duel with Oliver Kane, and Church's son Philip [Schuyler] "accompanied him to the scene of action." Shortly afterwards young Church was off to Philadelphia to marry the daughter of Walter

Stewart, the brilliant Continental they had all been so fond of at headquarters in the Revolution.

The friendship of twenty exciting years went affectionately on except for one incident which brought to light that even the successful capitalists were not able always to settle their accounts with each other.

> You know well, my dear Friend [Church wrote at the start of 1800], the affection I have for you and how much it must cost me to say anything to you that may in any way hurt your feelings, but I can no longer be silent on the subject of Symons mortgage. I did imagine you had long since obtained payment of it and am very much surprised indeed to find you have taken no step to procure the payment. I must therefore in the most decided manner insist on your taking the most effective steps the law will permit. . . . You must get the money and our old account must be settled as soon as possible. . . . I am,
>
> Ever affectionately yours.

Church was a great speculator himself and may have been under pressure, but there is just a hint, under the sincerity of the affection, of fear that Wadsworth, already in ill-health, might die before the books were cleared between them.

There is a letter from that stout Federalist, George Cabot, to Timothy Pickering two years before which in many ways is the best evidence of the confidence men had in the strength and stability of Wadsworth's character.

All the Federalists were concerned about the fate and behavior of Henry Knox, one of the most insatiable speculators of them all. He and his spendthrift wife had lived extravagantly for years on the brittle edge of bankruptcy, and in '98 there was fear he would end like Robert Morris and others in a debtors' prison. Furthermore his refusal to be second to Hamilton, in the reorganization of the army under Washington as war with France threatened, had caused a personal rift which Washington himself was unable to dispel, and served further to divide the Federalist Party.

Friends, ready to move to his financial assistance, were

alienated by his outburst against Washington. To Knox, plagued with debt, the preferment of Hamilton—who had been a lieutenant colonel when Knox was a major general—may have been simply the last intolerable outrage of fortune. What was to be done?

Cabot wrote Pickering from Brookline, "I can think of no person here who can tell [Knox] all he ought to know in a manner that would be well received. Colonel Wadsworth of Hartford could manage the business perfectly well if he were applied to for that purpose by Mr. Wolcott [then Adams's Secretary of the Treasury] and could afterwards see Knox. Colonel Wadsworth has been in the habits of friendship and intimacy with Knox for many years and has been accustomed to tell him of his faults with great freedom; and has, I believe, in some instances really served him by doing it." Behind the scenes Wadsworth moved accordingly.

With the "rearmament," James McHenry, Secretary of War, turned at once to Wadsworth with a variety of War Department contracts—"scabbards and belts for the Army," cartridge boxes, mess bowls and orderly books, and then an urgent shipment order: "Have as many as may be packed up and forwarded to Philadelphia by water as many of the shoes you have been attentive to procure as have passed inspection." History was repeating itself.

In many ways Wadsworth's closest friend was Benjamin Tallmadge of Litchfield, the Yale classmate of Nathan Hale and Washington's chief intelligence officer. He was a wonderful fellow. As he wrote happily of himself, he "never failed to lead the Second Light Dragoons, never had a dangerous wound or a broken bone, never had a duel . . . I would never have been guilty of this murderous sin." At the end of the Revolution Tallmadge had married Mary Floyd, a daughter of William Floyd, the Signer. Largely on credit from Wadsworth he opened a store in Litchfield, and shrewdly developed it into a substantial banker-merchant business, one of the fruits of which was the lovely house still standing.

Tallmadge, eleven years Wadsworth's junior, had been born in 1754 and lived to be eighty-one. (John Trumbull, born two years later, died in 1843.)

There is a mass of letters from Tallmadge in the Wadsworth Papers, all agreeable, all sensible and goodhearted, and on all sorts of subjects. One gets the distinct impression that Tallmadge was one of the very few completely happy men of the times. His affairs prospered. He was in love with his wife. He kept out of office though a staunch Federalist and he did a great deal to help the less fortunate. The letters report "the agreeable intelligence" of another son's arrival, describe humorously people like one Allen who "always talk in strong terms respecting Jacobins, Disorganizers and Dunces"; remind Wadsworth that they are delegates to the Cincinnati in Philadelphia in May 1800, as they had been in '87—"if you will persuade Mrs. W. to accompany you I will use my rhetoric upon Mrs. T. for the same purpose." He is sorry to report that "Daniel W. Lewis Esq. has eloped suddenly leaving a number of very meritorious debtors and no property to satisfy them. His condition has been very censurable for a long time. . . . I hear that his course is *westward*." No reviling the poor wretch by this creditor. He intercedes with Wadsworth for a debtor—"Do keep him out of the hands of an unfeeling creditor he has in Hartford."

Of the imminence of war with France he writes, "We have a report that the ship Four Sisters is taken by our *good Allies* [his italics]. . . . I believe we must have a war with France. Their government seems determined to have all the world under their control or be embraced by their *fraternal* hug. [How familiar one hundred fifty years later this sounds of another former ally.] It is doubtful which is to be preferred, the perfidy of their friendship, or open hostilities. I most heartily and sincerely deprecate war but I really feel almost willing to have a war rather than be so abominably insulted and abused by them."

And there is this charming note of introduction. "This

will be handed to you by my little son, Master Harry, who has a curiosity to visit Hartford during his vacation from school."

Peace and plenty had descended on Connecticut and the graces of the Carolina grandees sat easily on her solid men.

In the year before his death, Wadsworth received the last word from Catherine Greene. Phineas Miller, once his agent, later the tutor she had employed for her children, had become her man of business. He wrote Wadsworth in February that a mortgage General Greene had given Wadsworth was still open in court. Would Wadsworth sign a satisfaction? The letter went on to say somewhat cryptically that Miller would "once have sacrificed all save honor to please [Wadsworth]." Wadsworth sent the satisfaction.

In September Miller wrote again. Mrs. Greene and he had been married and "Mrs. Miller and family join in respects."

Wadsworth died April 30, 1804, and the family chronicler records that "he provided liberally and kindly for his widow."

There might well be a longer epitaph to this successful life.

Sources: The Jeremiah Wadsworth Papers, Connecticut Historical Society, have mainly supplied the letters to and from Wadsworth quoted herein. The Wadsworth Athenaeum in Hartford, Conn., has additional letters. Colonel Trumbull's letters are quoted in Theodore Sizer's *Trumbull's Troubles* (Yale University Library, 1950). See also *Friendly Club and Other Portraits,* by Francis Parsons (Hartford, 1922); *The Elizabeth Whitman Mystery* by Charles Knowles Bolton (Peabody, Mass., 1912); and the *Virginia Quarterly Review,* Spring, 1943.

CHAPTER III

Two Fantastics:
LITTLEPAGE *and* RODNEY

THERE were few fantastics in our Revolutionary-Federalist period. A large part of the genius of the leaders was their practical good sense. There is a comic irony in the fact that John Jay, one of the most cautious and conservative of the leaders, possessed of great wisdom and balance of mind, should have been involved for five years with one of the rare fantastics.

Lewis Littlepage was born in Virginia in 1762, became an orphan at an early age, and lived under the guardianship of his uncle, Colonel Benjamin Lewis, an acquaintance of Jay's. In 1779, as Jay was setting out for his mission to Madrid, Lewis had a talk with him about his nephew. He said he was an unusual and gifted boy who desired to pursue his studies of law, politics, and foreign languages abroad, to rub off, as Gouverneur Morris had put it at Littlepage's age, "a few of the many barbarisms which characterize a provincial education." He then asked Jay whether he would allow young Littlepage to join his household in Madrid, guide and counsel him, and advance him such money as he would need to pursue his studies. A special point was made of the last, only *money needed to pursue his studies.* Jay would be reimbursed by Colonel Lewis in due course.

Jay consented. It was the sort of request which had long been customary, the placing of a young cadet in a nobleman's house, or the attaching of him to a foreign mission where he could see the world under proper supervision.

Apparently neither Jay nor Colonel Lewis saw anything unusual in the fact that Littlepage, in the words of a poem by Colonel Humphreys, had no desire to "go to Washington and glory." The Signer John Witherspoon, the eminent Virginian George Mason—and many others—intended their sons, as they said, for peaceful pursuits. Besides, this boy was said to have remarkable gifts as a poet, and our principal younger poets of the time, Joel Barlow and Philip Freneau, had no desire to fight. Such soldier-poets as Sir Philip Sidney or Sir Walter Raleigh were not their idols.

In any event Jay and we have a picture of a studious, gifted "boy of seventeen," as Littlepage later described himself, about to complete his education abroad under Jay's paternal eye, as after the war General Greene's son was to do under Lafayette's. The matter turned out far differently. For five years Jay, envoy to Spain, Peace Commissioner in Paris, Secretary of Foreign Affairs in New York, was bedeviled by a young monster of deceit, exaggerated egotism, and general wrongheadedness. His most exasperating quality may well have been the fancied insult to his "honor," though in that he differed little from Washington himself at the same age.

Jay's direct relations with him began on April 3, 1780, when, having learned that he had reached Bordeaux, Jay wrote him from Madrid, congratulating him on his safe passage, inviting him to join his household in Madrid and to draw on him for his expenses.

In July Littlepage replied that he had found it would take him a year to learn French and that he had decided to live with a French family in the country until he had at least some fluency in the language. But very shortly he found country life boring, became ill, and had to go back to Bordeaux.

Almost all letters of the time have so much to say of their writers' ill-health that one perhaps unfairly finds them full of hypochondria. Frequently the writer who sounds like a complainer and malingerer was unquestionably ill with malaria, and the diet and badly washed dishes and pots and pans very likely afflicted them with a type of chronic ptomaine poisoning. But Littlepage was very young to wail so loudly.

Not until November did he find his health such as to permit the arduous journey to Madrid and he arrived there with his poems on the twenty-first of the month.

Jay and his family received him as a son. He paid no board and Jay provided him with spending money, kept an eye on him, gave him fatherly advice, and presented him in court circles. Like any sensible father, Jay did not take his poetry to be that of an immortal genius.

Within a few days of his arrival, Littlepage began, as he considered, to make himself invaluable by telling Jay what a dreadful fellow his secretary, Carmichael, was. To Jay, already plagued by the petty domestic intriguing of his young brother-in-law, Brockholst Livingston, this talebearing by a still younger member of the household must have seemed a little gratuitous.

The winter and spring of '80–'81 passed, however, in relative calm until June, when Littlepage *wrote* him—in the same house—that everyone was treating him coolly "because of an insidious enemy. Your secretary, Mr. William Carmichael, is the person to whom I allude." Because of this he said he must get away from it all and with a great parade of self-importance announced that the Duc de Crillon had invited him to join his staff on a secret expedition aimed at either Minorca or Gibraltar.

Having felt no urge to fight in or for his own country, he was fired to fight for Spain and asked that Jay advance money for his outfit, traveling expenses, and upkeep, as the duke had not indicated what pay if any he would receive.

Jay protested firmly but patiently. He said that Littlepage's guardian and friends had asked him to stand *in loco parentis* while Littlepage studied law and politics and learned two foreign languages. While he, Jay, could not forbid him to join Crillon, he had no authority to advance him money for it or indeed to help him to do so.

Howls and rodomontade followed from Littlepage. Jay, who was supposed to "help" him, was proposing to ruin his career. He demanded that Jay advance him any sums he himself considered necessary, and referred to his own "honor," family inheritance, etc., as all that Jay need rely on.

As far as actually preventing his going, Jay could do little, unless he took the extreme step of saying no to Crillon personally, or of canceling Littlepage's passport. The result of either would be to raise new problems. One can well believe that the lovely Sally, his wife, said, "Dear Mr. Jay, for goodness' sake, let him go and we shall be rid of a nuisance." So he gave grudging assent but said the allowance for expenses ought to be restricted to fixed limits.

Such an idea was an insult to Littlepage, who borrowed some money from another American, Harrison, and went off with Crillon to Cádiz.

On the way he became "ill," had to hire a carriage and servant, and learned at Cádiz that he would have to have a great deal of money to live like the young Spanish grandees of Crillon's staff.

The letter he wrote Jay about it had all the wonderful plausibility of the chronic borrower and contained a prudent forecast of necessary expenses. Littlepage added that he had drawn on Jay to cover the budget.

To this Jay replied patiently, repeating his basic reasons for opposing the adventure, saying that he had paid Harrison for his loans but had himself declined to accept the bill drawn on him. As to the fact that Crillon's young Spanish A.D.C.s were spending such amounts he said, "Sums which other officers might spend, measured by their fortunes, might be very moderate to them [but] with your funds very extravagant."

The injection of this puerile wrongheadedness into the great affairs with which Jay was dealing must have been more than exasperating. It was now the month of Yorktown but Jay, with his great sense of guardian duty, wrote more wise advice, couched in the long but wonderfully clear eighteenth-century sentences. "I have known many gentlemen with ten times your allowance in daily distress for want of money; and yet it would not have been proper to indulge them with more. Thus, sir, I have, by a full and temperate answer treated your letter with a degree of respect which it would not probably have received from many others. I forbear making any remarks on its improprieties, being persuaded they are rather to be considered as the incautious violences of a generous mind, revolting against narrow though necessary restraint, than as the virulent efforts of a bad disposition to give unmerited pain. My doors, my heart, and my purse are still as open to you as ever. [As to your statement that very large inheritances will be yours] I rejoice to hear that you have been left above dependence and I advise you to take care that that consideration does not reduce you to it."

To Master Littlepage this was an intolerable affront to his "honor." More than that, all his misfortunes were not of his own making. "I still affirm you was the cause of my leaving my friends and my country"! Jay answered, "You would do well to recollect that politeness is very consistent with spirit [courage] and that self-respect may be maintained without doing violence to good manners."

Meanwhile Port Mahon had fallen to Crillon's expedition and Littlepage had been in the show. Crillon returned to Cádiz and Gibraltar was the next objective. After it, Littlepage had had enough of foreign glory. Cornwallis had surrendered and it appeared that his own country was more important than he had supposed. He returned to Madrid to find that Jay had left for Paris to join Franklin and John Adams as a Peace Commissioner. Instructions had been left with Carmichael to make reasonable advances to Littlepage but, according to the latter, he refused to do so. The two of them had strong reasons for disliking each other and Carmichael, though not yet the victim of his later alcoholism, may well have been difficult. Nonetheless, Littlepage remained in and around Madrid until July of the next year, 1783.

He then went to Paris and agreed with Jay on the total amount of his indebtedness, without, however, being able to make any payment. This was on July 6.

Ten days later he went to Jay with the request that he be allowed to carry the definitive treaty with Great Britain to Congress.

In the circumstances of the times, this was an incredible piece of effrontery. To be made such a messenger was always a reward for unusual service. The bearer of good tidings, of military or diplomatic victory, received the thanks of kings or congresses. A certain immortality was given his name and there was likely to be a tangible reward as well.

But this pushing young man saw nothing improper in proposing himself. Jay might well have told him, "Nothing could be more ridiculous," but out of kindness and doubtless a natural desire to avoid an explosion told him the selection of the bearer would be a joint decision of his colleagues and himself. John Adams proposed Thaxter, his private secretary, and Jay and Franklin assented—though Littlepage did not.

He went to see the aged, weary, easygoing Franklin (seventy-seven) and reported to Jay that Franklin said he "had no predilection for Thaxter and if it would do [Littlepage] a pleasure he should have his vote." No doubt Franklin did say it to get rid of him.

Jay replied that Thaxter had served long and well in the diplomatic service and would not be superseded. Littlepage went off in a temper and the next day wrote Jay that he was a liar, and that he must "complain of the ill-usage" to which Jay had subjected him. Then he added that "as you well know" he had been left in Madrid to spy on Carmichael. For perhaps the only time in his life, Littlepage decided the next day he had gone too far and made an apology.

There was apparently no further contact until March 16, 1784, when Littlepage wrote the immemorial letter of the evasive debtor. It asked for a copy of his accounts with Jay (which he had received and agreed to eight months before) but pointed out he had "no actual obligation for sums advanced to me during my minority upon the credit of my guardian." He then demanded to know what Jay had done in the United States to collect them. The same day Jay sent him a copy of the account, adding that he had made no effort to collect. At this point Carmichael arrived in Paris and told Jay that Littlepage had told him he had been left in Madrid to spy on him. "Oh, the boys, when will they be men?" Jay must have wondered as he came back to America to be the last Secretary of Foreign Affairs under the Confederation.

The next year Littlepage also returned. On December 3, 1785, in New York he wrote Jay demanding a full investigation of what had passed between them! Receiving no reply by the next day, he wrote again imploring Jay to save himself "before I proceed to the last extremity, that is an appeal to the public [regarding your design] to injure and disgrace me."

Jay then replied go ahead and appeal, but the paper reported: "Mr. Littlepage was arrested at his lodgings in New York at the suit of Mr. Jay for the sums due him by [Mr. Littlepage's] late guardian, Colonel Benjamin Lewis."

Littlepage then challenged Jay to a duel and advised the public that he had "called Jay a coward in the street and Jay had saved himself in flight."

Thereupon the story behind the story appeared. The last Congress of the Confederation had before it a proposal from Littlepage that the Congress recommend him to the King of

Poland as chamberlain and secretary of the royal Cabinet! Jay, he alleged, had persuaded Congress to take no action. It was an act of unparalleled injustice and malignity toward a man who, so Littlepage described himself, had been "the first citizen of the United States ever recognized by Spain . . . the first Protestant ever authorized to serve in the [Spanish] Army. In a word I had been placed in a situation which insignificant as I was had attracted the attention of part of Europe." (Here at least he is more modest than Lafayette, on whom, so he said, the eyes of Europe were fixed.) In the face of such glory, Littlepage went on, "Jay abandoned me, deprived me of all credit and resources . . . such is the duplicity, such the want of honor and probity for which a President of Congress, a Minister Plenipotentiary and a Secretary of State has arraigned a boy of seventeen [Littlepage, was now twenty-three] before the tribunal of the American Public."

In this unresolved state the Jay-Littlepage imbroglio subsided but not Littlepage's incredible career.

Within three months this "boy," with every outward attribute of the *chicaneur*, was in Warsaw as chamberlain to King Stanislaus, the Polish monarch, later becoming the Polish envoy in St. Petersburg, and fighting from 1792 to '94 in the Polish Army during a Russian invasion.

From Warsaw he published an open letter to Jay, which contained nothing new. Even a friend of Gates, sending him the reply by "your waggoner," wrote, "I conceive that Jay has been very ungratefully repaid for the kindness he had bestowed on this polish [sic] Chamberlain, for it is plainly evident the American plenipo [sic] kept him under his roof, in the bosom of his family gratis."

Leaving the Polish service, after more foreign campaigns, Littlepage was a "secret agent" at various times for various masters in France and Spain, coming at last to Hamburg—like Gouverneur Morris and Aaron Burr—and thence home after Jefferson's first inauguration.

In November 1801 he wrote Rufus King, still our Minister in London though a Federalist. The letter is typical, cryptic and self-important with allusions to the great:

I have never forgotten the important conversation which passed between us the last time we met in St. James's Park. In a conversation which I had with the President about a week passed [sic] I mentioned the affair in a question to him. He told me he had been informed of it *for four months* [his italics] but that it would be unfortunate but what were the means of prevention? That question you may suppose I was ill prepared to answer, totally ignorant as I am of the politics and resources of my own country. I have here met with our vice-president, Colonel Burr, with whom I spoke a little on the same subject. He assured me that he had long studied it, had conversed upon it with Ternant and Talleyrand in this country, had his opinion irrevocably fixed upon it but could not declare to me what that opinion was except *in presence of the President.*

So far for external politics. With respect to our internal affairs the President thinks himself sure of a majority in both houses. With respect to changes he is less precipitate than many expected. I believe he does not mean to descend to the lower offices.

I was happy to hear him speak in high terms of you and can assure you his opinion of you is general in this country. I am surprised at the conduct of peace between England and France. For heaven's sake let me know how it came to pass.

Has Mr. Pitt sent you the paper for which he promised me to make enquiry. Should anything positive come to your knowledge, respecting the *great political affair* in question, let me know confidentially and a proper use will be made of it.

It was almost his last letter. He died in July 1802, at thirty-nine, leaving instructions to burn all his papers.

It is evident that under any flag but his own he served bravely, one of a long roll of men in history who can serve what is far but not what is near.

Thomas Rodney was a fantastic of a wholly different and much more amusing sort. It will come as a surprise to many to learn that he, whom it is unlikely they have ever heard of, was the savior of our country and the chief architect of its form of government. In these achievements he received some help from Almighty God.

Thomas Rodney was born in Delaware, June 4, 1744, youngest brother of Caesar Rodney, Signer of the Declaration. It must be admitted that Thomas is sole witness, as well as judge and jury, as to his genius, and had he not confided the facts to his *Journal* they might never have been known.

His original intention was to have the *Journal* contain only his poetry, but discovering at fifty-two that he could write prose as well as poetry—Le Bourgeois Gentilhomme in reverse—he began his entries.

As a record of country life in Delaware at the time the entries are pleasant reading. "Full moon. The morning clear and bright and a cool wind to the east," as he went for his walk, or friends stopped at his farm for dinner—the sort of entries Washington made at Mount Vernon. But such small change was not Rodney's main interest.

In addition to his poetry—perhaps no worse than Joel Barlow's—there are entries telling of his Visions (his dreams), which appear to have occurred once a year. He refers to them as "My Vision of 1785" or "My Vision of 1777." The dreams are not remarkable, and to the layman the subjects and symbols appear to be the normal material of a countryman's subconscious. It must be said that in describing them Rodney is as terse and vivid as a modern case history in psychiatry.

On January 10, 1797, he went to a banquet given by Governor Bedford of Delaware. "The tenth toast was to the House of Representatives in Congress assembled," and this set him thinking about his Vision of 1785 in which a great tree on his farm had fallen. He now saw clearly that "the Fall of The Great Tree meant the fall of the Old Congress." It had taken a long time to reach this solution but, as he says, "the seer of Visions cannot always interpret them, nor can I, but sometimes I can the figuration."

He had been disappointed in the defeat of Thomas Pinckney for Vice-President by Jefferson the previous fall and in his *Journal* he quotes a man "who favored Thomas Pinckney for prudence, moderation, sound judgment, great coolness and discretion, calm, steady firmness of character and uniformity of character." He himself believes "Mr. Jefferson to be greatly deficient in most of these qualities." He puts his view of Jefferson very well: "He has too much scientific knowledge, least useful for a statesman whose business it is to judge and act not to write books; no one will deny him the praise of considerable literary genius . . . but [he is] a weakly, wavering, indecisive character, deliberate when he ought to act, and frequently acting when he does attempt it without steadiness or perseverance, rashly engaging in attempts the difficulties [whereof] he ought to have foreseen. Thomas Jefferson is fitted for a President of a College, President of a Philosophy Society, and even Secretary of State, but not for First Magistrate. . . .

"It was then [1776] said and still is," he continues, "that Jefferson drew up the Declaration," and Rodney then proceeds to have his brief say about that sacred document. It has always, he says mildly, been commended "but for my part I always thought there was a *puerile continuance* [author's italics] in the charges exhibited against the king."

After the Declaration's magnificent preamble there are eighteen paragraphs beginning "He has . . ." which list the iniquities of the King. Some are famous "watchwords of democracy." *He has affected to render the Military independent of and superior to the Civil Power. . . .* [*He has*] *sent hither swarms of Officers to harass our people. . . .* Nonetheless, if one reads them behind locked doors safe from prowling thought-police, one does become confused as to whether there is or is not a good deal of *puerile continuance* about them, and to wish Thomas Rodney had either not raised the question or had written the Declaration himself.

He could have easily have done so, one gathers from the

entry: "I may here recapitulate a few important instances of that judgment and wisdom which Heaven has been pleased to bestow on me. . . . In December, 1776, when Congress, the people, the Army and Washington were on the point of surrendering, my counsels, especially enlightened by the messengers of the Most High God, prohibited the surrender and animated our Generals to those glorious successes which immediately followed–and when Corn Wallace [sic] was taken and Britain had solicited peace, myself and General Gates acting as it were as agents for Congress and the Army . . . concerted to plan the Association of the Cincinnati *and the Federal Government*, and both those plans being approved by the wise men of America have since [1796] been carried into execution.

"I do not descend here to detail other instances [of my judgment and wisdom]. I only mention these because they have not only had a supreme control on America but on Europe. Yet on me heaven bestows not the honor of their kings, for I am personally impoverished and depressed. I have been but an instrument in the hand of the Mighty God to do these things and to Him is the honor due [but] toward My Country indeed he has made me a guardian-angel."

For one man, with the slight help of God and Horatio Gates, to have held the cause together from Trenton to Yorktown and to have singlehanded done the work of the Fifty-five Men at the Federal Convention was surely reason for some pride on his part, but Thomas Rodney was without vanity. He admitted that his brother Caesar, the Signer, "was often astonished and frequently said he heard nothing in Congress or elsewhere equal to my reasoning and particularly on the question of Independence." From this we see that Thomas did himself an injustice in dating his help to the cause "late in '76." It was evidently at work as early as the spring before when the Declaration was being debated. "He [Caesar Rodney] said with a degree of wonder that what he heard from me excelled all he had heard in Congress from Adams, Dickinson and all the rest. . . .

"I thought my brother partial," Thomas concludes.

Sources: The Whole Correspondence between the Hon. John Jay, Esquire and Mr. Lewis Littlepage (1786) is in the Rare Book Room, N.Y.P.L. The letter to Gates "by his waggoner," Gates Papers, N.Y.H.S.; Littlepage to Rufus King, King Papers, N.Y.H.S. The *Journal* of Thomas Rodney (Mss.) is in the Historical Society of Pennsylvania.

CHAPTER IV

The New Yorkers:
JAY *and* LIVINGSTON

In contrast to drolls like Thomas Rodney or debtors like Robert Morris stand the characters and careers of two New Yorkers, John Jay and Robert R. Livingston. Jay was born in 1745, the year before Livingston, and from boyhood through King's College and the first five years of the Revolution they were the closest of friends, each seeing in the other qualities which he admired but did not himself possess. Both from young manhood were ornaments of their state and country. Both had active parts in the framing of the New York Constitution. Both served in the Continental Congress and Jay succeeded Livingston as its Secretary of Foreign Affairs. Livingston was long chancellor of New York, administering the presidential oath to Washington, and Jay was the nation's first Chief Justice. Both became envoys of their country at critical times. But the fierceness of "party spirit" in the Federalist period drove them into opposing camps.

"You were formed," Jay wrote to his friend early in '75, "for a citizen of the world. I for a colonist or villager . . . .

You were naturally easy of access and in advances. I in neither." In a time when brothers might begin letters to each other "Dear Sir," Jay's to Livingston were always begun "Dear Robert" and usually signed:

I am, dear Robert,
Your friend. . . .

In '82 Jay wrote from Bordeaux that Livingston had been named godfather to his new daughter and hoped Mrs. Livingston would soon put him under the same obligation.

Livingston's mother, perhaps a prejudiced witness, wrote of his "unequalled sweetness of disposition" among her ten children. In Jay's ardent devotion to his wife, the exquisite Sally Livingston, a cousin of the chancellor, the same sweetness is evidenced, but to the public he appeared stern and austere, obsessed with a sense of duty, as a Huguenot Calvinist might be expected to be. Livingston made no secret of the love of indolence "of which Gouverneur Morris so often reminded him." "The government has been weak and indigent," Livingston wrote Lafayette in '88, "but the people easy and happy." And so was Livingston himself. There was a great amateur touch in the pleasing sense about his attitude toward life, and the superb achievement of his life, the Louisiana Purchase, came about in the burst of prowess of which only champions are capable.

Most men of the time loudly protested their indifference to public office, but to a degree greater than most Livingston meant it. In '85, Lafayette wrote him, urging that he come to France to succeed the ailing Jefferson. "I have little thought of going abroad in any character," Livingston replied. "I have already been nominated for Spain (and withdrawn at my own request). I was against my consent opposed to Mr. Adams and Mr. Rutledge for England. Happily Mr. Adams's interest [supporters] prevailed, saving me the pain of refusing an honor which I knew to be above my merits, and though I could have had unanimous consent of all states to succeed

Mr. Adams in the Hague, I peremptorily refused." When the letter was written on June 1, Livingston apparently did have the "unanimous consent of all states" but an interesting side light is thrown on the situation and the strength of local loyalties by a letter to him from Charles Pinckney (cousin of C.C.P.) on August 28 following. They were friends and correspondents for years, of course increasingly so after Livingston's complete swing to Republicanism in the early nineties.

Pinckney says, "Mr. Rutledge declines going to the Hague and Wednesday next is assigned for election of a Minister to that court. . . . We are desired to nominate and push Mr. Ralph Izard [of South Carolina]. . . . I feel it unnecessary to assure you that was not a gentleman from our state a candidate for this office I know of no one who would more warmly meet my support and approbation than yourself."

It seems quite clear that Livingston did not want a post abroad which would take him away from his beloved seat at Clermont and his family and friends. It is likely, on the other hand, that he would like to have been something more than Chancellor Livingston. It is a deceptively sonorous title, but the presiding justice of a court of equity was not after all comparable with a Chief Justice, a governor, or a Cabinet member. One wonders whether he was disappointed and whether he was thus led away from Federalism.

In his papers there is a puzzling and fascinating letter to him up the Hudson at Clermont from his older sister, Janet Livingston Montgomery. She did not date it but it was plainly written in New York in 1789 and prior to September 29. She was devoted to her brother and ambitious for him and wrote in forthright fashion—calling men by their last names only:

"Armstrong has by this time informed you that Morris has convinced the P—— of the Independence of W—— and that in consequence he will have the appointment he wishes—but a very long conversation with Lear—which gave me the opportunity of carelessly throwing out this report convinces me nothing of this kind could take place—as he said Wil—— was not within six of the place."

What she has said so far means that while their brother-in-law John Armstrong, Jr., claims that his crony Robert Morris, senator from Pennsylvania, has cleared with the President the appointment of the Signer, James Wilson, to the Supreme Court, she has learned from Tobias Lear, Washington's secretary, that Wilson is "not within six of the place," which presumably leaves it vacant for the chancellor.

She then appears to say, "Mrs. K I have seen only once," but the difficulty is that K may be H or may even be R. It appears to be K and one thinks at once of Lucy Knox, wife of the Secretary of War, held over from the Confederation. In any event she has seen her only once but "with her husband I had a long and interesting conversation in which I was mostly the listener. . . . He began with the friendship he had for you, with the wish of the P—— how to serve you and have you in place—that nothing could prevent this but the fear of making so many appointments from this State. This gave me the opportunity of supposing H in the Treasury—he answered immediately 'or the Chancellor' which he said was the present idea."

"He" may have been Knox but in the line reading "Mrs. K [?] I have seen only once," Mrs. Montgomery has added, "Her child has [sic] and is still very ill." The Knoxes had so many children that it seems unlikely that her "child" would be referred to. Rather does it seem that Mrs. K is Mrs. Rufus King, wife of the New York senator and herself an Alsop, whom Mrs. Montgomery would naturally know. The Kings were married in March '86 and at the time had only one child.

Mrs. Montgomery continues, "This confirms me in the notion that he [K] had advised this measure to the P—— rather than take up H—— whome he fears—whoever it is, he seems to have much friendship for you, and yours to him I assured him—he told me he did not doubt it as he had proof of it from several confidential conversations . . . on the whole it appears to me he had much of the confidence of the P——— at least as much as any man."

Still the question, Who was K? and now the doubt that it is either Knox or King. The latter was then but thirty-four, nine years younger than the chancellor—it all sounds a little patronizing for him. Yet Knox was, until '95, Hamilton's disciple and would never have supported Livingston against him, or said that the President "fears" Hamilton. From whom would such recommendation come most naturally? Surely from Jay, but Mrs. Montgomery continues, "I am constantly at General Washington's and am each time very kindly received. . . . Jay [the Chief Justice] and his wife very formal —I have been to see her [a first cousin] and met him at the President's. When I dined there—he was closetted more than an hour."

So it is all very elusive. The last line of the letter, though, is wholly clear: "I thank you for the pigs" from the farm at Clermont.

There were three special occasions from 1782 to 1795 when Livingston wrote to or about Jay, as an American diplomat. The first was in April '82 as Jay was about to leave Madrid for Paris as a Peace Commissioner. The "leisure" of the letter drives the reader today almost frantic with impatience that it will not be finished in time. It is from Philadelphia. Someone has just come in to tell Livingston, then Secretary of Foreign Affairs, that there is a vessel ready to sail for Europe and that if he will hurry there will be just time to get a brief dispatch aboard. It explains to Jay in what haste it must be written, that there is scarcely time to say more than that "your conduct has been particularly acceptable to Congress." But on and on the "indolent" writer goes in a triumph of smooth composition, sequence, logic, and advice. Six legal-cap sheets are filled without a correction—though the messenger is waiting and word comes the ship lines are about to be cast off. There is a concluding paragraph pointing out that "as Spain has made the cession of Gibraltar [to her by Britain] a preliminary to peace" (How familiar today) "she can hardly expect that mediators, if they gratify her in that, will add to it other countrys to which she has claims." But at last it is done and signed and the reader sighs with relief—and with admiration of the force and clarity of our foreign policy. But when Livingston signed it he was only a third done. The Secretary of Foreign Affairs must then copy it. And when that was done encipher it: 312. 108. 425. 325. 509. 18 . . .

By July the next year Adams, Franklin, and Jay had agreed in principle and in detail with the British diplomats on the terms of the Treaty of Peace, and a draft had gone over to London from Paris.

Livingston wrote Jay, taking him to task very strongly, on behalf of Congress and himself, for not referring the draft treaty to the French Foreign Minister in advance. In effect the criticism by Congress illustrates at that early date the split between the so-called pro-French and pro-English sides of the government. In a general way it may be said the pro-French party became Jeffersonian Republicans who felt that the original French aid entitled that country to some general sovereignty over our foreign affairs; that we should not act without her prior knowledge, advice, and consent. They seemed to feel that the aid had been the generous gift of a benevolent French people. It was a misnomer to apply the term "pro-English" to the Federalists, Washington, Hamilton, and Jay, except as in general they feared England far less than France, after our independence—believing us capable of holding our own against either—and saw from 1778 on that French aid, however welcome, was given only out of deep self-interest, more to bring England down than build us up. Thereafter we were to be a French satellite.

Jay's reply to Livingston is a brilliant and convincing account of why he and his colleagues acted as they did. First: the French thought our demand that the British treat with us as an independent people (as she did) was premature and should arise from and not precede the treaty. Second: that France was disappointed at our securing British agreement to boundaries contrary to certain views of Spain which France favored. Third: that France considered our demand to rights in common in the Newfoundland fisheries (which Britain granted) "too extensive." Fourth: that as to our prevailing on Britain not to insist on our reinstating the Tories, France thought they should be reinstated.

It was clear, Jay continued, that French plans for a treaty between America and Britain "were far from being such as America would have preferred. As we disapproved of the models [of the French Foreign Minister] we thought it imprudent to give him an opportunity of moulding our treaty. Whether he was influenced by what he really thought best for us or best for France is doubtful but not very important. Whatever his motives they were such as opposed our system and in private life it is deemed imprudent to admit opponents to full confidence."

But even so, Jay continues, you may say, why didn't we show the articles to the French before signing? We acted under what we believed was "the necessity of speed. We felt sure Lord Shelburne was determined to put a period to the war" or quit his place as First Minister. If we had shown France the unsigned articles they would have said at once, "Wait until the French-Spanish-British articles are settled." That was far too great a risk. It presented every chance for Britain to change her mind toward us.

Of course it is true that Congress had said no separate peace, no peace except in confidence and concurrence with France. Jay's answer to that is specious reasoning. Of that there is no doubt. It is logic-chopping of a sort we condemn in our present-day enemies but it is also informed with the common sense without which we should have been lost in the "formidable politique" of Europe.

It was true, he wrote, that no separate peace meant "we should mention to and consult with France, but it is most certain that it was founded on a mutual understanding that France would patronize [support] our demands and assist us in obtaining the objects of them. . . . France, by discouraging our claims, ceases to be entitled to the degree of confidence respecting them specified in the Resolution."

However "Congress positively instructed us to do nothing without the advice and consent of the French Minister and we have departed from that line of conduct—but I apprehend that Congress marked out that line of conduct for their own sake and not for the sake of France. The object of the instructions was the supposed interest of America and not of France. . . ."

The long, sensible, convincing argument—written when Littlepage was at his most troublesome—ends with another matter. Jay had been away nearly four years. He was the head of the family, some of whom just then able to return to New York after the war in financial distress. "Tell my brother Peter he may share with me to the last shilling and so may Nancy"—all but the words of Charles C. Pinckney to his brother Thomas in similar circumstances. Deep family attachment among the leaders was one of the most marked of their qualities—Jay asks Livingston to draw on him for £150 and divide it between Peter and Sally. "If you find that more would be convenient, be pleased to supply it and draw on me."

As the nineties began the two friends began to drift apart. The chancellor's sister Janet, widow of General Montgomery, had gone to Ireland about his estate and wrote from there to her brother July 19, 1790, "Jefferson I see is Minister of Affairs and the papers tell me that Washington is ill . . . and Jay may now I suppose look for the Crown—or is it the great Hamilton as they call him—would to Heaven you had kept your old place [Secretary of Foreign Affairs under the Confederation] for now is not the reign of your friends."

Jay was then Chief Justice. The papers had evidently expressed the fears that the carbuncle on Washington's leg would be fatal and Mrs. Montgomery, overlooking Vice-

President Adams, appears to foresee Jay as his successor. The significant thing seems to be that it far from pleases her that her brother's most intimate friend should succeed.

On Independence Day, '92, Morgan Lewis, husband of Livingston's sister Gertrude, wrote him of Jay's arrival and acclaim in Albany, saying, "I have reason to suppose [Jay and others] are adopting measures subversive of the State Government. [Jay a *subversive!*] This is not bare suspicion. . . . I am persuaded I have called the great outlines of the Plan."

In 1794, Jay went as special envoy to London to make a new treaty with England enforcing terms of the Treaty of Paris (1783), particularly as to trade and the evacuation of the Northwest Posts. The decision to send any envoy and particularly Jay was the subject of most bitter senatorial party debate, and the Federalists drove it through by the narrowest of margins.

It broke the Jay-Livingston friendship definitely and finally but they parted like gentlemen with this extraordinary exchange of notes, May 11, 1794:

"The Chancellor presents his compliments to the Chief Justice of the United States. Tho' political differences have excited a coolness between them perhaps inconsistent with the liberality of both, the Chancellor is not so unmindful of past friendship as not to be sincere in wishing the Chief Justice a safe passage, a happy return to his friends and a successful issue to his mission."

It was Sunday and Jay replied that night: "The Chief Justice of the United States presents his compliments to the Chancellor of the State. It is now late at night and want of time imposes brevity. He assures the Chancellor that while he regrets what is, he will always remember with pleasure what has been their relative situation to each other. Time here or hereafter will correct errors. He thanks him for the kind wishes expressed in his note and without hesitation reciprocates them."

Jay's Treaty is regarded as one of our major diplomatic

defeats and it appeared for a long time that the Senate would not ratify it. Outside the Senate Livingston was one of its most violent critics, through the newspapers and in private correspondence.

He wrote Washington in a mixture of outraged patriotism and alarm that so great a man, for whom he had such devotion, could even consider signing it. Washington replied, "For myself I freely own that I cannot discover in it the mischief you anticipate . . . on the contrary, altho' it does not rise to all our wishes, yet it appears to me calculated to procure to the United States such advantages as entitle it to our acceptance. [As to what you say of your previous regard for me] I can merit your good opinion . . . only by a conscientious discharge of what I conceive to be my duty."

As in 1783, one of the great objections to it, on the Republican side, was the allegation that the French had not been consulted, nor shown the articles as they were negotiated. Monroe was Minister to France and the violence of his Francophilia concerning it led to his recall and to the publication of his *A View of the Conduct of the Executive*. Livingston wrote his brother Edward that "Monroe complained bitterly of the manner in which the negotiations had been conducted. Jay refused to let him know the contents of the Treaty. . . . The French Nation are extremely hurt."

The Republicans contended that Monroe, in Paris, should have been advised of each step Jay took as he took it and that the French government had some "right" to know what America was doing.

To understand the situation clearly it is necessary to read Monroe's *A View of the Conduct of the Executive* and Washington's own scathing marginal notes on it. When Livingston read the pamphlet he said, ". . . it places [Monroe's] character and the vices of the Administration in so conspicuous a point of view that I think it bids fairer for opening the eyes of the public than anything." It led also to a deepening of party strife and, to Washington's shocked amazement, to

Monroe being elected governor of Virginia, the month of Washington's death.

Livingston attributed it all to Jay's character. "I sincerely condole with you," he wrote extravagantly to Madison, "on the ratification of the Treaty which sacrifices every essential interest and prostitutes the honor of our country. I confess that I had little hope from the moment of Mr. J.'s appointment of his rendering us any service. His inveterate hatred for the French Nation and the violence with which he entered into the system of the ministerial party gave me reason to apprehend that want of energy which our situation required. I fear that French anger over the Treaty will make them force us into war either with Great Britain or themselves."

Reference to Jay's "inveterate hatred of France" has become a commonplace in historical writing. It is said to have arisen from the fact that his Huguenot ancestors were driven out of France by the Revocation of the Edict of Nantes—in effect Louis XIV's abrogation of the freedom of worship guaranteed by his grandfather, the great Henry IV. As to that, two things must be remembered: first, that there was in colonial America a deep contempt for the Catholic despotism of France and Spain and all they stood for; second, that the ancestors of most Americans of the time had come here as victims of religious persecution. Catholics were of course in a minority yet no one doubted the patriotism of Catholic signers, like Carroll and McKean, or supposed they were not to be trusted to place the interest of their country above anything else. To suppose that Jay's long diplomatic career, in the main one of great success, was motivated by a vindicative feud with France is to disregard his balance of mind, his ability to compromise and to achieve the maximum possible. However, Barbé-Marbois, writing after John Adams's death, said Adams's *Journal* for 1783 would show that "Mr. Jay likes the French as little as Mr. Lee and Mr. Izard. *He says they are not a moral people.*"

But the world went up and down. One of the first acts of

President Jefferson, in 1801, after the long balloting in the House to break the electoral tie, was the nomination of Chancellor Livingston to be Minister in Paris, where our diplomacy had been so unsuccessful in spite of the famous men who had been its agents—Morris, Monroe, Marshall, Pinckney, and the rest. While the Chancellor was only fifty-five and in excellent health, he was extremely deaf. In spite of that and his attachment to home he accepted at once, going out to what was to be perhaps the most conspicuous success an American diplomat ever achieved—the Louisiana Purchase.

It appears that he suggested to Joseph Alston of South Carolina that he go with him as private secretary. Alston was twenty-two and two months before had married Theodosia Burr. It would seem an ideal arrangement but on April 20 the new Vice-President thanked him for his "obliging overtures to Mr. and Mrs. Alston." They could not "go to Europe at present but were sensible to the honor done them by your politeness."

There was supposed to be another charming young couple aboard. Just before he was elected Jefferson had promised Thomas McKean that if he were elected he would do all possible to prevent the transfer of the Spanish Minister, the Marquis d'Yrujo, who had married McKean's daughter Sally. When the election was settled Jefferson wrote one of the unctuously modest letters of which he was so fond to McKean, saying how much happier he would have been if Colonel Burr had defeated him since as president of the Senate he, Jefferson, could have been at Monticello eight months of the year, but since he was so unlucky as to be Chief Executive he would do all he could about Yrujo. McKean replied, thanking him for his "polite and friendly conduct toward the Chevalier," adding in very human fashion, "Nothing would be more agreeable than his remaining in this country, for I love him as a child and never expect to see my daughter after their departure for Europe—happy should I be if your kind interference should arrive in time at Madrid to prevent his removal. [If not] he has expressed a wish for a passage with wife and family in the frigate that will convoy Chancellor Livingston to France—he means to pay the Captain the same as if in a private vessel and I have reason to believe it would be very agreeable to both Ministers."

Jefferson's efforts were successful for the time being so the Livingstons finally sailed without the Alstons or the Yrujos. The Chevalier supposed that an effort would be made to buy Louisiana and with fine Latin cynicism wrote his father-in-law:

"I wish Louisiana was at the bottom of the sea for the good of Spain and of the United States and of myself. . . . I have had three crises all originating from that —— Province. Whatever may have been the result I always had a great deal of trouble and I consider trouble as an evil. . . .

"We are all very well though not yet reconciled to the unconvenience of Washington City. . . . Sally offers her duty on [sic] you and Narcisa and Charles send their love to Grandpapa and Grandmamma."

The frigate with Livingston sailed finally in October 1801 and on January 10, 1803, Monroe was ordered again to Paris, this time as special envoy to consummate the great Purchase.

He arrived in April, rested five days in Havre, and reached Paris only to sign a *fait accompli*, the swift bargain made by the "indolent" Livingston, not merely for Louisiana but for the whole western side of the Mississippi, at five million dollars more than he was authorized to pay. "I trust," Gouverneur Morris wrote him with the pride of a fellow New Yorker, "it will not be pretended that the application of money could not be as safely entrusted to your care and intelligence as to those of a Monroe."

Of course the Purchase was primarily possible because Talleyrand wished to "cut his losses." Nonetheless Livingston responded to a mere intimation with amazing alacrity and resource. Two things may have influenced him—one, that Jay, as a special envoy, had gotten the credit (or discredit) for the groundwork laid by Thomas Pinckney, the regular Minister to London; and Pinckney then as special envoy to Madrid had done the same thing to William Short. Livingston was a proud man, far more brilliant and intellectual than Monroe. He can hardly have failed to be piqued, to put it mildly, at Jefferson sending Monroe. But the second and perhaps compelling reason for his swift disregard of instructions may have been the feeling that the unlucky, contentious, cautious, and melancholy Monroe might well lose the whole game if he waited for him.

The world did indeed go up and down. Livingston had this great success after three times refusing diplomatic posts abroad. Jay, who had responded to every call for foreign duty, against his own wishes, is said by his treaty with England to have made one of our greatest failures—and now his beloved wife Sally, the light of his life, was dead. And the morose Monroe, once recalled from France, had come back to share Livingston's victory, and would go on to be Secretary of State and finally to be President in the Era of Good Feeling.

Of his own achievement Livingston very properly did not think badly. He wrote his sister Janet Montgomery in July 1803, "But as it is I have accomplished a work which will never be forgotten in America and this, time shall discover . . . that I shall be counted among the most fortunate if not among the ablest of my country's benefactors [there is no punctuation in the whole paragraph] let the politics of the statesmen take their own course I may retire with honor and I hope with satisfaction to myself and to my friends and live the rest of my life for both." The last were almost the exact words he had written Jay at the end of the war twenty years before. Actually he had never been overburdened by public cares. He came back in 1804 and did live exactly as he wished, very valuably but very independently. His letters had been full of mechanical inventions of all sorts for years and soon after his return Fulton's and his *Clermont* steamed up and down the Hudson.

He lived sixty-six years, Jay eighty-three. Both were patriot leaders and great gentlemen. As to whether they were good men or bad, there is an infallible test of men of the times which gives the answer. Was he consecrated—no lesser word will do—to the *improvement* of his herds, his crops, his trees, his fruits and flowers, and did he feel an inescapable obligation to share knowledge of how to improve even with his bitterest political foe? If so, he was a good man, part of the special freemasonry. If not, he was someone like Aaron Burr.

Livingston, violently protesting the Jay Treaty and Washington's support of it, still sends Washington the latest *Transactions* of the Society for Promoting Agriculture. President Washington thanks him for his "goodness" and encloses in turn for Livington's "perusal a pamphlet on the culture of potatoes."

In 1799, Pickering, the Secretary of State, embodied all that Livingston considered politically evil. But Pickering was one of the founders of the Society for Promoting Agriculture and to him with a cordial letter went word of an agricultural improvement. Similar instances could be cited from the Jay Papers.

There is hence no doubt that these able patriots were good men.

Sources: All letters by members of the Livingston family are in the Robert R. Livingston Collection, N.Y.H.S., as are John Jay's letters to R.R.L. Barbé-Marbois on Jay from Charles Thomson's Scrap Book, Historical Society of Pennsylvania. Thomas McKean-Jefferson Correspondence, McKean Papers, H.S.P.

CHAPTER V

Have Done with Folly:

A LOOK AT PATRIOT WEDLOCK

HAVE done with folly, wife," the father of *Hugh Wynne, Free Quaker*, exclaims in Weir Mitchell's novel of the Revolution. This sober admonition has often been taken as characteristic of the marital relations of the time. Most biographers and historians have implied that the Founding Fathers, great, noble men, were fired by patriotism to the exclusion of all tenderer passions. It is admiringly recorded of the rich Jeremiah Wadsworth that "he provided liberally and kindly for his widow."

Certainly it does appear that no comparable group of men enjoyed such a degree of marital happiness. In considerable measure this may have been the result of their belief in the old adage that, when poverty enters in, love flies out the window. It was the accepted thing to seek the hand of a girl with "a handsome portion" of money. Girls were advised that a "pretty fortune" in a suitor was as much to be desired as a kind and affectionate nature. Such marriages turned out well. It was the spendthrifts, the gamesters, and the drunkards who, then as now, were unhappy.

It might be supposed that marriages based on such worldly considerations would have been lacking in tenderness or the pleasantries of love. The evidence to the contrary is overwhelming.

Elias Boudinot, not a great man but a rich and valuable one, had, so Benjamin Rush said, an almost canine appetite for money. Yet who has better expressed the love that changes not than he to his wife December 1785? "To tell you I love you is an old story you have heard a thousand times—to say I wish you to be always with me is no more than what you know by twenty odd years experience."

And Benjamin Rush himself, with his biting pen and tongue—married to the daughter of the Signer, Richard Stockton, as Boudinot was to Stockton's sister—wrote, "My dearest Jewel, I begin to sicken for your company"; "My Dearest—I awoke . . . no Julia near me"; "My Best Beloved, I think, write, talk, work, live only for you." Those are scraps from the letters of fifteen years. Years later when Meriwether Lewis went westward Rush asked him to find out if suicide was common among Indians, and if ever for love.

There was no soberer or outwardly more prosaic man of the time than Philip Schuyler, but long past sixty his letters to his wife begin "My Dearest Love" and he is "Yours forever."

Edward Hand, commanding the riflemen of the Continental Army at thirty-two, addresses his "dearest Kitty" as "My Dearest Creature" and "My Dearest Life." He had not heard from her in three weeks: "For God's sake my Dear let me not have that to say again." For the five years of the fighting they were seldom together. In July '81, just before the rush to Yorktown, she was very anxious to join him at headquarters in Dobbs Ferry. He could find nothing. "Those who have by accident got into houses find nothing but the walls and roof. You can't have a just idea of the distress of the neighborhood." All through the years he sends her "presents," cloth and trifles. But they were all that way. Wellford, going out as an army surgeon to the Whiskey Rebellion in '94, entered in his diary, bivouacked in the meadows where Braddock had made a stand, "In the evening wrote to my dear Mrs. W."

Levin Jynmes, a colonel of the Connecticut Line at twenty-eight, while a prisoner of war wrote his wife, "What filth it is that what passes between a man and his wife should be so exposed [to the curious eyes of the Commissary of Prisoners]."

In the letters of the younger husbands like Theodorick Bland, Tallmadge, and Oliver Wolcott, Jr., there is much amusing marital banter. Wolcott, a Yale classmate of Noah Webster and Joel Barlow, was married to the beautiful Elizabeth Stoughton from his home town, Litchfield, Connecticut. When Wolcott was Secretary of the Treasury at thirty-five, Liston, the British Minister, met her and said to Senator Tracy, "Your countrywoman, Mrs. Wolcott, would be admired even at St. James's." "She is admired even on Litchfield Hill," Tracy replied.

The Wolcotts had to be separated a good deal, much to their mutual displeasure and to her pretended alarm at his wandering. "Mr. Ellsworth [Chief Justice of the Supreme Court] will tell you how well I behave," Wolcott wrote back. "Indeed *I* think I am rather more steady than usual; it is certain I am not less so."

And then when he heard that she had "sent to Miss M and Miss W to inform you how I behave," he wrote her, "Miss M has gone to the country and Miss W cannot give you much information. I know more than both of them respecting the matter and if I did not fear this letter would fail of a direct conveyance would give you a history of all my proceedings. In general I have behaved well, but to enumerate my good actions would savor of vanity for which reason I am prevented from affording a great part of the history of my conduct. As I know you cannot have done anything which is not praiseworthy and as the ladies are permitted by custom to compliment themselves, it will be perfectly proper, and will be a satisfaction to me to know how *you* have behaved which I doubt not you will be good enough to inform me."

He writes her from Gray's Landing, a popular riverside "resort" of the time, the bored letter of a modern man. "I feel much as Adam did in Eden before he lost a rib. The place is mighty pretty and that is all. After a man has gone around the walks one way, if he pleases he may go round again; or he may return back upon his tracks or he may sit down or go upon the bridge and see a lazy fellow hold a line for hours in the river without taking a fish. . . . In the evening the scene changes. Then we have Eves in plenty of all nations, tongues and colours, but do not be jealous. I have not seen one yet whom I have thought pretty."

A friend of Gates put the same thought more ponderously. "Man is a forlorn creature without a companion into who's [sic] bosom he can pour the warm obsession of the heart with safety and from whom he is sure to receive the most tender endearment and affectionate good offices with full return."

Nor was it lonely husbands only who were forlorn creatures without a companion. Full of the lovely intimacy of happy marriage is a letter to "O My Tallmadge" from his wife:

It is Christmas Eve, O My Love will we ever live to spend one together. Good night, my dear, our darling babe is a-crying and wants her supper. I continue to have plenty of milk. I thought she would take so much of my time that I should not be as lonesome as in your former absences but I find I miss you more than ever.

A Christmas Kiss.

A month later she wrote, "When nine o'clock comes and the children are gone to bed it is then my best friend is missed. I look often at the bed and dread to undress. And think if I could sleep only this night with you or know that you were well I could go to my widow-bed contented."

Nor did wives have done with folly. Esther Edwards Burr, daughter of the theologian, wrote a girl friend in Boston,

"Pray what do you think everybody marrys in or about winter for, 'tis quite merry, isn't it? I really believe 'tis for fear of laying cold for want of a bedfellow"—a gross conclusion which occurred to John Marshall in writing to James Monroe at the same time, and which John Adams expressed to Abigail as he rode through Connecticut on his way to his inauguration: "This cold weather makes me regret the loss of my bed and fireside, and especially the companion and delight of both."

It is interesting that the letters of John and Abigail Adams should be the most human and charming of all the husbands and wives of the time. Perhaps it is only because more of them have been preserved. In the twenty years from the signing of the Declaration until his inauguration these married lovers had to endure long separations. "The hymeneal torch," Abigail wrote him, "yet burns with unabating fervor. Old Ocean has not quenched it [while he was abroad alone] nor old Time smothered it in this bosom."

In his absence at the First Continental Congress she wrote,

> My much loved Friend
> I dare not express to you at 300 miles' distance how ardently I long for your return. . . . The idea plays about my heart, unnerves my hand, whilst I write—awakens all the tender sentiments that years have increased and matured.

She wrote him in Paris in '82, the fourth year of their separation, "Life is too short to have the dearest of its enjoyments curtailed—the social feelings grow callous by disuse and lose that pliancy of affection which sweetens the cup of life as we drink it." As President he wrote her that he wanted to go home to Braintree: "I want my horse, my farm, my long walks and, more than all, the bosom of my friend."

When she finally was able to join him in France, after the peace with England, she must have wondered whether he had been faithful to her those long years amidst the follies of Paris. There is no evidence one way or the other but there is an amazing breadth of view toward folly on the part of this provincial, Puritan lady.

She wrote the Reverend John Shaw in Boston, "Can we suppose that of the many thousands whom the religion of this country obliges to celibacy [even] one quarter part of her number can find its [religion's] influence sufficiently powerful to conquer those passions which nature has implanted in men, when the gratification of them will cost only a few livres in confession."

The "disgust" she first felt at seeing "the visible garters and drawers" in the French ballet quickly wore off, she said. "I see them now with pleasure . . . yet when I consider the passions they must excite . . ."

As has been said, the high degree of marital happiness among the patriot leaders is indisputable, marred only by those cases, rare yet even then too frequent among the leaders, where wives were forced to invalidism or early death by excessive childbearing. Charles Carroll of Carrollton lived fifty years after his wife died at thirty-three, "driven to laudanum," her health ruined by childbearing against her doctor's orders. A man as enlightened and devoted as John Marshall, to name but another, begat ten children in twenty-one years of his beloved Polly's desperate ill-health. In the main, however, the relatively small families of the leaders are significant, the more so as most of them came from very large ones.

There was no case of divorce or desertion by husband or wife among the leaders. The gaunt, stern Timothy Pickering was as much in love with his wife as the gay grandees of South Carolina or the handsome Rufus King of New York. Mrs. Robert Morris's vow "for richer, for poorer" was not broken when her husband went to a debtors' prison and their great possessions were sold on the block. Chastellux was astonished to hear an innkeeper call his old wife "honey," and after seeing the little house of Colonel Peck in Providence "where comfort and simplicity reign" and his "young wife pleasing but not striking" was given "an idea of that serene and sweet state of happiness which appears to have taken refuge in the New World." Even Benjamin Rush believed there was something special in a New World republic that subdued men's lusts. It was royal courts which created "servility, insincerity and vice of every kind including seduction."

That marital happiness was general throughout all classes in the thirteen states would seem true, if it were not for the fact that the newspapers of the time have about as many advertisements for runaway wives as for runaway slaves.

One gets the impression that the bereaved husbands–none of whose names is otherwise known–were well-meaning fellows who were, as one of the delectable Tilghman girls described a beau, "What the Philosophers have long been in search of, a perfect vacuum." They would certainly have said, "Have done with folly, wife!" to someone like the lovely Jewess of Lancaster, Mrs. Elijah Etting, "the life of all the gaiety that could be mustered in the village, always in spirits, full of frolic and glee," or Mrs. Beatty, who went "in the country frollicking in December" and came home pleasantly drunk to write Mrs. Gates that "the man had oysters, turkeys, tarts and wine and none but his dear self and two ladies" to share it with.

The advertisements about leaving bed and board were slightly more personalized than their counterparts today. Each husband characterized his wife's conduct in individual terms. To cite a few:

George Dalzell's wife Nancy "behaved in a very indecent manner which renders it impossible for me to live with her etc. etc." Anna Benjamin "behaved in a most vile and absurd manner." Isaac Woodruff's wife Ann merely "behaved in a very unbecoming manner" but "Phoebe Weare refuses my bed and board and behaves in a very undutiful and un-Christianlike manner." Mr. Brown's wife Rebecca, having left his bed and board, "says she has another husband." One cannot blame Mr. Brown for refusing to pay "one farthing of her contracting."

When Benjamin Jacob's wife left his bed and board he published the usual disclaimer about paying her debts in the *New York Packet.* In the issue of the next and following week Mrs. Jacobs spoke for herself. No person that knows him, she advertised, would trust him even with a shilling. "I am happy that the law protects me from being obliged to pay his debts."

Of such varieties happy and unhappy marriages were made up, with the former far more frequent. As to the standards of sexual morality at the time, there was probably a similar variety, though charges of libertinism against the leaders—in a period when calumny was reckless—are relatively few, aside from Burr and Gouverneur Morris.

It is all but impossible to decide how much truth and how much hypocrisy there were in protestations of virtue. Mrs. Kirby, in giving "young Mr. Lovett" a letter of introduction to Horatio Gates in '96, said he "is warmly alive to all that is pure, noble and generous. There's a bijoux, my dear General, in these times of sensuality, villainy and almost universal depravity." But this is scarcely more than a "sensible man" might have said in the accepted idiom of the time.

Chastellux said a neighbor's young daughter had no objection to being looked at "or even to receive a few caresses" if they were given "without familiarity or libertinism." His translator said they saw a great deal of public love-making by boys and girls of sixteen. "Both sexes arrive early at puberty, their constitutions are warm, there are few restraints and they lose no time in completing the great object, the populating of the country." But that may well be as faulty a generalization as most, or as a French observer like Simone de Beauvoir makes today. Certainly his much-quoted innuendo at finding old Sam Adams "tête-à-tête with a young girl of fifteen who was preparing his tea" is of no significance at all. Besides, the customs of foreigners frequently amaze the oldest traveler. Charles Biddle in '83 saw high French ladies "wet the quarter-deck before us." He had "heard and read of it as being common [usual]" but as a patriotic American he points out that "the most common street-walker with us would not have done it." But Biddle had a capacity for surprise even in Philadelphia. When he went to look for runaway slaves of his he "found parties of whites, blacks and mulattoes all dancing together."

There is little question that the seaport towns had many drabs. Anthony Wayne warned his Pennsylvania Continentals in New York not to go "strowling" alone, lest the whores murder them. General Charles Lee—not a paragon of morality—was surprised to see General Armstrong, Sr., "strowling" with a colored one in the streets of Philadelphia. Benjamin Rush, noting that William Penn, great-grandson of the founder, married a prostitute, said, "he wanted [lacked] an understanding of life . . . two of his wife's sisters were prostitutes . . . her mother a washerwoman."

But withal there was the traditional American respect for virtue and womanhood. The *New York Packet's* Charleston, South Carolina correspondent sent the story of three ladies there who walked out in the country and stopped at an inn for a glass of water. The men present suggested they take gin instead, which they did. When they left, under its influence, the men followed and saw one of them fall into a pool. They immediately offered to help her out, but the ladies said no one but a married man might approach. Fortunately there was one such. The others turned their backs and he went forward, "giving the lady his shirt, handkerchief, etc.," to cover her.

The "handkerchief" of the time was an accessory of dress of many uses. As First Lady in Philadelphia, in spite of all she had seen in Paris, Abigail Adams was shocked by the immodest dress which "Without a handkerchief [left] the rich luxurience of nature's charm fully displayed [while some] not content with the show which nature bestows, borrow from art and literally look like nursing mothers."

Perhaps it was one of the latter whose "rump with 1 eyebrow and entire bosom" an advertiser in the *New York Journal and Weekly Register* found in the street and said that "whoever can prove her property may have them."

There were not only whores but many rogues roaming the country and particularly the back settlements. "Vile and impudent fellows would come to a Planter's House, and tye him, lie with his wife before his face . . . and a dozen fellows in succession. The villains had their confederates in every colony . . . and their concubines in the woods," someone informed the Bishop of London.

Gangs, which sound very modern, "were associated for the object of plunder," Goodrich wrote Wolcott, Secretary of the Treasury; "the conflagrations of our town is a mysterious business [but] no doubt seems to be entertained of their being infested with incendiaries." The mails were held up and waggons, carrying cargoes inland, were hijacked. Statesmen were charged with being in the pay of foreign powers, the Federalists with wishing a monarchy. Vermont and Kentucky wished for separatism. It would take thirty years to force Spain to open the Mississippi to American traffic and trade. In short the new nation was in a bad way, though it seems to have survived.

And as to a generalization about family life, it was apparently then much as now.

Have we not all, in our own families, read this letter from the daughter of John Jay to her brother as to the treatment she has received from her troublemaking sister-in-law? Bliss Perry once remarked that few good letters had been written by angry men, none by women.

The old gentleman [her father-in-law] this morning received a letter from his daughter enclosed to Mr. Lansing with a request that *he* would read it to his family in my presence—in which I am spoken of in the most contemptuous, bitter and harsh terms I ever knew applied to a woman of character and in which totally disregarding veracity she accuses me of the most *interested* [self-seeking] and overbearing conduct and in consequence of a letter Cousin Peter saw and can inform you of the contents. . . . [She was going to visit the old gentleman] and insist upon an explanation and investigation of my conduct. . . . I cannot endure the idea of thus being insulted with impunity. . . . However the conscious integrity of my conduct and firm trust in that God who doubtless for wise purposes has permitted me to suffer so many trials . . . I will hold fast my integrity and look forward with hope to that world where the wicked cease from troubling and the weary are at rest.

Maria B.

P.S. Aunt Symmes arrived yesterday. [Her mother's sister, who married John Cleves Symmes, of Ohio fame, and was the stepmother-in-law of President William Henry Harrison.]

Sources: Hand's letters to his wife, Edward Hand Papers, Historical Society of Pennsylvania, Wolcott's, Oliver Wolcott Papers, Connecticut Historical Society. Advertisements about errant wives, contemporary newspapers, N.Y.H.S.

CHAPTER VI

The Patriot Financier:

ROBERT MORRIS

FEW people realize the personal price Robert Morris paid for the riches he was supposed to have. The general view is that he, a Signer of the Declaration of Independence, was the Patriot Financier, the wise counselor of Washington, the genius who largely out of his own resources provided the money to support the Revolution. It is considered tragic that an ungrateful people should have allowed him all but to end his life in a debtors' prison.

It is quite true that without his know-how and resourcefulness it might several times have been difficult to carry on the war, and very many of the warriors were carried on his books for the sums on which their families lived. Yet it is also true that his services to the country practically ceased with the loan of $20,000 he secured from Rochambeau's military chest on the way to Yorktown in 1781. As early as December 1783, two weeks after the British evacuation of New York, he wrote Robert R. Livingston, then Secretary of Foreign Affairs, that only "want of money" had prevented his coming over to witness it.

It had not been long since Morris had written him with the breezy, reassuring generosity so characteristic of his prosperity, "Make yourself easy as to the transaction at the Bank. I have already enabled Mr. Lewis Morris to discharge the greater part of the note and will provide him with the balance a day or two hence when it falls due."

Thereafter, though many continued to regard him as the wealthiest man in the country, practically every important man, from Jefferson and Madison in the opposition to Wadsworth and Gouverneur Morris, his friends and fellow Federalists, knew that his affairs were on a razor's edge.

In his correspondence of fifteen years (1785–1800) there is almost no letter of wise counsel or of insight or interest in the nature of the future Republic, except as it affected the financial interests. His letters all those years are about schemes and deals and the minutiae of collections, payments, and market prices. Most of them could be dated any one of the years, and are full of either overblown optimism or uncertainty, self-deception, and vague promises of future payments.

Most men of the time made no secret of their love of indolence but Morris was like the modern businessman who boasts he has not had a vacation in twenty years and who gives his personal attention to every detail—asking Tench Tilghman if three hundred pipes of good Nantes brandy lying in New York could be sold in Baltimore, telling Wadsworth his offer for the tea cargo "squeezes too close," airily asserting the protest of his drafts on Paris had "nothing to do with me really."

In 1785 his partnerships included one in the merchant-banking business which Tench Tilghman, of Washington's staff, had opened in Baltimore. The capital, supposed to be Morris's, was actually Tilghman's, Morris's contribution being his name and a first refusal to Tilghman on any business for Baltimore. When Tilghman died in '86 Morris wrote two letters to young Thomas Tilghman the same day, one of hasty condolence, the other telling him "candidly of many pressing applications and advantageous offers made by intimate friends and acquaintances and by well-established houses in Baltimore to obtain the preference of my business. . . ."

There would be something ghoulish about the letter if it were not for Morris's innate friendliness and generosity. A man like him could only have written it under great financial strain. Even when he wrote creditors for more time he did so with aplomb. With others he was still the Maecenas of the Moneybags.

Fittingly enough, almost the only "sharp" letters he ever wrote were three to Horatio Gates, whom he disliked from recollections of the old Cabal. Gates apparently wrote him in the mistaken belief Morris would be pleased to be of service.

In October 1784, Morris wrote, "I have not seen Mr. Willing [his former partner] nor could I spare time to apply to him respecting the certificates you lodged in the bank." In February '86 he wrote he was glad to have Gates as a stockholder in the bank. All Gates had to do was to pay the subscription to William Alexander and Company in Richmond and they would draw on Morris. "I cannot spare the time necessary to supporting a regular correspondence." The next year he wrote he could not collect interest for Gates. He wished for ease for himself "as much as anybody can do."

How does it happen that a man of Washington's discernment offered the Treasury post in his Cabinet to this tired, overburdened man, up to his neck in debts and deals, his Revolutionary accounts still unsettled, and the stories of his private enrichment from the war constantly spreading? He was bound to be unpopular with the agrarian opposition. He had not spoken at the Constitutional Convention, having no grasp of the great issues with which the delegates were concerned.

The *Dictionary of American Biography* says the offer was made. The author of that sketch, Professor Oberholtzer, had said so in his Morris biography, as had Professor William Graham Sumner in his. Of such "authorities" there could surely be no doubt, and earlier William C. Rives in his "standard" *Life* of Madison had said, "In the organization of the new government [Morris] was invited by the president Washington to take the important post of Secretary of the Treasury which his impaired health compelled him to decline." The story comes down to the present-day Nathan Schachner, writing in his *Alexander Hamilton,* "The logical man was Robert Morris. Washington took the logical step and offered him the post. But Morris declined. . . ."

Yet the more one thinks of it, the more unlikely it seems that Washington could have done so foolish a thing, however much personal regard he had for Morris. Further research revealed that apparently no one of the time had ever commented on the offer in a letter, and there was strong negative evidence that no one knew about it. Senator Maclay, Madison, or Monroe would surely have had his say about it. The Washington *Writings* do not mention it nor is there reference to it in the Morris Letters and Papers at San Marino.

Looking back, however, we find a footnote on page 204 of the second volume of Sumner's biography of Morris. It reads *Custis, 349.* The reference is to the *Recollections of George Washington Parke Custis,* that book which perhaps, next to Weems's, has contributed most to the myths of American history.

On page 349 we find one of those conversations which never took place. It is worth quoting in full in view of its wide acceptance.

In 1789 when the first president was on his way to the seat of the new government, he stopped in Philadelphia at the house of Robert Morris and while consulting with that eminent patriot and benefactor of America as to the members of the first Cabinet, Washington observed "The Treasury, Morris, will of course be your berth. After your invaluable services as financier of the Revolution no one can pretend to contest the office of the Secretary of the Treasury with you."

Robert Morris respectfully but firmly declined the appointment on the ground of his private affairs and then said, "But, my dear General, you will be no loser by my declining Secretary of the Treasury for I can recommend to you a far cleverer fellow than I am for your Minister of Finance in the person of your Aide de Camp, Colonel Hamilton."

Custis says the President was amazed and continued, "I always knew Colonel Hamilton to be a man of superior talents but never supposed that he had any knowledge of finance." Of such incredible nonsense has the myth been made.

During the Constitutional Convention, to which he was a delegate, Morris was the host to Washington. He sat silent during the whole great proceedings, even then, as he wrote Gates, "A man teazed with a great deal more business than I like." Yet to the general world he managed still to present his breezy, assured front—a prince of good fellows over wine and cigars. Few travelers of note passing through Philadelphia failed to crack a pot with him. "I had a joyous evening with him at Ben Levy's who keeps on at the old, idle way, merry and hearty," Richard Carson wrote Gates. With Anthony Wayne and Thomas Fitzsimons, a fellow banker whom he ruined, Morris characteristically stood out against the suppression of theaters in Philadelphia. They were, Morris said, "rational, instructive and innocent amusement. I cannot but deem it rather hard that gentlemen of the Country should wish to debar citizens of an amusement of which they bear the whole expense."

With the formation of the national government he went to New York as senator from Pennsylvania. Jeremiah Wadsworth, going to the House from Connecticut, warned Edmund Randolph, the Attorney General, that Morris was already "in want," a prophetic warning for Randolph, as it turned out.

To the other Pennsylvania senator, Maclay, the diarist, Morris was "the greatest blackguard in the way [of depravity] I ever heard open a mouth," and John Adams, seeing him at "The Republican Court," was revolted by him and his cronies, though it must be said for little better reason than that in the evening they sat and smoked, drank and gossiped about the ladies like the traditional clubmen of a century later.

In Morris's mind there must have been considerable business sagacity but it was "teazed away" in speculations which were "sure things" that never paid off. Had he been content with the profits of his merchant-banking business, he would have left a considerable fortune. But almost uniquely among the patriot leaders, "he carried his arrogance and pride of wealth and his habits of display and luxury to a degree of assumption unbecoming a private man"—as Plutarch said of Philotas, Alexander's officer.

His senatorial career was mainly notable for his unsuccessful effort to have the national capital built on land he owned along the Delaware. Very shortly his time was consumed in new promises "to pay with interest," or borrowings from Peter to pay Paul. Yet remembering all the Continental officers and members of Congress, including Washington himself on occasion, who were carried on his books during the Revolution, there is pathos in a letter of his of 1790: "I must confess that my feelings are equally wounded. I lent money very freely to my acquaintances whilst I had it to spare but now when I want it back, my convenience is not consulted."

It is a measure of his decline that, having been a partner of the always rich and eminently respectable Thomas Willing, he sank by 1794 to a partnership with John Nicholson.

It is a commonplace of psychiatry to say of a suicide that he has been committing suicide for twenty years, meaning that the final act was not the impulse of a moment. It perfectly applies to the quarter of a century during which Robert Morris committed moral and financial suicide. And doubtless its origins were much further back.

In June 1776, happily married to a beautiful wife, a partner of Willing & Morris, merchants and bankers, Morris, at forty-two, had only, as credit reports say, "to give strict attention to their affairs" to be a man of stable wealth and renown.

Instead he began that summer, while a Pennsylvania delegate to the Continental Congress which was framing the Declaration, the long course of tangled scheming, of big deals, the details of which even today are all but incomprehensible.

Fifty-six famous men signed the Declaration that summer, but two of them at least, Morris and Carter Braxton of Virginia, were far more engrossed in their own than their country's interests. The "scheme" which they set up was a matter of mutual dispute and distrust, until finally in 1788 it became a matter of suit and countersuit, in which neither jurors nor arbitrators could establish what were the facts.

Braxton, born in 1736, was a Virginia gentleman two years younger than Morris and a man, so Sanderson said in his *Biographies of the Signers*, "of mild and philanthropic disposition . . . never as happy as when associated with his wife," by whom he had nineteen children. In February '76 he was appointed to the Continental Congress, to fill the place of Peyton Randolph, and except for this accident of being a Signer had no other claim to political prominence. His first term was his last.

In the briefs which they filed against each other in '88, the two men said a great deal about each other and each tried to make clear that he had been the somewhat naïve victim of the other's wild plans.

Morris said the connection began in the summer of '76 and was entered into by Braxton "with a view to his benefit."

It is extraordinary to think of their scheming as the Declaration was debated. Fittingly enough, their signatures to it are adjoining: Braxton's the last of the Virginia delegation at the bottom of the third column; Morris's heading the Pennsylvania delegation in the fourth column, Rush and Franklin following him. One almost feels, studying the facsimile, that both of them had to be squeezed in; in Morris's case that the Delaware signers had left no room for him except at the top of the Pennsylvania group.

If their correspondence is attentively read, Morris says, "One fact must have struck the attention . . . [that on the part of Morris] there was the utmost and most unsuspecting confidence and in consequence of it an easy (too easy) acquiescence in proposals of any and every kind from Braxton . . . the correspondence abounds with professions of esteem and attachment and contains every assurance that all funds [advanced by Morris] were duly applied to proper objects and *combined with equivalent of C.B.*"

Before the end of June '77, Braxton had become possessed of funds from Morris "of above 16,000 pounds paper, equal to 12,500 pounds specie, besides $40,000 sent him by Morris for the use of the [United States]."

In spite of this his calls for money had been "loud and urgent" by the end of '76 and on January 3, 1777, he "declared his money and credit were almost exhausted." By March, Morris says, Braxton was in arrears over £7500. By June there had been time for money to be coming back to Braxton but "he was under the necessity of borrowing from Mr. Harrison (which in other words was borrowing from Willing, Morris and Company, Mr. Harrison being their agent)."

The brief then makes clear that the original plan had been (put briefly) for Braxton to act in effect as a government purchasing agent in Virginia. Morris, in Congress, would secure the contracts. Congress would advance the money to Morris (no doubt after he had loaned it to them), who would advance it to Braxton.

But, declares Morris, the wicked Braxton "was drawing for supplies bought for the United States, altho already paid in advance."

As to that, Morris righteously declares that although he "neither claims nor wishes any convenience, much less *any advantage* [his italics] from the Public Money placed with Braxton he may justly insist that he should sustain no loss thereby, but yet this has happened." Braxton's debit balance or overdraft or unaccounted-for advances was and is now £16,000.

The brief was, of course, long after the event. There can be no doubt that at the start both parties desired every "convenience" and "advantage" from the public money and that had the scheme gone as they planned, with only quick profits to divide, the pair would have remained fast friends.

Braxton's reply begins calmly with the well-put statement that "the papers are so complicated and separated that it is with difficulty the matters contained in them can be brought into view at one and the same point." The papers referred to are the transcripts of ledger pages from both sides, from which it appears that from 1776 to 1781 there was never an agreed balance between the two. The bookkeeping was partly on an account sales (i.e., charging all direct expenses to a transaction, determining the profit or loss, and transferring it to an account current; in other cases expenses, such as weighing, grading, packing, were charged to the account current with no reference as to what they applied to). Prior to the case going to the courts, one of the two or three brightest minds in the country, Gouverneur Morris, went to Virginia to try to get an agreed stipulation of facts. Braxton thought well of this, "it being the object that right may take place effectively and without delay."

Besides all this, it is obvious both parties commingled their own, the other's, and the public's funds, and that the latter, though earmarked for a specific purchase, were used for a "quick turnover" to be replaced later. It is not too much to say that thieves fell out.

Braxton, in an explanation which does not explain, says airily, "It has frequently happened that we differed as to the quantum of advances." Before making his case, Braxton demurs at Morris's claim that Braxton went into it originally "with a view to his benefit."

In righteous anger he writes, "The remark ushering in his whole reasoning and being so plainly intended to deceive and divert your knowledge from the true state of things is pursued by similar attempts thro' the whole of his voluminous production and it shall be my task to detect and expose them."

In December 1776, Braxton says, "I was appointed to purchase tobacco for the Army," and then continues, "As to Robert Morris's insinuation that I paid a part of this money . . . to answer my own ends and all the reasoning therefrom of fine-spun deductions I shall say they are hatched by the fertile brain of a gentleman well versed in specious and gilded argument but will not bear the test of truth."

He then refers to Morris's claim that, outside the contract, Braxton received "separate advances and friendly offices" *ex gratia.* Well, says Braxton, "if they are to be called favors, aren't they such as can be repaid merely with thanks?"

"Is it not melancholy," he asks, "to see one of the first characters of America practicing so much evasion, such elusion to vacate a most solemn contract?"

And what, he asks, of these irregularities Morris charges him with? "In '77 [Morris] endeavors to sacrifice my interest by making me expend *my own money sent by Congress* [author's italics] to answer his joint purpose of paying for Flour, Pork and then to account to Congress for the value at that date in tobacco."

In that sentence he puts his finger on the business methods and morals of his partner, the Patriot Financier. During and after the war, whether in government contracts or land speculation, Morris's ability to complicate a simple transaction, to postpone settlement by the addition of ancillary deals, defies understanding except as chicanery. Yet there is small doubt that his purpose was never deliberately dishonest —and if all had gone well would have shown that "extra profit."

Braxton says further that in August '78 (when Morris was re-established in Philadelphia after the British evacuation) Morris "purchased some protested bills of mine from Virginia which he says increases his advance and instead [as a friend and partner might have been expected to do] of settling them as paper at the time. He now demands them as part of a Bond for Sterling money with accumulated interest altho it will appear he was then greatly in my debt."

And then "to crown the whole after all these things he assumes a right of converting Paper Money into pounds sterling—then by his process of trans-substantiation, gold is turned into paper and paper into gold, as if he had the power of Midas himself and having done all this he tells you his money is secured by a fictitious Bond and is out of your reach."

Braxton deserves no sympathy but in that sentence he has summed up Robert Morris. He died in 1797 or he might also have set G. W. P. Custis right about Morris.

His brief in his own hand is thirty folio pages, all so complicated by cross reference as to be insoluble from an accounting point of view. Toward the end of it, one senses how outrage has exhausted him. As to small items or differences in dispute, phrases such as "normal error" or "this is merely an error of clerkship" are used. Anything to get it over with.

Thus two of the Founding Fathers, Signers of the Declaration, sent their charges and countercharges of fraud, duplicity, and malfeasance to arbitration. Men of opposing views like Monroe and Gouverneur Morris knew that the worst was true of both. Through the turnover of everyday business in cargoes and currency—and by the outward impression of wealth from his way of living, Robert Morris was able to hang on, making "great progress in taking up such bills as are most pressing on him," Richard Carson, a Baltimore businessman, wrote Gates. Washington himself wanted his nephew to join Tench Tilghman, who was not in a "piddling way being associated with Mr. Robert Morris." Thomas McKean, Chief Justice of Pennsylvania, recommended Peter Whitesides, a man of Morris-Braxton money morals, to John Adams in London because "he has been concerned in trade here with Mr. Robert Morris and is reputed a skillful merchant and a good citizen." Tench Coxe, pressing John Nicholson, shortly to be Robert Morris's partner, "to send in any part of his debt which he can make it convenient to pay today [May 5, 1788]," assured Madison the next year that Robert Morris would be favorable if Madison proposed Coxe for Postmaster General. Failing in that, he was sure of Morris's backing (and sure it was important) to be Assistant Secretary of the Treasury. Actually when it came up Senator Maclay recorded that Morris "spoke against Coxe with great asperity."

The dissolution of Morris's partnership with Thomas Willing and his subsequent one with John Nicholson is a good deal as though he had, at the height of their power, left J. P. Morgan and Company under pressure to go in business with the comptroller general of New York, under indictment for malfeasance in office.

Seen in retrospect, a whole process of what is now called after-education, the re-creating of an individual, would have been necessary to save Morris from ruin as early as 1781, and even if he had been able to become a new man, someone like Gouverneur Morris would have had to achieve financial miracles in clearing up his affairs.

While there was no hope for him, he went to his final ruin with the worst possible associate in the person of John Nicholson, a man like him in every defect of character but evidently without the breezy, rather attractive front which Morris was so long able to maintain. The two of them deceived their creditors, deceived each other and above all lived in a Mulberry Sellers haze of conviction that "something would turn up," wherein they completely deceived themselves.

And with the inevitableness of Greek tragedy they involved Edmund Randolph with them in the fatal year, 1795, and, it appears, made it impossible for him to vindicate himself because of what had happened between them.

The federal government had moved to Philadelphia when,

in 1791, the Pennsylvania legislature brought charges against the state comptroller general, John Nicholson, for improper conduct of a financial nature.

Nicholson immediately asked Edmund Randolph, the Attorney General of the United States, to act as his counsel. This was not preposterous as under the law at the time, and as an offset to his salary of $1500, half that of the other three Cabinet members, the Attorney General was allowed to engage in private practice. On July 31, Randolph replied with a remarkable combination of honor and good sense. It is a splendid letter, in tragic contrast to those of four years later.

"I am much indebted to you for your politeness in selecting me as your counsel and I greatly regret that I do not feel myself at liberty to give an opinion upon the subject you hinted to me.

"Being the law-officer of the United States I must weigh the use to which my opinion is to be applied. If it is destined to influence the Secretary of the Treasury I ought to reserve it until he shall consult me. If it be intended as the basis of a suit against the United States it is my peculiar duty to defend them. So that upon either ground, it would seem improper in me to yield to your wishes on this occasion."

Nicholson acquiesced and there was a long postponement of his trial. There is no corpus of Randolph papers, but the Gratz Collection, from which the above is taken, has one more letter from him to Nicholson. It is utterly trivial, declining an invitation from Nicholson to a "Philadelphia Dancing" on Washington's birthday, 1792. Yet, taken with all that follows, one has the feeling of Nicholson's desire to ingratiate himself with Randolph—a feeling he evidently never had except for ultimately selfish purposes. And it seems significant that the only record until then of Randolph's contacts with him should be to decline doing what Nicholson asks.

Randolph's private debts were already known to many. Nicholson may well have thought him purchasable. Nicholson's reputation was not of the best. Randolph doubtless thought it best to avoid all involvement.

Two years later Nicholson came to trial with William Bradford, who later succeeded Randolph as Attorney General, among his counsel of three. The trial began on February 26. That wonderful livery-stable man, Jacob Hiltzheimer, the intimate of all the great of the land, attended the trial. In his view Nicholson's counsel were each "smooth and elegant and masterly" but he said, "Arguments without facts seldom prevail." To his amazement they did and Nicholson was acquitted. On April 11, immediately afterwards, he resigned to join Robert Morris in his speculations and on the side to run a store and a glass factory of his own.

Sources: Braxton-Morris Briefs, Carter Braxton Papers, Historical Society of Pennsylvania. Morris to R. R. Livingston, R. R. Livingston Miscellaneous Mss., N.Y.P.L. Morris to Gates, Emmet Collection, N.Y.P.L., and Gates Papers, N.Y.H.S. Morris to Tilghman, Robert Morris Miscellaneous Mss., N.Y.P.L. Wadsworth to Randolph, Jeremiah Wadsworth Papers, Connecticut Historical Society. McKean to John Adams, Thomas McKean Papers, H.S.P. Randolph to Nicholson, Gratz Collection, H.S.P.

CHAPTER VII

Aristotle's Tragic Hero: EDMUND RANDOLPH

As Edmund Randolph set out for his post on Washington's staff at Cambridge in 1775, he typified the great young men of the future. Twenty-two years old, possessed of a profound and brilliant mind, a handsome presence, and the social graces of the Randolph blood, none of that marvelous group born in the fifties surpassed him. Who indeed at the time equaled him? Yet twenty years later he was forced by circumstances he could not explain to resign as Secretary of State. By then he was the counterpart of Aristotle's tragic hero—a man highly renowned whose misfortune is brought upon him not by vice and depravity but by some error of judgment or human frailty.

Debt was the incurable cancer that destroyed him. Given "a competence," as they called private means, it seems almost certain he would have left a name in the first rank of renown and honor. On the other hand, how could a man of such talents and opportunities fail to achieve a competence? The excuse of an invalid wife has been offered, but when has a real man offered it?

Debt, domestic affliction, ill luck—none fully explains his downfall. Rather do we see at the very start of his career the error of judgment, at work in an otherwise sensible man. And in what in effect was the second great occasion of his life in 1787 we see it again, until he was caught in a Niagara of decisions where all judgment was lost.

In the first months of the Revolution no army problem was more pressing than competent staff work at headquarters. Two of the four original A.D.C.s—Moylan and Baylor—were brave but not very good soldiers, and at headquarters were worse than useless. Reed was capable but badly balanced. Webb, "fond of company, of gaiety," was of no consequence. When Randolph, with his trained mind, his ability to write and think, joined them he was indeed an answer to the Commander's prayers. But before Christmas, 1775, his uncle Peyton Randolph died and this young man resigned at once, returned to Virginia to take care of the estate, and never bore arms again. Seldom has a man thrown away such chances and never has a country more greatly needed their young men. Contrast the act with the careers of Hamilton, McHenry, Tilghman, Harrison, and the others who saw the British evacuate Boston that St. Patrick's Day and Cornwallis's troops lay down their arms at Yorktown. In 1776, Randolph married Elizabeth Nicholas of Virginia. His non-combatant war record was as valuable as such careers are, but for a man in his early twenties it was a disgrace.

In 1787 he came to the Federal Convention as a member of the seven-man delegation from Virginia, of which he was then governor. He, more even than Madison, was the author of the Virginia Plan, from which so much of the Constitution was finally drawn. Then, doubtless from principle, though it would seem a capricious one, he refused to sign the Constitution, though his fellow delegates, Washington, Madison, and Blair—together with thirty-six other patriot leaders—considered that its merits outweighed its defects. Nor can his opposition have been profound, as he immediately worked to have Virginia ratify it against the opposition of such men as Patrick Henry and George Mason.

It is interesting to see how meticulous as to propriety Randolph was even then in his official papers, in later contrast to his private ones. There is no reason to suggest hypocrisy in this. There is small if any doubt of his desire to do "the right thing," though one does get the feeling that he is somehow compensating, as the psychologists say.

There is a letter from him to Thomas McKean, Chief Justice of Pennsylvania, written while the Convention was in session. "I concur with you," he writes, "in thinking that the trial of the pirates now in your gaol will be conducted with a better hope of conviction in Virginia. But I consider myself as wholely divested of executive authority while I remain out of my own country [i.e., I cannot authorize the expense of sending them there but urge you to continue them in custody while I write to the lieutenant governor]." Certainly it shows a fine sense of the limitations of authority as to "expense," but certainly also it is a refinement of hairsplitting.

With the inauguration of the federal government, Washington appointed him to be Attorney General, a post a shade below Cabinet rank though above the Postmaster General, who was a purely administrative officer.

As Randolph was about to leave for New York he wrote a letter of guidance for James Madison, who with three others were to act as his trustees. In it he said, "I consign to the humanity of James Madison [etc.] the protections of my poor slaves in and near Williamsburg." It is a rather fine touch for the times, though qualified by the careful next sentence: "By protections I mean only that they should see justice done to them in case they shall be ill-treated by persons having no authority over them."

As Attorney General, Randolph said he was "a sort of mongrel between the States and the U.S.," adding that he would have been wiser to keep "at home to encounter my pecuniary difficulties there, rather than add to them here." His work was well done. He tried in vain to bring the federal district attorneys under his instead of Jefferson's authority and "in advance of his time" wished his office to be "the federal agency for the enforcement of Federal law."

When the Supreme Court told Washington, who had asked its advice on a series of legal problems, that advice was not a judicial function but that of the Attorney General, Jefferson demanded that a separate board be established. Randolph insisted successfully that it be attached to his office and Jefferson complained that "in plain language this [makes] him sole arbiter of the line of conduct of the U.S."

Despite these contests, Randolph in general Cabinet opinions frequently sided with Jefferson against Hamilton and Knox.

Nonetheless, Jefferson seems to have had that sneering contempt, so characteristic of him in private, for Randolph, "the poorest cameleon I ever saw having no colour of his own and reflecting that nearest him." "The fact is [Randolph] has generally given his principles to one party and his practice to another . . . whether his conduct is to be ascribed to a superior view of things, an adherence to right without regard to party, as he pretends, or to an anxiety to trim between both, those who know his character and capacity will decide."

As to trimming between them both, Jefferson himself had great trouble when Washington, through Randolph, recalled and dismissed Jefferson's protégé, Monroe, as Minister to France, only to have Randolph's resignation as Secretary of State drive him into uneasy alliance with Monroe.

Nonetheless, on his own earlier resignation Jefferson recommended Randolph as his successor. He quoted Washington as saying, "I do not know that he is fit for it," and he himself spoke "of the serious embarrassment in Randolph's private affairs," alleging that even his merchandise creditors had deprived him of all independence.

But, in 1794, Randolph became Secretary of State and was

succeeded by William Bradford of New Jersey, son-in-law of Elias Boudinot, as Attorney General.

With fatal portent one of his first messages was to Thomas Mifflin, governor of Pennsylvania, reading, "It gives me pain to inform Your Excellency that Fauchet [the French Minister] believes he has reason to complain of the treatment French prizes too often receive."

Meanwhile in Philadelphia Robert Morris and John Nicholson pursued their incredible business. None knew better than they the financial plight of the Secretary of State, but it is doubtful if he had any realization, until late in the spring, of the even greater desperation in which they were living.

On February 4, 1795, Morris wrote Nicholson, apparently at his house nearby, "If you can, step hither for ten minutes that we may fix on the two hundred thousand acres of Pennsylvania lands and on the other tracts for the schedule. I think it would greatly forward our friend's project.

"You must come instantly or I shall be gone."

This was evidently a day when there were "millions in it," and the pot of gold was visible. The skies were darker in March when Morris wrote, "A new storm is rising that if not allayed may revise our *Plan* [his italics]. No time is to be lost. The blame will be yours but the sufferings we shall all feel—— Consultation is necessary and that immediately."

We turn now to John Nicholson's Letter Books for March ten days later. On the twenty-fourth he writes the Secretary of State that a vessel of his has been attached at Alexandria and asks him how under the laws of Virginia the cargo can be sold.

Three days later he sends him the bylaws of the Association of the Asylum Company "which we talked about this morning." There is good reason to believe the Asylum Company and the North American Land Company comprise "our *Plan*" in Morris's second letter and that Randolph was "our friend" in the first.

The contemporary booklets setting forth the purposes and bylaws of both are in existence (both, incidentally, printed by Aitken, who printed the Journals of the Continental Congress and was so mysteriously involved with their sequestering during the British occupation of Philadelphia in '78).

The Asylum Company is an "impressive" agreement between "Robert Morris, Senator from Pennsylvania in the Senate of the U.S., and John Nicholson, former Comptroller General." It contemplates "the settling and improving of one or more tracts of Pennsylvania lands" up to one million acres. Stock units are for two hundred acres at one shilling. The company will have a Board of Managers (the president and four others) and a quorum shall be the president and any two. The Managers *may* employ a secretary, treasurer, and surveyors, buy and sell lands, but *must* issue financial statements every six months, on which dates dividends are to be declared. The life of the Association is to be fifteen years. While the Managers may do all that may be necessary, it is clear they are the servants of the investors and as such promotional schemes like to do, then and now, it is pointed out that moneys received and land titles are in the custody of eminent and disinterested trustees–in this case Thomas Willing himself, Jared Ingersoll, the state attorney general, and Matthew Clarkson, the mayor of Philadelphia.

Four days after he received the brochure, Randolph was asked by Nicholson to become a trustee, with the proviso that if the federal government were in any way involved he would not be asked to continue.

The trusteeship was a sinecure with handsome fees but no participation in profits. Even so Randolph apparently hesitated. He was very busy those weeks over the Jay Treaty, which he was so cogently defending to Monroe, the Minister to Paris, as being neither offensive nor defensive, nor in any way to the detriment of France. However, on April 21, Nicholson reminded him that "you had said you would go ahead if there was no impropriety [and not having heard to the contrary] I have so designated you and you have acquired title therefore to about 300,000 acres near Knoxville."

The next day Nicholson bought out Robert Morris and his associates and the whole control was vested in him. The reason for this is not definite but reasonably clear. For one thing the only "up to one million acres" was a limiting factor. In February, Morris, Nicholson, and James Greenleaf, "ex-counsel of the U.S. in Amsterdam," had formed the North American Land Company, which could go "up to six million acres" in Pennsylvania, Virginia, the Carolinas, Georgia, and Kentucky. Its corporate form followed the Asylum Company's. Among the trustees was David Rittenhouse, and on May 9, Nicholson wrote Randolph he had spoken to him "on the subject we this day mentioned. He is very reserved in naming any person he would prefer to succeed him." Evidently Nicholson intended that Randolph should be on both boards.

One cannot of course be sure of exactly what objects Randolph and Nicholson had in view. Getting an eminent man to serve as "trustee" was a normal piece of good business, but it so quickly became something else, it is hard to escape the conclusion that both men contemplated improper advantages. Certainly the hard-pressed Secretary of State did not go into it to befriend an even harder-pressed promoter. More was afoot but exactly what we cannot be sure.

However, on May 21, Nicholson wrote Randolph, "In case the bills are paid which I believe is the case, will it suit you to pay the remainder of the sum due for them. [Had Nicholson allowed Randolph to have some of his creditors draw on Nicholson who had accepted or endorsed on long terms, gotten the drafts discounted, thus satisfying the creditor?] I am in extreme want or I would not now trouble you. [This must have been a shock to Randolph. There had been no intimation of it from Nicholson.]"

On the twenty-seventh he wrote again. "Any money you can give me today, be the same more or less on account, you may class as given to charitable purposes—do let me have a check from you for some. I am in great distress."

On the thirtieth Nicholson writes again. "If you can help me to the $3,600 this morning you believe [sic] if you give me any part you serve me so far." This is the first mention of a definite sum. Later the same day he wrote again, "Will it be in your power to send me some mo [sic] this day?"

Randolph made no reply. It was the day he was writing thirty magnificent, lucid pages of legal cap in his own hand to Monroe, pointing out that the complaints being made to him by Hammond, the British Minister, and Fauchet, the French, about the Jay Treaty were identical and that therefore neither side had been favored. Strangely fitting is the end of the letter. The President wishes to know if Madame Lafayette received the money he sent her from his private purse. (Lafayette had deserted to the Austrians and been imprisoned by them. The marquise was in peril and penury in France.) "We shall endeavor to do something for her out of the Marquis's money [here] if it has not been absorbed."

The dispatch went on the thirty-first. Apparently on the next day, June 1, Randolph sent for Nicholson and told him he had no funds with which to pay him or to loan him money, whichever it was.

In spite of the calm reasoning and judicious argument of the dispatches to Monroe it seems obvious that in private he was in desperation, because he proposed an incredible alternative, whether to save himself or to assist Nicholson we cannot be sure. Nor is it crystal-clear what he did propose but on June 2 Nicholson wrote him, "I find it will be an advantage to me to have the bill on Mr. [Thomas] Pinckney [American Minister in London about to leave there as special envoy to Madrid] which I did not consider when I saw you. . . . You will let me have it if you please."

It appears almost positive from a subsequent letter (July 1) that the words "bill on" are a slip of the pen. A "bill on" in the nomenclature of the times is a bill or draft "payable by," and it is difficult to find a normal reason why Randolph or the government should draw *on* Pinckney, but every natural reason why they should be remitting *to* him for salary, legation maintenance, and travel expenses across France to Madrid.

It is conceivable that they drew on him for accumulated "consular revenues"—that is, fees for visas, ship clearance, etc.—but it seems most unlikely that they would bring sterling home only to remit it to him again. As will later be seen, it is reasonable to believe Nicholson meant to write "letter of credit" instead of "bill on."

If that is true, what Randolph evidently said to him on the first was, "I have no funds I can offer you but I have this letter of credit ready to go to Pinckney. Is there any way you could negotiate something under it temporarily and let me have it back in full shortly?"

Nicholson apparently saw no way that day but on thinking it over, possibly talking it over with Robert Morris, a method of misuse occurred to him. Just what it could have been is hard to say but what hard-pressed men can do with money is sometimes miraculous.

He wrote Randolph the next day, "If you will prepare the Bill for the $6,000 in the morning I will thank you as I want it for the [packet] William Penn—and on your giving me your note for the stock I will pay you the $3,000." We are still in the dark as to the details of this arrangement, but it appears that Randolph had committed himself to the purchase of stock (in the Asylum Company?) for $3000 and that, having no funds with which to pay, he offered Nicholson a bill on, or a letter of credit in favor of, Thomas Pinckney for $6000. It would appear that the only way Nicholson could have gotten money under the letter of credit was to have forged Thomas Pinckney's name on a draft. While he was quite capable of it—always in the belief he would put it right in time—he evidently did not do so, or the fact would have later arisen. It seems likely that he took the credit to some second-rate dealer in commercial paper, telling him with much éclat that he was now the issuing agent for State Department funds abroad and casually getting a note of his own discounted while he talked. "Oh, by the way, just discount this, if you will."

Early on the morning of June 5 he sent a messenger to Randolph. "The [mail] bag of the William Penn goes away at 12 o'clock today. If the Letter be ready, the Bearer will receive it." It was not ready. In midmorning he sent again. "Excuse my urgency—the ship is fallen down [the river] and I am to send a person down with the letter. If you will send it I'll thank you and when you send me your note for the stock as agreed I'll send you the $3,000 cash I am to pay you and thank you."

Still no answer, and at noonday another incoherent note:

If it can't be sent till the cash be sent—say $3,000—I can't take the bill by the William Penn for I must have it [the cash] this afternoon—but I depended on the note as agreed to raise the same in part.

P.S. I'll make a statement of the stock by tomorrow morning but that will be too late unless you can entrust me till tomorrow for the balance of the bill.

It seems evident that he must have the bill, the credit, at least to show if he is to raise any cash.

There is a final note of frantic repetition from Nicholson that day: "I received yours just now but it will be impossible to raise the $3,000 tonight. If I were now in the possession of the note—[which Randolph has evidently refused]—I will make the statement of the stock in the morning."

Whatever the skulduggery was, it is clear that Randolph improperly "loaned" Nicholson a Pinckney document but as late as June 16 had not given his note for his stock. Nicholson wrote him that day: "Enclosed is account of stock at the market price. Your note at 60 days per bearer will help me out for $780.23." Until now all the pressure and importunity appears to have come from Nicholson, but on the eighteenth Randolph wrote him, "E.R. prays Mr. N. to deliver him from the difficulty which he incurs every half hour. He knows that E.R. would not urge him but for reasons which are *officially* indispensable."

What can this letter mean? *Officially* is in Randolph's italics. It suggests very strongly that "every half hour" someone has been in to ask, "What was the disposition of the Pinckney credit? Did it go by the *William Penn?* Have you found it? Was it mislaid?" But if so who was the person? It would be natural to suppose it was Wolcott, Secretary of the Treasury, or a member of his staff. It would solve a great deal if that were true. But unfortunately—as regards a solution—it was not Wolcott. Under the law of the time Randolph himself "personally disbursed the funds provided for diplomatic and consular services." And as to those funds, after Randolph had left the Department, an amount of $49,154.89 was found to be unaccounted for. The fact of its being open did not mean he had stolen it but how much of it was lost at sea and how much was misappropriated is still not clear.

To Randolph's note in the third person Nicholson replied on the twentieth, "I delayed . . . intending to make the payment and answer together. This I am not able to do today and am sorry it is so."

Not until July 1 was some sort of a balance struck when Nicholson sent Randolph this statement of *Balance Due for Letter of Credit received of you.*

June 6	1,285 pounds, say		6,000
	By cash	1,000	
	By cash	1,600	
	In note	3,000	
	Balance	400	

In all old accounts of this kind, care must be exercised to be sure there is not a transposition of debits and credits but this appears to say Nicholson received a letter of credit worth $6000 from Randolph and credited him with it. That Nicholson made two cash payments totaling $2600 against it and gave a note for $3000. (Was the note he wanted from Randolph a wash-transaction, a piece of check kiting?) But it does not say what became of the letter of credit.

The next day Nicholson wrote, "I hoped to have sent the $400 balance but alas all my resources failed me. I hope to send it today."

On July 28 he told Randolph of some local land he had had to mortgage "to secure the payment of some bills *in Calcutta in Asia.*" The italics are his and one feels he is telling Randolph that time and place are so remote everything will be arranged by the time the bills come home.

Actually time was running out very fast for Randolph. That very night Secretary Wolcott was telling Pickering of what Hammond, the British Minister, had told him two nights before.

The Cabinet were alone in Philadelphia. Following the long-delayed ratification of the Jay Treaty by the Senate, Washington had left for Mount Vernon at 8 A.M. the morning of the fifteenth. Jacob Hiltzheimer saw him drive off and himself went sea bathing on the Jersey coast. Had he not, and his heirs not destroyed most of his diary, we should be less in the dark on all this.

At dinner the afternoon of the twenty-sixth Hammond had given Secretary Wolcott a dispatch of Fauchet, the French Minister, written the October previous and taken off a French packet by a British cruiser in the Mediterranean. In it Fauchet told his government that Randolph, the Secretary of State, had opened the way to receive a bribe from Fauchet in return for influence Randolph would exercise in favor of France. Hammond left the original dispatch with Wolcott.

It will be noted that Wolcott waited until the second day to tell Pickering, the Secretary of War, and that they in turn waited another day until they went to the house of William

Bradford, the Attorney General, to tell him. There is every indication that they were reluctant to believe Fauchet, but that all three of them, strong and decent men, were sure Randolph was guilty. One wonders whether the business of Thomas Pinckney's credit was known to Wolcott. They talked to Bradford on the twenty-ninth, and apparently frequently to each other the two following days. On the thirty-first Pickering on their behalf wrote Washington "in extreme solicitude" that he must return at once "for a special reason. This letter is for your eye alone."

On the twenty-ninth Randolph, "in spite of an enfeebling disorder," wrote Monroe "by the vessel that will carry Fauchet" back to France from Newport. He strongly denounced Fauchet as an intriguer. Fauchet had dined with him on the day Hammond dined with Wolcott.

Washington did not reach Philadelphia until August 11. On the seventh Randolph had written Nicholson, "You must excuse me but upon my honour I am embarrassed and tortured by the situation into which I am thrown by the omission to satisfy the balance. My confidence was and is great in you but I have no resources and as a public man you ought not to leave me in this predicament." This must mean that Nicholson still owes the $400 of the July 1 statement, and may well also mean (sixty days having passed) that Nicholson's note for $3000, part of the offset to the letter of credit, has not been paid.

It seems apparent that as soon as Washington heard the accusations he believed they were true. According to Pickering, writing twenty-odd years later, he learned of them in this way. Hearing that he had arrived, Pickering went to his house to find Randolph already there, having a glass of wine with the President. Washington "rose, giving me a wink. I rose, and followed him into another room. 'What,' said he, 'is the cause of your writing me such a letter?' 'That man,' said I, 'in the other room,' pointing towards that in which we had left Randolph, 'is a traitor.'" It must have been a bitter blow to

Washington privately to have two New Englanders bring such charges against his fellow Virginian, charges paralleled only by the West Point betrayal. There is no evidence that Washington said, "But this can't be true." We do know that what he did was to prepare one of his typical plans of action in his own hand. "At what time should Mr. F——'s letter be made known to Mr. R.? What will be the best mode of doing it? In the presence of the Secretaries and the Attorney General? What immediate steps are necessary to be taken, so soon as the removal of Mr. R. is resolved upon . . . with respect to the archives of that office?"

On the thirteenth Nicholson appealed to De Noailles, the rich French émigré, for $3000 for Randolph. Noailles replied, "I would lend you the sum you wish with the greatest satisfaction but I am obliged as you will see by the enclosure to pay this day at the bank $2,980–I feel really distressed I cannot do what you desire."

Not until the nineteenth was Randolph faced with the charges. That morning it was known that the *Thisbe* had sailed from New York for London on the seventeenth and that Hammond was aboard with the ratification of the treaty. Randolph's signature had been necessary and they had not dared move against him lest they risk his refusal to sign. On the fourteenth Washington, according to Randolph's advocate Conway, "disregarding the etiquette so carefully observed" as to visiting no one, went to Randolph's house and "dandled the children on his knee," to flatter the Secretary so that he would sign. Randolph must have been puzzled at what there was in the air to keep the President in Philadelphia in the very week of the wedding of his former secretary Tobias Lear to his niece Fanny Bassett Washington.

According to Randolph, writing a few months later in his *Vindication*, he went to the President as usual at nine in the morning on the nineteenth. He was asked by Mr. Rawle, the chief usher, to return at ten-thirty. He did so and then learned that Colonel Pickering and Mr. Wolcott had been upstairs for some time. Randolph supposed a Cabinet meeting had been called of which he had not heard, and he went upstairs himself. The President and the other two were there and "all rose with much formality." The President handed him a document of some fifteen pages of large paper and asked for an explanation.

Few scenes in our history can have been more truly tragic than this. Randolph above all must have wondered which of his many secrets was out.

As Wolcott recalled the scene, writing to John Marshall ten years later, "Randolph commenced reading paragraph by paragraph and though a great part of it contained nothing interesting to himself yet he commented on every part. His remarks were very desultory and it was evident he was considering what explanation he should give of the most material passages. As he was not interrupted it was, however, impossible to speak with precision on one subject while his reflections were employed on other subjects. He asserted, however, that he had never received or proposed to receive money for his own use or that of any other person. . . . [He asked for a moment to consider in private and left the room.] Mr. Randolph returned for a short time but he must have felt that neither this manner nor the matter of his explanation could afford any degree of satisfaction. . . ."

According to Randolph, the President then asked Pickering and Wolcott to question him. They declined but in any event, he said, he would not have replied to such a humiliation. He pointed out to the President that there were missing pages in those given him, but it appeared to him that Washington had been "worked up to prejudge the case" and that argument was useless.

In his subsequent writing about the charges, he several times stressed that he was being called upon "to defend a negative." By this he presumably meant that in an ordinary criminal trial the accused is presumed innocent until he is proven guilty, whereas he was being called to prove he was *not* guilty.

He therefore left, went to his offices, had his "room locked and the key given to a messenger," and sent his resignation to the President.

Was his behavior that of an innocent man falsely accused? Was he the premeditated victim of party strife and personal jealousy? Would an innocent man have "resigned under fire"? Was the resignation a matter of honor? The answer to any of these questions is very difficult.

It is incredible to the present writer that Randolph was a traitor as Pickering charged. As to whether he solicited a bribe from Fauchet, the answer is more difficult, though far more than reasonable doubt of his guilt appears to exist. On the other hand, it is equally incredible that Pickering and Wolcott desired and contrived his downfall, and preposterous that, as Moncure Conway wrote, "Oliver Wolcott was picked by Downing Street to run down Randolph," on the instructions of Hammond.

What seems most likely is that, weakened and distraught by the things such as the Pinckney-Nicholson credit which hung over him, Randolph could never do justice to his conduct. The President, Pickering, and Wolcott either knew of Nicholson or of so many similar things that they felt a presumption of guilt in the Fauchet matter. Whether strict justice was done him no one can be sure. Certainly rough justice was.

With his resignation, received August 20, the Administration was satisfied and made no effort to publish it. On the twenty-first, Randolph left for Newport, hoping to see Fauchet before he sailed.

What is said to have transpired we shall see later. Meanwhile press and public were both puzzled, unaware as they were of his resignation.

On September 14, the *New York Argus* carried the following:

Various conjectures respecting the journey of the Secretary of State to Rhode Island and his reception there have been hazarded in Boston papers. He is said to have been ill and well received by

Fauchet. It was said [Randolph] embarked and sailed for France on the Medusa—this we know to be false as he arrived in this city [New York] last Thursday [Sept. 10] and went to Philadelphia. Some say he had to impress some opinion on Fauchet but we *know* his official capacity ceased on the day it became his duty as Secretary of State to countersign the Treaty. He may have gone to add private letters or to possess papers he had no copies or a thousand other things. . . . We learn that Mr. John Bartow Prevost, accompanied Mr. Randolph from this city to New York to embark to take post as private secretary to Mr. Monroe.

On the seventeenth, the Boston correspondent of the *Argus* wrote, "We learn from good authority that Mr. Randolph was at Newport and conversed with Mr. Fauchet the whole evening previous to his sailing. Fauchet sent word he had sent answers to Randolph's question to Adet [the new Minister]. What these questions and answers are time will develop but we cannot at present conjecture."

This week, meanwhile, Nicholson was busy on his own affairs but his letters are characteristic. He writes George Beckham, "I am ashamed your debt hath lain so long—still I am money-less but I can draw Bills now on London at 90 days. Will a bill suit you?" Beckham took one the same day for £182.11.9.

Then on the nineteenth Randolph wrote the papers from Germantown, "According to the course of the mail, the original of the enclosed letter must have been delivered last night to the President of the United States. I request you therefore to publish it in your paper of today."

The letter, dated September 15, was addressed to Washington at Mount Vernon and read: "In my letter of the 19th ult. I informed you of my purpose to overtake Mr. Fauchet if possible. I accordingly went to Newport in Rhode Island where I had an interview with him. . . . I trust I am in possession of such materials not only from Mr. Fauchet but also from other sources as will convince every unprejudiced mind that my resignation was dictated by considerations which ought not to have been resisted for a moment and that everything connected with it stands upon a footing perfectly honorable to myself.

"Having passed thro' New York on my return I am under the necessity of remaining at the distance of 5 miles from Philadelphia until Saturday next [September 19, because of plague]. This circumstance prevents me from immediately consulting my private and other papers [but I shall quickly do so] as malicious whispers have been more than commonly active and absurd upon this occasion."

To this Washington replied, "No man would rejoice more than I should to find the suspicions which have resulted from the intercepted letter were unequivocally and honorably removed." His letter was dated the twenty-seventh and of course could not have been known to the *New York Argus*, which on the twenty-eighth went to the then unusual lengths of publishing its own editorial on the situation.

The resignation of the Secretary of State appears in the Gazette of the United States. An incident so unexpected naturally excited surmizes and rumors as no reasons for his removal were publicly assigned . . . his journey to Newport gave colour to reports that altho' Mr. Randolph had for wise reasons evacuated his place he was still in the President's confidence . . . [but] the public was still in the dark when a very extraordinary letter dated from Germantown the 19th September addressed by Edmund Randolph to the President of the United States appeared in a Philadelphia paper with an unceremonious request to the printer to publish it, a copy of which was in ours and we presume has been inserted in almost every newspaper in the Union. . . . It casts but "a glimmering light" upon the subject . . . maybe a threatening one as in submitting it to the inspection and judgment of the public it evidently indicates that in case of need the whole business shall be brought before their tribunal.

That "people will talk" is no new thing . . . but that it should have been malicious whispers appears to be a rather singular imputation. We certainly have no enmity to the gentleman, private or public—on the contrary we incline to a favorable opinion of him in both capacities . . . it is no derogation from this sentence to give the public what is said upon a tolerable respectable authority to have been the subject of the rumor or malicious and absurd whispers alluded to—having no doubt that Mr. R. will ere long come forward and positively clear the gloom by explaining the hidden cause of his letter.

There follows an account of the capture of the *Jean Bart* by the British near Toulon, the failure of the jettisoned dispatch bag containing the Fauchet dispatch to sink, and its salvage by the British.

Meanwhile Morris and Nicholson were going their incredible ways. Morris had sunk to a point where, on September 21, Nicholson could write him, "I wish you to agree that in case we share our wharf, the rent of any of our houses, etc., you will agree to rent or sell as I propose," and the pleas to all and sundry for petty loans (petty against the millions of debt piling up) went on: to Hopkinson for $200; to General Brodhead "to ask you to add $200 to what I owe you already seems extravagant . . . repay it and more before the close of next week"; to Mr. Tanguay: "I would I could have sent you the $40 on Saturday. I hope two days more will put you in possession of it"—of $40 while the same letter reports the purchase of 750,000 acres of land in Georgia; and the next one sends Mr. Edwards $60 "on account, more before tonight"; and two notes for $3434 each go to Robert Morris for him to endorse, saying, "Send me yours that I may endorse them"; to Higbie: "You will oblige me much if you can lend me $450 or any less sum this afternoon"; to Robert Smith: "Will you give me credit for $600 worth of goods for 6 months—I will give you Robert Morris's note and mine"; to Governor Mifflin: "I propose to contract for improving the navigation of the River Schuylkill above Reading"; and an invitation to the rich Walter Stewarts and Clement Biddles "to a small party."

Like all men of their type, Morris and Nicholson always deluded themselves that a flood of benign miracles would occur in each new day. There is an extraordinary fixed pattern to it: during each forenoon they are sure money will be coming in before the close of business: as the afternoon dies away and they see it is a question of "another day," their hopes sink and then revive for the morrow. Apparently every night they sent out a batch of requests for loans, sure that some were bound to "pull," and with them sent assurances to creditors of payment—and then such letters as these:

"I have waited today in anxious expectation of the money I was to have sent to you at half past three but it is now 5 and I have not got it. I hope I shall get it by evening but if I do not I shall certainly have it early on Monday morning."

And to another man that same day: "I am yet waiting for the money—I begin to fear it will not be rec [sic] tonight as it is now past 5 o'clock—however if it comes I'll send you the sum to pay half the note."

And again: "It is now near 9 o'clock and I am yet without the money I expected to pay you this morning. My expectations were from a person who is not returned to town. . . . I was told the notes I gave you on Saturday to deposit were for sale in the market. I hope it is not so."

Again the same day: "I was not able to send you the money or any part of it on Saturday. My expectations are to do it in all this day."

A few days later: "At half past 3 o'clock I should absolutely have the money today when I shall send it to you."

All the above are examples from the Letter Book for the two weeks September 26–October 10. To consider that the Secretary of State was involved with such a pair makes it abundantly clear why his resignation was so important. The business of the Pinckney credit must have hung over Randolph. The *Vindication* he prepared quickly moved away from all questions of bribery and money into fields of political philosophy. But not until he had received the following letter of October 2 from Wolcott: "You may be assured however, that nothing has been at any time concealed by me to your prejudice [and I know of nothing further to come up against you]" could he be sure the Nicholson business would not rise. It seems almost certain that Wolcott must have known of it, and informed the President and his colleagues. Apparently those remarkable men agreed the public interest was best served by saying as little as possible.

Washington wrote Randolph that he was at full liberty to publish any and every private and confidential letter he had ever written—and every word he ever uttered to him or in his presence from whence he could derive any advantage in his *Vindication.* He wrote it after Randolph (having Wolcott's letter) published in the *Philadelphia Gazette* his "request for a particular paper" from Washington.

Yet, on October 24, Randolph wrote Samuel Bayard, then serving on the American Claims Commission in London, "I shall quickly send to you a statement of my controversy with the President whose hypocrisy and perfidy are unexampled but in Tiberius."

It is interesting, though entirely a coincidence, that Bayard is addressed in care of Tom Paine, who might well have written the last sentence.

In the last month of 1795 the *Vindication* was published. Chancellor Livingston had written his brother Edward, then a member of Congress, on October 30 that he longed to see Randolph's publication. "The circumstances you mention with respect to the signature of the Treaty is very extraordinary and will show the astonishing influence of some men over the President. . . . So disgraceful and unconstitutional an act is impossible and just how to notice it a matter of much delicacy. I would advise you to form no plan till you advise . . . with Madison."

The fact was that, greatly as the Republicans would have liked to make an issue of Randolph's attesting the ratification of the treaty, unaware of the charges hanging over him, they did not want him in their camp. At the time the *Aurora* in Philadelphia was carrying a series of violent attacks on Washington and Wolcott signed "A Calm Observer." Randolph in Alexandria heard that he was considered the author and wrote an open letter saying, "I think it is important to my other vindication that I should not be supposed to carry on any attack that does not carry my name." There is about it the decency and dignity of Randolph at his best. Few stories are as tragic as his—a man of great mental and moral potential, brought down by inability to "manage financially" and then by ill luck. At his worst one feels sympathy for him, whereas for Morris and Nicholson it is difficult to raise any—until the last curtain falls.

As for decency and dignity, the three men who distrusted Randolph also behaved well. All that the Administration said in announcing his successor was that "Timothy Pickering of Pennsylvania has been appointed Secretary of State vice Edmund Randolph, resigned," and coupled it with "Charles Lee of Virginia has been appointed Attorney-General, vice William Bradford deceased."

As soon as the *Vindication* was off the press, Wolcott sent a copy to the Signer, William Ellery, then Collector of Customs at Newport, requesting him "to ascertain as soon as possible whether Mr. Randolph was or was not for some time in private consultation with Mr. Fauchet at Newport." It is puzzling, as is the whole matter, that three months after the event, which Randolph had made no effort to hide, Wolcott should have felt he'd better have a record of it. "It has been stated," he continued, "to me in a manner which admits of but little doubt that Mr. Randolph was in fact closeted with Mr. Fauchet for the greatest part or whole of one night. If this be true you would much oblige me by obtaining an affidavit of the fact from some creditable person."

On January 11 (1796), Ellery replied that when Randolph had reached Newport in September the boardinghouse was full and he took lodging in a private house with a separate entrance. "The front door was left unlocked so that he might go in and out at what time he pleased without observation."

Fauchet was in another house. "The Marshal of the District can add nothing to Mr. Randolph's story of hiring a boat to pursue [Fauchet aboard] the Medusa except that Mr. Randolph appeared to be much agitated." Ellery said Fauchet had told a Newport hostess that "Mr. Randolph was a damn rascal and deceiver," but the conversation was in French and Ellery could not swear the words "damn rascal" were used.

Ellery's account hardly varied from the story given by Randolph in the *Vindication* except for the latter's naturally greater detail.

The *Vindication* said that on arrival in Newport Randolph saw Fauchet and demanded an explanation of his dispatch. Until then the relations of the two had been cordial, while Hammond, the British Minister, had been close to hostile, and certainly closer to Wolcott at the Treasury, as had been the situation when Jefferson and Hamilton were at State and Treasury.

Randolph said that after his first talk with Fauchet he had returned to his boardinghouse to write out his questions. While doing so he learned to his dismay that the *Medusa* had sailed and he tried to pursue her. When her pilot returned to Newport he brought a message from Fauchet saying that he had sent a covering reply on the whole business to his successor, Adet. Fauchet said he was "bound to no explanation of my communications to my government . . . but I owe Mr. Randolph full and entire justice. . . ."

Fauchet's letter pointed out that in talks with Randolph he himself always spoke French, while Randolph spoke both English and French. He said he believed there had been a misunderstanding of some Anglo-French conversation and that "I was mistaken in the proposition which I supposed to have been made to me." Then in a triumph of sanctity he added, ". . . further the morals of my nation and the candor of my government severely forbid the use of money in any circumstances which could not be publicly avowed."

He added–one of the points at issue–that Randolph had

always assured him of Washington's "fairness" between England and France, while Randolph said that his alleged invitation to be bribed by Fauchet arose from a frank talk they had had at the time of the Whiskey Rebellion (1794) when it appeared to lie in the power of a few men to plunge the country in civil war. He felt Fauchet's explanation sufficient.

At Rose Hill Farm in New York, as Ellery was writing Wolcott, Horatio Gates read the *Vindication* and of course agreed that Randolph had been unfairly dealt with, and Joel Barlow shortly wrote Monroe in France, "On the face of Fauchet's letter . . . Robespierre never sacrificed a man on slighter grounds."

There is apparently only one more letter of Randolph's to Nicholson extant and it is of no relevance to the summer's events. Randolph quickly acquired a large law practice in Richmond but even it did not suffice to clear his debts. It is somehow fitting that he should have been chief counsel for Burr, another great debtor, at his trial for treason in 1807. In a message to Congress at the outset of the trial President Jefferson declared that Burr's "guilt is placed beyond question."

Before Chief Justice Marshall, Randolph rose to say that the President's declaration of Burr's guilt was unconstitutional and then, surely speaking for himself as much as Burr, added that it is not the business of the President to give an opinion concerning the guilt or innocence of any person.

Sources: It was the chance discovery of Randolph's letters to Nicholson of June 18 and August 7 in the Manuscript Room of the N.Y.P.L. which led to the examination of the seven volumes of Letter Books of John Nicholson at the Historical Society of Pennsylvania from which all other Nicholson-Randolph correspondence has been taken. Randolph to McKean, McKean Papers, H.S.P. Randolph to Mifflin, Frank B. Nead Collection, H.S.P. Morris to Nicholson, R. Morris Miscellaneous Mss. N.Y.P.L. Plan for the Asylum Company and North American Land, Nead Collection, H.S.P. Randolph to Monroe, Monroe Papers, N.Y.P.L. Wolcott to Marshall, Wolcott Papers, Connecticut Historical Society. Randolph to Bayard, Gratz Collection, H.S.P. Wolcott-Ellery exchange, Emmett Collection, N.Y.P.L. See also *Vindication* of Edmund Randolph, 1795 (and Richmond, 1855); *Omitted Chapter of History* by Moncure Daniel Conway (New York, 1885).

CHAPTER VIII

Third Act–Debtors' Prison:

ROBERT MORRIS *and* JOHN NICHOLSON

WHATEVER the date, whichever the writer, the letters of Morris and Nicholson during the years of their final ruin, 1796–97, are the same. It seems impossible that men could have gone on as they did in such illusion and self-deceit. How could they possibly have stood the strain of it? When did they sleep?

Seventeen ninety-six begins: "I am almost certain of sending you the money yet this afternoon and it shall be done if possible." The writer is Nicholson. His transactions are in millions of dollars and acres but he puts a postscript to this letter, "I have a quantity of snuff-bottles for sale . . ." And while he writes, Morris writes Parish, his agent in Hamburg, "I have lately formed a plan for selling fifty to a hundred thousand acres [which will cover everything]. *This is not visionary. This is certain as fate*," and then, like Nicholson and the snuff-bottles, he has "cotton samples" for Talleyrand, then a refugee here, which will turn out a profit.

Nicholson writes to Jonas Philips, "Please let the bearer have the notes of $10,000 or if they are not done, keep the $3,000 as pledge I will send you $520 tomorrow," while Morris writes another man, "I will cheerfully comply with your request to remit $1,500 in this envelope if . . . [but in any event] if certain things I am working at succeed, I will pay you sooner than you expect."

During that summer Harman Blennerhassett arrived in Philadelphia with a comfortable fortune of which Aaron Burr was to relieve him. Writing to a friend in England, he said, "Now for the land hits. They are going on every day not only in England but in America on principles no better than horse-jockeying. In this play, also, many fortunes are made or lost, the adventurers purchase on credit and a presumption of re-selling within a certain time their former acquisitions at an advance equivalent to enable them to make good their former engagements. But they have found their calculations to exceed dreadfully the capital settling this country and now the paper of a Mr. Morris of Philadelphia who in the last war had more credit than the Union altogether is selling at four, five and sixpence in the pound, though he still continues proceeding with a house that cannot cost less than 200,000 pounds. There is not one cipher too many."

By the end of the year Chauncey Goodrich wrote Oliver Wolcott, Sr., that "Mr. Morris is greatly embarrassed. 'Tis said that Nicholson has fled to England."

The last was not true. He was in Georgetown, watching the capital city starting, on behalf of Morris and himself, practically a fugitive from creditors. What a Christmas week that was for them. On December 21 he wrote Morris, "Carrington is in ill humor about his account. I invited him to dine with me today on hopes to reconcile his temper. He writes coldly declining."

The next day he wrote, ". . . between two and three in the morning. I have sent late last night into Georgetown and my servant returned at 4. *Mr. Scott not yet come* home, his presence here was necessary to sign for the indorsers. . . . I have been reflecting on the insufficiency of my means to meet Carrington's demands by $8,000 and have therefore drawn $200,-000 in notes and sent them to William Moulder to get them endorsed . . . send me all you can."

On the day after Christmas he wrote to General Brodhead, "Just be assured my affairs are not in the situation to prevent my fulfilling my wish and my promise of securing you for the money for which I am indebted to your friend. Would to God I could come with money to your aid."

The next following letter in his Book is to Robert Morris and begins, "Would to God I could do anything towards working your assistance. . . ."

As 1797 began he was "still in an unpleasant situation here, obliged to be denied to everybody. . . . I find my destruction is counted on. —— has applied to everybody to be my bail. They all would be happy to serve me *but* a but always intervenes to prevent it." Such flashes of cynic wisdom as the last is all they ever seem to have learned from their experiences.

William Moulder worked for Nicholson as manager of his store, and apparently as a "name" in his countinghouse. Before this pathetic donkey they dangled a carrot for years, but on January 8, 1797, Moulder must have eaten rose leaves and was no longer a Golden Ass. In Nicholson's own Letter Book, Moulder pressed a copy of his letter to Robert Morris: "I once more apply for the $2,000 I lent you Thursday night and which you promised me in the most sacred manner to return on Saturday last, likewise for part (at least) of the $72,000 notes last sent me by Mr. Nicholson not having enough in the house as will meet the demands of Mr. Nicholson's family."

Nicholson was still in Georgetown. From there he wrote Morris that he had "had Scott and Forest to dine" (how familiar that entertaining by the desperate promoter)—and then he adds, as though figures had lost all meaning, "I send on $400,000 in notes as desired. Mr. Moulder will supply you, if anything can be gotten on them." And there is a postscript: "Hallowell is hovering around me with $30,000 of due paper."

Three days later he informed Morris that he slipped out of

Georgetown, so that "the Prince George [County] or the Montgomery sheriff should not take me there." If I took the wings of the morning, he continues, and flew to the uttermost ends of the earth, "even there should my debts follow and my Bills and Notes oppose me . . . both sides of the Potomac are alike insecure. You remember when I thought a trip to Mount Vernon might expose us to a landing at Alexandria. I will digest my route from here as prudently as possible. . . . I am sorry the Banks plague you. Tell them to have faith like a grain of mustard and . . . Adieu, fellow sufferer, may He Who . . ."

On the nineteenth, he heard that Morris "has attached $2,000 of Moulder's money" in Morris's hands. Evidently Morris, borrowing the $2000 from poor Moulder "under sacred promises" to return it, found something against which to offset and wipe it out. Nicholson said, "So I find you will have your domestic attachments against me too."

A week later Morris proposed "the dissolution of the North American Land Co." Nicholson would not agree, saying, "Mr. Camp has got $9,000 of your notes out on a flanking party."

Yet with all this mutual distrust they trusted each other and made plans to "prefer" certain friends. With Mr. Camp out on a flanking party $9000 strong, Nicholson writes to Morris the next day, January 28, in the most equable tones. "Charles Weyman mentioned to me that he holds your notes with my endorsement *due next August* [author's italics]. He begged I would mention it to you believing you would, when it fell due, be more attentive, from what has passed with him, to make provision for it in his hands than some others."

Nicholson knew Morris could no more "make provision" for the following August than he could loose the belt of Orion —but apparently some going-through-forms helped in the day-to-day tension. Just as one can see Morris "making a fresh start" on February 1, when after the years of confusion he asked Nicholson to number his letters; he saw in the numbering a symbol of order and regularity amidst the disordered irregularity.

But Nicholson replied, refusing: "My letters like my *printed* notes are become numberless–i.e. innumerable."

This failing, Morris wrote, as men in his state do, of "decided measures" he must now take for the sake of his family. Nicholson replies, "I know not what answer I can make to this. I know of nothing on my part which I can reproach myself with and whatever be the measures you contemplate I am sure they will be governed by prudence." The last is perhaps in answer to the familiar hint of suicide men make.

On February 8 things took a sudden turn for the better. The sheriff arrived at court to arrest Nicholson but "all my friends turned out and I returned home rejoicing, escorted by my friends (not by bailiffs) who partook of a cold supper with me." But he adds, though the writs against him were thrown out, he presumed he "should not make a triumphant return to Babylon" but that Morris and he must confer in private.

It turns out that one of the "friends" above was Light Horse Harry Lee, himself in debt to many. Nicholson wrote him March 7, "If you will give me a list of the dates and sums of the notes you have of mine including the $6,000 you took up to prevent suits against me by Wilson at Alexandria, I will make the best provision I can for them and inform you what I can do. Of some of my notes Robert Morris is to be payer. However when I get your list I can tell."

He wrote the same morning complaining of the general abuse he was being subjected to and saying that Lee was "making a merit of saving me from arrest" and deranging the notes. An hour later he wrote Morris again: "Brenton was here and if I don't pay $1,500 by 1 o'clock he will give up the deputation to Thompson so that it will be Satan let loose on me–and the vendition will be ordered against you tomorrow and yet I fear I can't raise this $1,500." He evidently did raise it, perhaps from Tench Coxe, to whom he wrote, "I have hopes of getting you a note this day if you [sic] I'll send it to you tomorrow morning."

On the tenth there is a line to Elias Boudinot: "I am anxious to know the fate of my business today at the Bank," where he had asked for a twelve months' extension on all his paper.

Boudinot, director of the Mint, a director of the Bank of North America, was not a man of conspicuous ability. Yet while others went down to ruin he made his sure-footed, level-headed way to increasing wealth. He had the same sort of common sense and prudence as Washington had—or Jeremiah Wadsworth. During the Revolution he had been Commissary General of Prisoners and conducted the early exchanges with the British. His wife was a sister of Richard Stockton, the Signer, and at Elizabeth, New Jersey, where his fine house still stands, Boudinot had been leader of the bar. Hamilton had lived in his house before entering Columbia. In 1782 he had been president of Congress and he had written his wife, "I ardently wish some person of superior talents was in my room. I am not so humble as to suppose I am not as equal to the task as many . . . but their deficiency does not give me capacity." He was not a nobody in '82, but compared to Robert Morris, then Superintendent of Finance, he was a very minor figure. He must have thought of all this as he read Nicholson's letter. Perhaps he concluded that the reason they were such poor moral risks was that, unlike him, they had not been baptized by George Whitefield.

On May 31, the anniversary of that day two years before when Randolph was writing Monroe while Nicholson waited, Morris and Nicholson met and sent joint letters to a number of people who owed them money, begging that exertions be made to repay as each was "in want of money even for the necessary articles of our families," and Nicholson, going through his papers of two years before, found that Thomas Fitzsimons had never credited him with "$1011.50 paid you in cash May 27, 1795 . . . can you explain it?"

There is a note to Morris that June as vivid as a picture. They did not like to be seen together in public. The note reads: "I was looking out for you and sorry to see you going homeward along the Canal this morning. If I could have seen you I should have been glad."

With midsummer gone, the inevitable end was coming very fast. The Letter Book, so beautifully written originally in the copperplate hands of many clerks, is by now all in Nicholson's hasty scrawl.

The letters are a series of illusions, "little plans," terrible unrealities, yet twice these harried men turned on their pursuers and wrote with a dignity which only great suffering can bring about. Here are some of the other letters. To James Higbie: "In part to secure you of the balance I owe you . . . accept an assignment of the enclosed inventory . . . two Shakespeares, one General Wayne . . ." Another: "When Mr. Eichbaum removes, please receive the key of the house. There are eleven barrels of old cyder turned into vinegar. Could not you sell it, perhaps someone will buy it?" And then there is a note in the margin: "No Purchasers."

Perhaps the letters would not be so heart-rending if next to the unwanted barrels of cyder turned to vinegar there was not a letter of new hope and the hasty issuance of "notes for $140,000."

To a tailor in Philadelphia, Nicholson writes, "I owe the bearer, Mr. Sundcliffe, a greatcoat. If you will make him one on my credit I will try to pay you." Occasionally there came times when, in dismay at the vast promises he had made, Nicholson would limit a minor one merely to trying to pay. And again they would highly resolve on candor. "Let us be completely frank," one can hear them say to each other, so that both signed a letter to that brilliant sot, Luther Martin, "We expect to receive some money and we were desirous to pay the balance of your fee out of it . . . but . . ."

To a creditor named Garrison, Nicholson wrote, "If I can

satisfy you in [illegible] will you agree to issue your notes at three times the sums I owe you payable in six months to have your own debts paid out of them? . . ." The writing fades out, but the following letter is a hearty assurance to someone else: "I am more likely to be able to pay $2,000 than $1,000," and the next is a plan involving "$140,000."

In August their needs were frequently "in low two-figures," as banks say. But as their funds shrank, their "philosophy" about it all became more and more lofty.

They wrote jointly to General Uriah Tracy, ". . . we observe that you are dissatisfied. . . . As to our notes we may not have it in our power to secure you to your good liking but we have a security for those whose favour we receive that will never permit them to lose by us. [!] A sense of gratitude for favours received will not fail to establish the best security. . . . We were [it is true] unable to raise you even $150 or $100 . . . and it was with difficulty we could get what money was necessary to go to market for the support of our families. . . ."

And there is pathos—though almost farcical—in the "gentlemanly" way they can accept some new person's inability to loan them money. To a William Christian Smith, Nicholson wrote airily, "I have received your letter which breathes that spirit of affection which brings the glistening tear into the eye—I wish you were more pleasantly situated for cash. Mr. Morris and I are safe and even in our exile we enjoy some satisfaction in recognizing the good wishes of those for whose good will we are desirous."

The next day, dropping the lofty tone, Nicholson wrote a Mr. Gibson, "You would render me an essential favor by lending me $20 today. I hope soon to return both it and what you have already obliged me with."

In the Nicholson Letter Book that same day there is a letter to one Beckley in Robert Morris's hand. There is a simple dignity in it that is very moving: "If you had spared some of the epithets in your letter it would have been less offensive to us and of no injury to you. If we had money, you should be paid but we have no money nor can we get any."

That month Morris had been appointed one of the commissioners for a treaty with the Indians in western New York. Jeremiah Wadsworth (whose success Morris must so greatly have envied) was to be another commissioner. It was a last chance, as it were, for Morris to be among his peers as the man he should have been. But the risks were too great. He wrote Wadsworth, "I did intend to have attended myself at the Treaty but after considering my present situation and circumstances I found that by going I might not only expose myself to malicious attacks but also put my friends [how the lost man comforts himself with the fallacy that he still has friends who will "stand by him"] to certain inconveniences to which they should not be liable and, above all other considerations, that my absence from here would subject my affairs to greater inquiry than my presence at the Treaty could counterbalance."

One wonders where this worldly good sense had been all these years. The situation now was such that not all the sagacity and good will of Gouverneur Morris or Jeremiah Wadsworth could have done anything. Yet Nicholson and Morris somehow hung on until February '98 when on an action by a comparatively minor creditor they went to debtors' prison. Those men who needed $20 for food failed for something like $34,000,000 between them.

Many men were brought down with them but they were mainly those drawn more by greed than inexperience. The person on whom it fell most cruelly was Mrs. Morris. Abigail Adams, in December of '99 when she was First Lady, found Mrs. Morris "in a small neat room and at dinner with her daughter and youngest son. . . . Her feelings were evidently strongly excited. She endeavored to smile away the melancholy . . . and entered into conversation. I asked her to tea. I took her by the hand. She said she did not visit . . . she then turned from me and burst into tears."

In prison Robert Morris sent a remarkable note to his partner and fellow prisoner. It says better than anyone else can what happened. "You remember I am sure how I used to grumble and growl at the issueing of our notes. Little did I then know the fatal consequences. Gouverneur Morris tells me that my friend Mr. Parish [his business correspondent in Hamburg] and himself had set about a plan of raising there as much money as would extricate my affairs and would have done it but, upon being informed of the *system* [his italics] of our notes, they abandoned the pursuit.

"Thus you see fate determined that we should ruin ourselves and to be sure we have done it."

Source: Almost wholly the John Nicholson Letter Books, Historical Society of Pennsylvania.

CHAPTER IX

Penniless Leaders:

KNOX, LEE, DUER

THOUGH of a magnitude unequaled by any other financial disaster of the time, the pattern of the Morris-Nicholson ruin was followed in many lesser cases. John Cleves Symmes, the pioneer settler of the Ohio Valley, like his fellow townsman, Boudinot, once a magnate in New Jersey, died penniless, as did five general officers of the Revolution—Parsons, Sullivan, Lincoln, Moultrie, and Knox—to name but a few.

"Imprisonment for debt hung like a nightmare over some of the first families of Virginia," Edmund Pendleton's biographer remarks. Men still remembered the death of John Robinson in 1766, when it was found "that ruined men owed him 130,000 pounds, of which he had taken 100,000 pounds from the Colony's treasury."

Henry Knox, following the Morris pattern on a smaller scale, all but went under the summer of '97 when Morris and Nicholson were hurrying to their ruin—actually some mutual speculations were involved. George Cabot wrote Pickering, "I have so often seen men made desperate by pecuniary wants that I am always grieved to see men of influence reduced, on account of what they may do as well as what they may suffer." It was written in the months of the reorganizing of the army, in event of war with France, and Knox had written bitterly to Washington protesting his naming Hamilton as a major general senior to Knox. General Benjamin Lincoln, who took the surrender at Yorktown, came strongly to Knox's support.

"The principal reason for this extraordinary conduct," Cabot wrote again to Pickering, "is to be found in the peculiar circumstances of General Lincoln who is an endorser of Knox's notes which are floating in this quarter to a very great amount [believed to be $130,000 with Lincoln on for $50,000]."

A month later Knox was summoned to Boston by urgent creditors. "He does not pay his notes and General Lincoln's property is attached . . . even in Boston the number is small who hold [Knox] very high and those mostly table-friends or expectants of office [if Knox is field commander of the army]."

The financial collapse of Knox was not a sudden thing. He had been an inveterate speculator and a constant borrower, his enormous wife Lucy a gamester. As Secretary of War it "always [afforded him] pleasure to have the opportunity of serving" men later likely to help him financially. So he wrote M. N. Hays in '91. Like a troubled Micawber, he wrote him in '97, "If you are determined not to extend [your] endorsement beyond the sum which would cover the $2,500 you will please to put your name on another [note] payable to Henry Jackson for $3,000. The remainder [an extra $500] would be a real accommodation but if you decline it, I acquiesce. . . ." Then in a postscript he adds, "You will observe how perniciously your declining to endorse the $4,000 note will operate as Mr. Marston will know you refused for which he will suppose . . ."

Not only are the wild figures evidence of a man going to

pieces, "made desperate by pecuniary wants," but the letter and others like it are not in Knox's earlier bold, legible, well-spelled script. Even his note paper, so easily identifiable in manuscripts by its size, has shrunk to a scrap. He wrote simultaneously to Wolcott of "his stands of black spruce and white pine" in Maine which "must be sold" to ease his condition.

It was a terrible year in every way for this essentially well-intentioned man. In its first month he had written Washington, ". . . the loss of two lovely children on which you condole in your letter has been renewed and increased by the death of our son [George Washington Knox] of seven years old . . . the loss of eight children . . ." And as the year ended his hapless brother William, for whom he had tried to do so much, died, insane and penniless.

Henry Jackson, referred to above, was a Bostonian, three years older than Knox, who had been a colonel of the Massachusetts Line. There are many "Dear Harry" letters to him from Knox. On December 1, 1799, Knox wrote:

My Dear Friend,

If you are so locked up to be unable to pay $1,000 either to keep yourself or me from a gaol we are in a bad plight indeed. . . .

I had hopes that upon such an emergency you could by some means or other effect something. But if it is impossible the event must be met with becoming fortitude.

I feel all the deep regret than can be experienced by any mortal that my expectations have not been so promptly realized as to save my friends from the great evils under which they are laboring on my account . . . I am sorry that General Lincoln after your assurances continues to press you. I would to God I could [illegible] you and him.

Then the postscript "Cannot you speak to Gorham?" and the final one: "I would we could have a meeting with our friend Nicholson. Would it be possible?"

Nicholson was, we have seen, himself in a debtors' prison and would be dead within a few months.

So it went with many. Of 150 of the most prominent patriot

leaders 41 are known to have died in straitened or penniless circumstances.

When John Jay was Secretary of Foreign Affairs, just before the national government, Gardoqui, the Spanish Minister, was sure he could be influenced by discreet gifts or loans, and he wrote his government, "Jay is not the only one in his country who has the same weakness [needing money] for there are many poor persons among the governing body."

In Jay's case, his needs were temporary, following long years in Europe, badly paid, away from his affairs and his law practice, and he did not let the Spanish government alleviate them.

That government did, however, come to the aid of Light Horse Harry Lee—and to others. Lee is a knightly figure to many. In life he was perhaps less so. There is the ugly, little known incident of his beheading a mutineer, to Washington's horror, in the Revolution, there is the Spanish gift, and then a long record of debt in spite of opportunities of rehabilitation few men have had. Even the tolerant Gates lost patience with his promises to pay, and in a letter to Hamilton, written to him when first Secretary of the Treasury, there is evidence of an unpleasing craftiness in Lee.

Lee had written, asking for foreknowledge of the Administration's intentions as to assumption of the state's debts and currencies, and made a conventional disclaimer as to impropriety.

Hamilton wrote gravely back, "I am sure you are sincere when you say you would not subject me to an impropriety—nor do I know there would be any in answering your queries. But you remember the saying with regard to Caesar's wife. I think the spirit of it applicable to every man concerned in the administrations of the finance of a country. With respect to the conduct of such men, suspicion is ever eagle-eyed and the most innocent things may be misinterpreted."

It ought not to have been necessary for Hamilton to write

this to a brother Continental from one of the first families of Virginia.

Hamilton himself, though he died a debtor, was able to a miraculous degree to keep his private financial difficulties wholly separate from his official responsibilities. The Livingston Papers contain a note from him dated November 18, 1788, on which Walter Livingston, the addressee, has added some notations of interest.

It begins, "Mr. Hamilton requests the favor of Mr. Walter Livingston to lend his name on the enclosure." Below it W.L. has written, ". . . the note enclosed was for 300 pounds payable in 30 days drawn by himself in my favor which I endorsed and returned to him by the servant who brought it." Then on November 20, W.L. adds, "Colonel Alexander Hamilton sent a note of his to me by Mr. Duer for $3,000 specie to endorse which I did and sent the same to the Bank to be discounted for him." And finally, November 22, by W.L.: "Mr. Duer sent Mr. Remsen with a check for the $3,000 to sign, which I did."

At the time William Duer could have signed almost any check himself, living as he did in truly princely style, as Manasseh Cutler saw him, with the great and humble thronging to leave their money with him—as they did until the March day in '92 when he went to a debtors' prison from which he was only briefly freed, dying there in May 1799.

The night before his arrest he wrote in the desperate optimism of Morris and Nicholson to Walter Livingston, in almost as deep as he, "You do me wrong, my friend . . . there is more than sufficient [to cover everything]. . . . For Heaven's sake and for your own let Benson instantly raise funds to take up your note. . . ."

In the morning, March 23, he was arrested, and without a break, day after day, for months to come, he wrote Walter Livingston of plans and schemes to get free.

"Be calm, my dear Friend, above all things," he wrote Livingston when the latter found the Bank of New York had

$60,000 of Duer's notes with his endorsement, beside $19,000 on which Livingston was the payer. "I will assist you," Duer continues from his jail, "and if you will follow my advice ultimately bear you through, but a false step now taken may plunge you deeper than you foresee. Come instantly, Yours ever . . ."

The day after Duer's arrest Walter Livingston, heavily involved, issued a statement in which he said, "It is my misfortune to be a principal creditor of Mr. Duer and it is but too certain that I shall be the greatest sufferer by his failure. Nearly allied to Mr. Duer [Duer's wife was the daughter of Lord Stirling and hence a Livingston on her mother's side] and persuaded that he had been successful in business, I was induced to endorse his notes to a very great amount. . . ." The statement is manly and has that touch of noble martyrdom men so easily assume in such a situation. I am a man, he says, "whose own personal pursuits have neither been imprudent nor unprosperous." Reading it, one naturally feels sympathy for the man "persuaded" to this great involvement. There is seldom need to sympathize with a businessman so caught. They have become involved from a desire to make money. It had not in fact been long since Livingston, riding high, had written Duer, "I have received a better offer which you can take provided it is done immediately. . . . I wish you would call as soon as possible. My bargain with you is as follows: . . . to be at your risk if you do not underwrite it. The note you are to give me is to have a good endorser on it . . ."

Another of March '95, written while Duer was briefly at liberty, illustrates that pathetic preciseness which the bankrupt or utterly disorganized man will apply to some trivial thing which does not warrant it:

"A servant who brought the money to your house not finding you at home carried it back—he afterwards by my direction left it with Mrs. Livingston in bank notes, under seal, as my friend was disappointed in exchanging it for specie—

Mrs. Livingston has not known she had the money. . . . I went to your house, *Sent in Season* [his italics] the money to take up your note in Bank—which is done.

"I write this to relieve your anxiety.

"½ past four o'clock."

Then, May '97, an incoherent, half-illegible note to Livingston. "Let me entreat you for special reasons to pay [?] Benson, Carter's note—that he may try and settle it without a moment's delay for your protection [?]—I will advise him for the best you will be liable at all events for [?] Demand which is—and you risque the goodness of this note."

And then, May, two years later, he died.

Sources: Henry Knox's letters, Miscellaneous Mss., N.Y.P.L. Duer's and Walter Livingston's letters, R. R. Livingston Collection, N.Y.H.S.

CHAPTER X

The Hermit of Rose Hill: HORATIO GATES

THE life of General Horatio Gates did not end with either the triumph at Saratoga, the Cabal, alleged or actual, to make him Commander in Chief instead of Washington, or the disaster at Camden. These three events occurred between 1777 and 1780, his fiftieth and fifty-third years. He lived to be seventy-eight, dying in 1806, seven years after Washington, who was four years his junior.

But as a result of the events of 1777–80 he is still perhaps the most controversial military figure of the Revolution. People divide sharply in their feelings about him and in recent years he has had two strong advocates in the historian Knollenberg and his biographer, Professor Patterson.

Those who today most admire Washington see nothing great, competent, or distinguished about Gates. His admirers see almost no faults and regard him as the victim of great injustice. All his friends of the Revolution were "anti-Washington" and those of his later years were none of them of importance.

At the close of the war he was financially able to seek and

enjoy that "delicious retirement" which most of the leaders wanted. For this there can be no criticism, yet if there had been any spark of greatness about him his letters and papers in retirement would contain some trace of it. To the large issues of new government he and his correspondents appear completely indifferent. Nonetheless, the correspondence is of great human interest with its gossip and its oblique light on what ordinary men thought and wrote about, and how they lived.

Gates had originally come out to North America as a king's officer, garrisoned at Annapolis in Nova Scotia. There in 1754 he married his first wife, Elizabeth Phillips.

During the French and Indian War he was with Braddock and was wounded at the massacre. He was later commanding officer at Fort Stanwix, the successful defense of which against St. Leger in '77 so greatly contributed to his victory over Burgoyne. There he met Honikol Herkimer, later the American leader at Oriskany.

Back in London in '72, he was at a dinner given by Benjamin Franklin at which he met two later Signers of the Declaration, Richard Henry Lee and Benjamin Rush, both of whom wanted him as Commander in Chief instead of Washington five years later.

He returned to this country that year and settled in Virginia (near present-day Charlestown, West Virginia) at a "seat" to which he gave the charming name of Travellers' Rest. He had one son, Bob, born in '58.

Washington and he were correspondents, mainly on land matters, and Gates and Charles Lee were guests at Mount Vernon in the month of Lexington and Concord. In spite of his background, Gates immediately joined the patriot cause and with Ward, Israel Putnam, Philip Schuyler, and Charles Lee was one of the five original major generals commissioned by Congress.

He was sent to join the Northern Command in Albany, in June 1776, but as Washington's force retreated across the

Jerseys, November–December 1776, he was ordered to join him with a brigade. He and his force reached the west side of the Delaware in mid-December, just before the Trenton action, and Washington implored him to take command of the middle sector of the river and of the force which would cross simultaneously with his on Christmas night.

Gates declined, alleging ill-health, rode off to Philadelphia and on to Baltimore, to which Congress had moved.

General Charles Lee had just been captured by the British, the army was desperately short of general officers, and in view of Gates's subsequent activities with Congress, it is hard to believe his health warranted this refusal, or that it had been made except for personal and petty reasons.

However, the next summer, after the fall of Ticonderoga and Schuyler's eclipse, Congress sent Gates to command the northern forces opposing the Burgoyne invasion. There, whatever the conflict of evidence as to Gates's leadership, the fact remains that Burgoyne and his whole army surrendered to him, in a great triumph of American arms.

Meanwhile Washington had lost the Brandywine action against Howe and, on the very edge of victory at Germantown, the tide had turned and the main Continental Army fell back twenty miles to reorganize.

The contrast of victory and defeat seemed to speak for itself, if no weight was given to all the subordinate questions involved, and a considerable party of opinion believed Gates should supersede Washington.

The Cabal, as men of the time called it, failed. Gates disavowed its alleged aim to promote him. No man of proven good judgment believed that Gates had the qualities, moral, mental, or physical, of a commander in chief.

Thereafter Gates held various area commands, away from the "front," where, to put it mildly, he was difficult and unco-operative toward the headquarters of the Continental Army, getting himself involved among other things in bloodless duels with two unimportant men.

However, when Cornwallis invaded the Carolinas from the sea, Congress appointed him to the Southern Command and the American disaster at Camden followed, with Gates riding seventy miles from the field ahead of his routed forces. His worst enemies saw this as an act of panic and cowardice. It may have been mental panic—it was certainly not what a great leader would have done—but Thomas Pinckney, who was left badly wounded on the field, and who was a strong "Washingtonian," defended Gates's conduct at Camden then and thereafter. To add to Gates's sorrows, word reached him almost at Camden that his son Bob had died at twenty-two.

Gates was in retirement during Yorktown and his services there were limited to sending Washington a letter of introduction for a man who wished to sell meat to the army.

With the peace in 1783, his correspondence to and from Travellers' Rest was largely concerned with the normal interests of the time—land buying "on the north side of the Ohio, certainly the Land of Promise and the Garden of Eden," as George Weedon wrote him; with the uncertainties of having goods he had ordered from the seacoast delivered to him; with investments and the collection of interest on securities.

One of his former aides, "Charles" Richmond, wrote frequently. "With respect to your companions of the war I am sorry to give it as my simple opinion that few of them deserve to drink anything better than water—inasmuch as they have abused their friends." He goes on to say he cannot leave Philadelphia until he gets money to settle his debts there. He has collected some allowances due Gates and has had to use some of it himself, but will repay as "five months pay lies ready in Maryland for the officers of the Line."

Later he writes that "poor Clajon is no more—the money you were so good to procure for him came in time enough probably to satisfy his creditors and to bury him. Peace be to him. . . . I hope we shall not lose young John Armstrong [another aide to Gates] for many years. Clajon died of the gravel, which John Adams also has."

Clajon had been a sort of secretary to Gates through 1779. He was a pathetic character, foreign born, with the fixed idea that he had been deprived of a career by a question Gouverneur Morris asked about him in '77 as he was about to set off with Gates for the Northern Command. Morris had seen him, remembered he was somehow involved in a perjury case in New York prewar and, in present-day terms, wanted to know if he was a good security risk. Gates vouched for him and the matter was dropped, but as he failed to get anywhere thereafter, Clajon in 1780 threatened to sue and then to challenge Morris to a duel for defamation. His last years were spent largely in writing unsuccessfully to all and sundry to help.

Late in '83 Mrs. Gates died and before long the lonely Gates began to think about marrying again.

Richmond, writing from Congress, sitting in Annapolis, sent him regards from Alexander Hamilton and Thomas Johnson and his own to Adam Stephen and "the widow ladies of your neighborhood."

On the assumption that a man receives the sort of letters he writes, the following from Richmond to Gates is of interest.

I found, my dear General, you are got upon a wrong scent with respect to the beauteous Daphne for neither did I ever pursue or Daphne fly that I know of. Nor did I ever catch or was caught by —however the story is a good one. With respect to the fairer nymphs you speak of I think it not unlikely were I near them I might endeavor to stick a pin into one or both of their cushions. I hope you still keep up your ancient propensity for the fairest part of the creation—apropos I hear you are smitten with a fair widow erst yclept the wife of Mr. Drews. By George if you engage with her, she'll expect great doings as you may remember of prodigious things said to be done by said Drews in his lifetime. Therefore it will be necessary to examine carefully the state of your arms and ammunition before you engage lest you meet with a too powerful adversary—for this purpose you were to exercise and try your powers a little with these Blues and Etons [?] and if you come off with flying colors from them I think you may attack without fear the nation aforesaid.[1]

This letter, coming from a former aide to his general, is particularly distasteful. No one can imagine Hamilton or John Laurens having written it to Washington. Or for that matter Washington's receiving the one to Gates from an old friend in England: "It seems to me but yesterday when you was walking upon the Beach at Halifax among the train of Miss Cosby's admirers . . . [or] the pretty woman whom you bequeathed to me at your departure who by the way was with child whether by you or her husband is more than I or you either perhaps can determine. . . ."

The supposed license of the times does not account for these letters. Their counterparts are not in other men's papers, though perhaps only because other trustees were more careful than Joel Barlow, the trustee of Gates. Yet there must have been something coarse rather than immoral about Gates. Henry Cruger, about to go abroad in '84, wrote that he hoped to meet him in heaven "with your vision renovated and all those parts of the Body which formerly produced you such ecstatic delight in a perfect state of Juvenility and Vigour."

In or during the pre-Federal period, when men of ability were so needed in public service at home or abroad, the name of Gates seems to have occurred to no one, except Thomas Tillotson, Superintendent of Finance, who wrote him in '85, "I wish I could condole with you on what is your right, the appointment of the War Office. Knox is the fortunate person." On the other hand, there is no indication until later that Gates was disappointed or would have accepted.

His most frequent personal correspondent, during the rest of his life, was John Armstrong, Jr., the author of the New-

[1]In light of the intimacy of the Richmond letters it is amusing to find a postscript to one of 1791 saying, "My name is Christopher not Charles."

burgh Addresses—the proposed manifesto to Congress by the Continental officers in 1783 which in effect threatened the overthrow of the civil power by the army if their grievances were not met. It was the famous incident when Washington, by sheer force of personality and character, brought an end to the whole plan in an address to all his officers.

In June '85, Armstrong asked Gates, ". . . is there no fine girl in your neighborhood whom you can count for me?" Like most young men of the time, he wanted a wife with "a fine portion" of worldly goods. "The truth is," he wrote, "I am too poor to marry a woman without some fortune and too proud to marry any woman that I know who possesses one." Fortunately for him, he later recognized the sin of pride and married a lady of name and fortune.

The following June, '86, he wrote urging Gates to come up to Philadelphia, promising "a sight of your old friend Morris, from whom you may learn the whole science of Finance and Stocks and the joy we shall feel in common in cracking a pot once more with the old boy."

As it happened Gates was too busy on marital business of his own to go.

Two years previously he had set out to marry the widow of General Montgomery, killed in action at Quebec in '75. Mrs. Montgomery had been Janet Livingston, sister of Chancellor Livingston. Gates wrote her "wistful pensive words out of my dream-world's window." To him she was, he said, "soul-emptying" and "soul-bracing."

The lady would have none of it, writing him, "I have dropped a tear over your billet without being able to make the reply you wish. I should have deserved the reproaches of my own heart had I been capable of sporting one moment with the feelings of the man who in the offer he has made, does me the highest honor. But that heart would deserve it in a greater degree should it encourage hopes which it finds itself incapable of gratifying. . . . I would hope that in ceasing to love me, my unaffected candor may always entitle me to your esteem and that you may soon, good sir, meet with some more amiable woman whose undivided affection will continue to your lasting felicity."

This is surely as handsome a rejection as a suitor has ever had, and Gates rose to the occasion in the best eighteenth-century manner. "Nothing," he replied, "could so much enhance the value of the jewel I have lost as the politeness and elegant sensibility of your answer—suffer me to weep over it. . . ."

He finally dried his tears and on July 31, 1786, in his fifty-ninth year married Mary Vallance, a spinster of forty-six or -seven, said to be worth $500,000. Both were anxious to leave the provincial society of Berkeley County, Virginia, where old Adam Stephen, cashiered for drunkenness on the field at Germantown—possibly the cause of the defeat—was their "worthy friend."

Someone congratulated Gates on the "elligibel move . . . to the highly improved society of New York with the added convenience [and no small one then] of one of the finest fruit, fish and fowl markets in the Union."

There was one product of Virginia, however, in which New York could not rival her. John Mark, who bought Travellers' Rest, sent some of it occasionally to Gates in New York—"a keg of good old whiskey . . . contains near 6 gallons, distilled from the Domestic Materials of Travellers' Rest."

In December '87, Adam Stephen wrote Gates that "as soon as I get clear of the gout I intend to go to the Hague to congratulate the Princess of Orange"! This seems a rather impulsive proposal even for an alcoholic old Indian fighter and one wonders what could have provoked it. This may be the answer:

The *New York Packet* of the previous September carried a dispatch from The Hague quoting a letter from William, Prince of Orange, to his High and Mighty Lords, reading, "We have this instant received certain intelligence that Her

Royal Highness, our Dear Comfort, was stopt on the way to The Hague. . . . Indignities were offered her. . . ." Their High Mightinesses apologized. One can see Stephen, blear-eyed, reading the *Packet*, hear the drunken soliloquy that followed, and appreciate the chivalrous feelings it aroused!

The letters of job hunters and borrowers are many in the Gates Papers of those years. One Rutherford, "disappointed in every attempt to raise the most trifling sum by applying to those indebted [was] constrained to trouble [his] friends. Nothing [would] be more obliging than the lent [by Gates] of any number of dollars from one to ten." William Fiume asked Gates to help him get a job in the new government —"many friends wish to serve me particularly yours, Robert Morris." A year later "Your friend, Mr. Morris and many others here are strong advocates in my favor"; eight months later though, in spite of "Colonel Hammelton, Mr. R. Morris and many other gentlemen [who are] warm friends," the poor fellow was still unemployed.

Mr. Robert Morris was not such a great friend of Gates as the latter believed. He wrote Gates frequently and firmly he had no time for a correspondence or for collecting interest on Gates's securities.

Another debtor of Gates was Jesse Hollingsworth, who when pressed said that "Governor Lee [Light Horse Harry] promised me I should receive £1,000 from him by first October last. This promise has not yet been complied with owing as he tells me to Mr. Charles Carroll [of Carrollton] disappointing him of a loan he hoped to procure. If he complies in time I will lend you a part thereof. [Nice touch. He owed Gates.] Care must be taken to keep this a secret for if Mr. William Lee knows it he will not consider my wants as extream." In a lofty vein he concludes, ". . . there are few things more painful to a generous mind than not having it immediately in one's power to serve a friend in distress."

By November Gates was angry about it, writing, "You declare in your [subsequent] letter how anxious you are to pay the debt you owe me. I cannot think that anxiety corresponds with the purchases I hear you have lately made from ——— in Georgetown. If you can make so large a purchase you could pay me. . . . This with the indulgences I have already given for your Bonds have been near 5 years due is much more than I trust I should receive in the same circumstances."

Gates could have told Hollingsworth how futile it was to hope for money from Light Horse Harry as he was himself one of Lee's creditors. As late as '95, Gates wrote Richard Carson in Baltimore, "I am sorry to acquaint you I am again deceived and disappointed in Lee. Is it not a shame after a gentleman has for three years possessed the highest offices in the State [that] he should fail in fulfilling a simple promise made three years ago. . . . Either this man speculates or plays or has some way of disposing of his money rather than paying his just debts. I wish I was once clear of him for there is no end of such trifling."

Meantime a Mr. Alexander Robbins took both Gates and his new wife to task for the way they, evidently as trustees for a Mr. Booth, handled his affairs. "Permit me to ask you how you, sir, Mrs. Gates and Mr. Booth can possibly reconcile to your consciences to hold the real estate and £3,000 of a personal estate in your hands for three years, receiving the rent yearly, paying yourselves all demands and never offering Mrs. Robbins a single shilling."

Pleas for the loan of money at the time were written (by those who could never repay) in high-flown language, perhaps none more so than in the case of a man who began his to Gates in the third person. "Mordecai Booth having failed as a farmer for three years past makes a request that may be the means of making a fortune for my family." He would like Gates to give him a credit of £1/2,000 with which to set up a mercantile establishment. If Gates would do so "*I would forever acknowledge you a friend* indeed [his italics]. Trust this with your friendship and if I abuse it, then abandon me to infamy and ruin." Then back to the third person. "He has considered you and your amiable lady as his friends *whom he would feel honored by being obliged and delighted at owing his prosperity to* [his italics]."

On the backs of many such requests there are scribbled calculations in Gates's hand and a great deal of evidence that out of sheer kindness of heart he did his best, within reason, to help the unfortunate unless they were gamesters or drunkards. In that he and Washington thought much alike. Many of the borrowers, then as now, were blind to the endless importunities rich men are subject to, and failed to realize both that, if none of them ever paid, there would finally be nothing with which to help others, and that even capitalists, like Gates or Jeremiah Wadsworth, are not always possessors of ready cash.

Gates went to a great deal of trouble, and in an unassuming way, to explain to all borrowers why he could or could not make a loan. The following letter is certainly that of a kindly man: "Poor Backhouse has just been with me and has acquainted me with his disappointment and distress. I am truly sorry that it is not in my power immediately to relieve him as I wish, but not receiving two sums of money I had reason to expect . . . but to shew my good intentions to the man, I am willing to be bound with him to pay you the money by installments, ⅕ every year. . . . The heartfelt sorrow and distress of mind which so deeply affects the man convinces me that he is no impostor. . . ."

There are three letters in three months of '89 to Mrs. Gates which tell a really touching little tragedy. A Mrs. Jane Thomson from Virginia, a friend of Mrs. Gates and of Mrs. George Mason, had moved with her husband to Raspberry Plain near Johnstown, New York. In October 1787, Mr. Thomson had sailed for Dundee, well supplied with funds, and with the purpose of living there permanently. He was to get all "well-settled" and come back for her after she had sold some final property in Johnstown. No letters came from him.

On April 1 she wrote Mrs. Gates that her "Neighborhood is settled by the lowest class of people from Ireland, and Scotland and New England who are a turbulent set. My situation is very disgusting. The power Mr. Thomson left me being wrote according to the forms he had been accustomed to and [there is] some informality in it and advantage was taken of it. He did not call me his lawful wife but simply his wife Mrs. Jane Chapman [instead of] Mrs. Jane Thomson. Evidently the report spread that I had never been married to Mr. Thomson . . . the ladies started at such a report and withdrew visiting and stared and tittered and laughed. When they saw me they drew away particularly those of the streets sort same such as in Leesburg." She asks nothing but friendship.

On the twentieth she wrote again, "My dear Mr. Thomson is not returned it is now six months since the date of his last letter. I need not tell you what I suffer."

In July her last letter came. She was about to go to New York "but still waiting Mr. Thomson's letter."

Another romantic tragedy affected Mrs. Gates. The man Booth previously mentioned had "an unfortunate connection with Miss Drusy." She became with child and "all parties [were] in a distracted state."

A friend wrote Gates that "the principal object that gave [Booth] pain was his knowledge of Mrs. Gates's disapprobation thereto and his repeated promises to her on that account."

Amidst the trivia there is a letter of everlasting credit to Gates. His wife and he had leased Rose Hill in New York City and sold Travellers' Rest. The historian, Gordon, wrote him from London congratulating him on his marriage and added, "The reading of *The Gazette of the United States* brought me to the knowledge of what afforded me peculiar satisfaction, viz your summoning, [when about to leave Virginia] your numerous family of slaves and giving them their freedom. A fresh effort is to be made the next week for putting a stop to the British slave trade." In this manumission Gates was greater than many greater men.

In 1794 the old Cabal raised its now venerable head in a letter to Gates from one of its members, the Signer, Dr. Benjamin Rush, one of the most fascinating letter writers of the time. His letter begins:

> An old friend who admires and professes a republican form of government as much as he did in the year 1777 is very happy in an opportunity of apprising General Gates of the continuance of his respect.
>
> The name of that old friend
>
> Benjamin Rush

Rush had been perhaps the most vigorous and vituperative (against Washington) of any of Gates's supporters. He had probably the widest European education of any American of the times, was an eminent physician, a profound psychologist before psychology had been discovered, a devoted husband, an upright and patriotic citizen, and on the wrong side of almost every public issue.

In his letters to him Gates apparently confessed to disappointment that no one had asked him to perform any public service since Camden.

Rush replied that his heart reverberated to Gates's letter. "Little did we think," he wrote on December 26, 1795, "that the father of the discipline of the American Army in 1775 and the conqueror of Burgoyne in 1777 would be overlooked in the arrangement of that government which owes its existence in part to his exertions . . . only once have I been in company with the President of the United States since he came to our city [in 1790]. He himself is in a foreign country [Washington in Philadelphia]." Gates and his wife must come over for a visit. "We will fancy R. H. Lee and Sam Adams [of the Cabal] are part of our company."

(It is amusing to note that "the father of the discipline of the American Army" in 1778 as many believe, Baron von

Steuben, wrote Gates at the same time asking to have his field glass back.)

Thomas Mifflin, another leader of the Cabal, now governor of Pennsylvania, wrote "affectionately" to Gates, had them both over, and planned a vacation in the Narrows or in the Rockaways before which he would visit "you and your Mary." He came and Brockholst Livingston, the brother-in-law so troublesome to John Jay when he was envoy in Madrid, had them to dine "on Friday at three thirty."

In view of Mifflin's devoted support of Gates and his violent opposition to Washington in the Revolution, some aspects of his career and character are of interest.

He was born in 1744 and graduated from what was later the University of Pennsylvania at sixteen. He joined the army at Cambridge, was briefly an aide both to Washington and to Gates. At the Battle of Long Island, commanding a brigade, he was the victim of Scammell's or someone's terrible blunder ordering him prematurely to withdraw during the night of the evacuation, a blunder which all but led to the capture of the whole American Army.

During the November retreat to the Delaware he was appointed Quartermaster General, was charged by the Army with non-performance, and then sat in the Continental Congress, where late in '77 he was part of the pro-Gates Cabal.

He commanded the Pennsylvania Militia at Monmouth but was, in Washington's words about him that month, "one of the men who steps forward or retires as the sun happens to beam forth or obscure."

Postwar he was governor of Pennsylvania, 1790–99, during which terms he was an ardent supporter of the French mischief-maker, Genêt. He died bankrupt in the month after Washington. Chief Justice McKean of Pennsylvania wrote his daughter Sally, wife of the Spanish Minister, that he had seen Mifflin carried in delirium to the House to vote for a state treasurer—and back to his bed where he died next day.

"Had he fallen in battle," his fellow intriguer, Rush, wrote, "he would have ranked with Warren and the first patriots of the Revolution," though on his election as governor, Rush said he was "known to be a very immoral character [who] lived in a state of adultery with many women during the life of his wife and had children by some of them whom he educated in his own family. It is said his wife died of a broken heart . . . his conversation was profane and obscene."

In the spring and summer before Mifflin's death John Armstrong wrote Gates, "Mifflin is reduced by the bottle to a state of utter brutality," and Oliver Wolcott, Secretary of the Treasury, wrote, "The Governor is an habitual drunkard. Every day and not infrequently in the forenoon, he is unable to articulate distinctly. The effective powers of the [state] government are exercised by Judge McKean and Dallas."

That June, Judge McKean, "the Republican wretch," as the South Carolina Federalists called him, gave young Caesar Augustus Rodney a letter of introduction to Gates. Rodney "wishes to know the Conqueror of Burgoyne." McKean modestly adds that Rodney's uncle and father were in the Continental Congress with him (like McKean, one was a Signer) and assures Gates that the present Rodney "is a sound Republican in principle and practice."

And from the wartime governor of Rhode Island came another to "be handed to you by my son Mr. Horatio Gates Bowen." On the Republican side there were more namesakes of Gates than anyone else. A tally between the Federalist "George Washingtons" and Republican "Horatio Gateses" would be close.

Of all Gates's admirers none is so attractive as Kosciuszko, the irresponsible, happy Polish engineer who served with Gates in the war when Gates was in command at West Point. The foreigners, Clajon and Kosci, the Americans, Armstrong and Robert Troup, were devoted to Gates, as John Laurens, McHenry, and Tilghman were to Washington, or John Francis Mercer to Charles Lee.

In '78, Kosci, as they called him, wrote the first Mrs. Gates he would always see her "taking out biscuits from your portable magazine, where they are so neatly stored . . . and saying My Son, here, this is for you; come Troup, take this biscuit."

Nineteen years later Rush wrote Gates that Kosci was in Philadelphia. He said Kosci was not happy as there had been "a regression from the Spirit of '76. He speaks of some of the customs of the late administration [Washington's] . . . with surprise and horror."

Kosci himself wrote that he would "ron away from Philadelphia j propose to go see you and before hand j fell great satisfaction." (Rush said, ". . . he loves your very name.") He was "coming for one week onless you will lett your dogs at me and by force trow me out from your house . . . j have only one friend and servant with me and with such arms j will attack your house. . . . My best respects to your Lady hear j stop for fear you should not be jealous of me."

In his bread-and-butter letter to Mrs. Gates afterward he said he was "your friend forever and j send my respectful kisses."

It was the summer of Monroe's home-coming after his recall as Minister to France by Washington. There was "a feast of reason" to honor him in Philadelphia and Gates went down to sit around the board with such luminaries as Philip Freneau and Aaron Burr, who handled the considerable legal business which a man of Gates's wealth naturally had.

At the dinner for Monroe, Jefferson had been in the chair. Four years before he had written Gates that he was sorry not to have seen him in New York, "as my own plans of retirement rendered it hardly probable I should pass that way again." And the next year, after his resignation as Secretary of State, he wrote from Monticello that "the length of my tether is now fixed for life from [here] to Richmond. My private business can never call me elsewhere and certainly politics will not which I have ever hated both in theory and practice."

Gates, more farseeing or candid than he, replied as "the Hermit of Rose Hill," "If the best seamen abandon the ship in a storm she must founder and perish. . . . Make no rash promises [of permanent retirement] lest like other Great Men you should be tempted to break them."

Jefferson's letter had concluded with the fascinating statement that Gates's letter books were "sacredly safe" with him. It sounds more conspiratorial than it probably was. They were perhaps left with Jefferson, then governor of Virginia, when Gates was on the way to his brief command of the Southern Army in 1780.

In any event it was three years, almost to the day, before Madison wrote Gates that Jefferson had given them to him and that he was sending them along to Rose Hill by Edward Livingston. And meanwhile Gates had Madison's letters to him, and his letter book to Madison, "in a large chest of publick papers"—which Madison wanted back. Gates asked him why not bring Mrs. Madison to Rose Hill for the summer. "You statesmen should take all opportunity to relax your minds. The best bow will be spoiled by always being bent . . . the best time of the year to ramble is from the middle of June to the last of July." All very hospitable, but each wanted to be sure his letters were sacredly safe in his own keeping.

Both at Travellers' Rest and at Rose Hill, Gates's most frequent and friendly correspondent was John Armstrong, Jr. In '88, from Virginia, Gates sent him an old note to collect from Robert Troup, who, it will be recalled, had been one of the aides. It is worth noting that in 1780, when Secretary of the Board of Treasury, Troup had drawn $9500 for himself against an entitlement of $500 and was allowed to resign without restitution.

Armstrong reported that Troup said he knew nothing of Gates's note "but admitted the hand-writing and paid the money, or what was the same thing, gave me an order upon Rivington for the books." He then continues:

"I am not yet married—or likely to be so"—but eleven

months later he was able to announce to Gates his marriage to "the youngest sister of Chancellor Livingston [and hence of Gates's charmer, Mrs. Richard Montgomery]." "You have been prepared," he continues, "to hear that G.W. is President . . . even Roger Sherman has set his head at work to devise some style of address more novel and dignified than Excellency." He also enclosed a cartoon of Washington riding on an ass in the arms of his mulatto body servant Billy, with David Humphreys leading them, which proves, he added, that "there are people who will spare nothing neither Washington nor God and the former like the latter will have something to suffer and much to forgive."

Of Washington's principal appointments Armstrong wrote, "Jay, Jefferson and Hamilton are all very able men and promise as much as any man could do for the honour, consistency and firmness of the Government. I am glad [G.W.] has got into such good hands for alas he might have remained in those of Knox and Humphreys." (Gates's biographer, Professor Patterson, says he was satisfied "in the main" with Washington's Cabinet.)

Armstrong's marriage to a Livingston rescued him from poverty and obscurity, though Mrs. Livingston, his mother-in-law, wrote proudly, "Alida's husband, General John Armstrong, a captain at 16, a major at 18, a colonel at 20, Secretary to Executive Council in Philadelphia at 22, in Congress and a General at 25"–to say nothing of marrying a Livingston at 30. It must be said that his response to it was of the best. During the first few years he lived as a country gentleman–sleighing back to Clermont, the Livingston seat, from New York, he kept his ears warm with his wig and his body with burnt brandy and eggs–and, as Mrs. Livingston wrote Gates, having nothing to do in the summer "except to mow grass, to howe corne and potatoes–to hear the Chancellor say how many tons of hay or lucerne I forget which from an acre." He was a devoted husband and father, becoming senator from New York later on, Minister to France, but having the final official misfortune to be Secretary of War under Madison in the month the British burned Washington.

In 1790 "to her many other favors Mrs. Armstrong lately added a very fine boy" and by all her conduct "made him grateful." The boy was named Horatio Robert Gates Armstrong.

From Virginia before his move, Gates wrote, as one country gentleman did to another at the time, "I have entreated Mr. Jefferson and Mr. Madison to take beds with you on their way to Lake Champlain. They are entitled to and will receive your best attentions." Then he adds in not unattractive vanity, "Show them the field of Saratoga."

Armstrong was largely responsible for the move to New York rather than, as Gates had first proposed, to Wilmington, Delaware, or Long Island. Armstrong said that both those suffered "from a want of society. Wilmington is a mere borough of flour merchants, shopkeepers and carriers of the latter. [It] has not a gentleman upon it." A considerable part of Armstrong's gentlemanliness, in a caste sense, was acquired through his marriage and he was thereafter very class-conscious. In one of his last letters to Gates he told him, "Your new acquaintance [Jerome] Bonaparte is married to a Miss Patterson. Her father is one of those fortunate men who has risen rapidly from nothing. He was a clerk to Billy Bell of Philadelphia, a kind of one-half merchant, one-half peddler whom you may recollect. But *time and chance* happens to all men." Of the elections of '93 he wrote Gates, "Many of the candidates have neither sense or morals enough to represent North Carolina, which is the most concise method I have of saying they have none at all."

William Duer of New York, then in a debtors' prison, was no great example of sense or morals. His bankruptcy, as sensational as any in American financial history, followed a career of unbridled speculation and extravagant living, on other people's money.

Armstrong heard that William S. Smith, John Adams's

son-in-law, was back from Europe and personally "fortunate negotiations." He was sorry to hear that "he does not bring some relief to poor Duer. . . . Should [Gates] find however that Smith is to do anything for him I wish you [Gates] would try him in a confidential way upon the subject of Duer's bond to me. The sum is small (but £600) and I shall be glad to get even less than that for it just now." It might be noted that Duer's mother-in-law, the widow of Lord Stirling, and Armstrong's mother-in-law were both Clermont Livingstons.

Early in January '93, when details of the September massacres in Paris and the imminence of the execution of Louis XVI were known in New York, Armstrong wrote Gates, "That the majority of any nation has a right to rise up and change their form of government at *pleasure* is in my view totally void of all foundation in common sense or common honesty and is only a Bill of Rights for a band of robbers. Thank God, however, the influenza [of the French Revolution] cannot reach us. We have no kings to dethrone, no clergy to plunder, no nobles to extinguish." Then to this calm view he added a comment on Washington worthy of Tom Paine or Freneau at their most violent: "Our kings (that is the President and Government) are dross and dung and cannot be humbled."

Gates sent him, no doubt naturally, the Republican pamphlet, published in 1797, reopening the matter of Alexander Hamilton's affair with Mrs. Reynolds. Armstrong wrote he had already seen "Callender's attack on [Hamilton's] probity and have heard that to shield himself against this he has attempted to creep under Mrs. R.'s petticoats. A pretty hiding-place for a national leader." And an example of how "time and chance" affected his early favorable view of Hamilton in the Cabinet.

As to the Federalist charges against Monroe, as Minister to France, Armstrong wrote Gates, "Many of the attacks made upon him are I think quite unfounded–nor indeed do I see anything blameable in his conduct." He then puts the defense better than anyone did, including Monroe. "He has taken one way to accomplish his objective and the Administration would have had him take another. But in the great business of mankind modes are of little importance and it is only for such men as Pickering [Secretary of State] and [President] Adams to prefer the shadow to the substance."

He was distressed that Kosci was not going to settle in the Hudson River Valley and that there was no chance of seeing him for another spring "and whether we shall all or either of us see another is among the secrets of a Cabinet much more inscrutable than that of Philadelphia."

At the beginning of 1799 the Hermit of Rose Hill and his Mary decided to leave the country seat for a town house in New York. He agreed to sublease Rose Hill and its forty acres for £550 a year, and to sell all its furniture, farm implements, and livestock, "from next May." To protect whatever "view" there was from the town house he secured a lease on an adjoining property to run until the death of the survivor, Mrs. Gates or himself. In his application for it he settled the question of their ages, on which there was a question even in the *Dictionary of American Biography*. Mrs. Gates, he said, was in her fifty-ninth year and "I shall be seventy-one years old in April next," hence being born in 1728. In town, life went on much as before. One wonders at the absence of mention of Washington's death by his correspondents and himself, but in his Papers there is a draft of a rather pathetic letter of December '99, apparently addressed to Hamilton, written in a weary hand.

Dear Gineral [sic—unusual for him]

It is the wish of my heart to show the utmost respect to the memory of General W [sic] but my infirmities forbid my being exposed to the open air at this season so long as will be necessary to attend either the procession or the oration to [sic] St. Paul's.

I am much obliged by the Distinguished Notice taken of me by the Committee.

A month later Colonel Thomas Hartley of the old Pennsylvania Line wrote him, "General Mifflin has left us. Do not be disturbed at these numerous deaths. You have many years. . . ."

Aaron Burr, in asking his proxy as a stockholder in the Bank of Manhattan, wrote in December the next year that "all accounts agree that Jefferson will certainly have the votes of South Carolina—this will I think secure to him the Presidency." It did but only after Burr himself was tied with Jefferson at seventy-three electoral votes each—over Adams and Charles Cotesworth Pinckney with sixty-five and sixty-four respectively—and the House of Representatives chose Jefferson after thirty-six roll calls.

In a postscript to the proxy letters Burr asked, "Do you use the warm bath?" Bathrooms and bathing were prime interests of this man so fastidious about everything except his public and private morals.

It must have flattered Gates considerably to have a letter from Robert R. Livingston in Paris, though one suspects Gates had opened the correspondence. Livingston said it was difficult to write anything of real interest without a cipher though he had seen Kosciuszko frequently—"he is much respected and keeps himself aloof from the Court."

In 1803 an anonymous letter came from "A Person who has leisure and is desirous of writing General Gates history." He could be met "any morning at Mr. Taylor's at the New Bath in the rear of Trinity Church." But he waited in vain though Gates filed his letter.

It is pleasant to record that in the last week of the year a letter came to him from Mrs. Richard Montgomery after almost twenty years. She wanted some young horse-chestnut trees from Rose Hill and Gates roused himself to write a long letter as to the arrangements he had made to have them sent to her and also at length as to her brother, the Chancellor, then in Paris as Minister, busy on the Louisiana Purchase.

The letter ends "With the most unalterable esteem."

Almost the last letter by Gates, written in a fine clear hand three months before his death in April 1806, was to James Madison, then Secretary of State, enclosing a letter from General Moreau sent Gates by Lafayette. Gates added that "*War in Disguise* makes much stir here." He was referring to a pamphlet just published, as an answer to *The Frauds of Neutral Flags*, in London by Sir William Scott, holding that for neutral nations to insist upon "free trade" in their own ships in the circumstances of the Napoleonic War was "war in disguise" against England.

The answer, *War in Disguise*, protested most strongly, not so much the fact of British seizures of neutral shipping, as the inference that the aces England had up her sleeves were put there by God to insure "the liberties of mankind," and "if you pretend to dispute the conclusion," you could be "d—–d for a pack of rascals."

Most of the high Federalists knew at once that the author was Gouverneur Morris, who had been Minister to France during their Revolution and later senator from New York. Yet oddly enough Gates heard that another former New York senator and the then Minister to France—his former confidant, John Armstrong—was the author. He wrote Madison, "I never will believe Armstrong is treacherous to his trust unless it is better confirmed than by assertion." Perhaps he had heard the "assertion" from another former aide, Robert Troup, who, referring to Armstrong's "virulent and Jacobinial pieces" against the Federalists (to whom Troup had swung over), wrote, "I never have believed and I never shall believe after his attempt to create a mutiny in the Army at the conclusion of the Revolutionary War that he has a heart fit to be trusted with any important interests of his country."

It is difficult to find a modicum of greatness about Gates. There seems no evidence that any promotion or employment of him, beyond what he received, would have benefited his country. His admirers and advocates were practically all men who were ineffective in powers of leadership or of that indispensable requirement in governing men—conciliation—Sam Adams, John Adams, Richard Henry Lee, Rush, Mifflin. None was a man who could mold a team out of individuals. Jefferson's and Madison's notice of Gates came after the Constitution's adoption and had more to do with opposition to Washington as President than with any great admiration for Gates.

But if this Revolutionary war record is set aside, Gates's life was an amiable and valuable one. In a period when the lives of so many men were ruined by drink, debts, or speculation, the solvent sensible stability of the Hermit of Rose Hill is a rare and great relief. And with it he did a great deal of good. His ideas and his friends were mainly commonplace, but he was neither a hypocrite nor an extremist, a little wistful at times at being forgotten, perhaps overemphasizing the Hermit of Rose Hill but on the whole quite happy in his home and marriage, as indeed he had reason to be.

In a late letter of his to an unknown friend, he says of another, "He is fond of drink, not as you and I have been sometimes induced by the Pleasures of Society to like it—but fond of the Society for the sake of drink and not of drink for the sake of Society. The former if it be a disease it is one a man of honor can easily cure. The latter if persisted in is cured only by death." Many men of brilliant potentialities of the time, from Thomas Mifflin to Luther Martin, could have saved their names by taking this advice. Washington might have given it.

There is something of amusing irony in the fact that the Papers of this commonplace man should have been left by Mrs. Gates to the unstable, eccentric Joel Barlow.

Sources: The main source is of course the unpublished Gates Papers in the N.Y.H.S. which contain practically all the letters quoted, though Janet Montgomery's letter to him is in the Bancroft Transcripts, N.Y.P.L.

CHAPTER XI

The Dapper Little Gentleman:

ELBRIDGE GERRY

A DECADE after he had made his choice of the three special envoys to France in 1797, John Adams wrote, "I then called the heads of departments together and proposed Mr. Gerry. All the five voices[1] unanimously were against him. Such inveterate prejudice shocked me. I said nothing but was determined I would not be the slave of it." This, Adams continued, "was my first mortal offense against my *sovereign* [his italics] Heads of Departments."

The full Adamsian quality of these sentences is best understood if one considers how impossible it would be to find them in Washington's writings. If his five principal advisers were against a proposed appointment, Washington, like Cromwell, would have said to himself, "I may be wrong." Both Adams and Pickering, the Secretary of State, lacked the stature ever to be wrong. Pickering said they had no "hatred of Gerry," but were simply carrying out the duty of Cabinet members "to prevent the mischievous measures of a wrong-headed

[1]Pickering, Wolcott, McHenry, Stoddert (State, Treasury, War, and Navy), Habersham, Postmaster General.

President." And as to what was mischievous and who was wrong-headed, Pickering considered himself the sole judge. Adams said that Hamilton shared the sovereign department heads' "hatred of Gerry and of every other man who labored and suffered early in the revolution."

Certainly Hamilton was bigoted and uncompromising in his opinions but it is doubtful that his views of men were based on their pre-Revolutionary records. It is rather that Adams is speaking for himself, living in a Boston Massacre past, still contemptuous of those who had been Continental officers.

Elbridge Gerry was a Signer of the Declaration, a delegate to the Constitutional Convention, but not a Signer, a member of both houses of the federal government, a governor of Massachusetts, and a Vice-President of the United States. He was born in 1744, the third of twelve children, graduated from Harvard in '62, and at forty-one married the seventeen-year-old daughter of a wealthy New York merchant. He was a small man with a bad stammer, a patriot, without venality, but surely "wrong-headed" on most of the great issues which followed the Declaration—a suspicious and petty man, a man unable to get along effectively with other men, perhaps with Monroe the best example of how a man may hold the greatest offices without possessing a spark of greatness himself.

Neither the Adamses nor he were able to stifle a sense of injustice done them by the fact that other men, particularly the warriors, took over the management of the country which the Massachusetts zealots felt existed only because of their resistance to tyranny in Massachusetts before 1775.

In 1784, Gerry was filled with forebodings as to the Society of the Cincinnati (Washington's officers) and he wrote Sam Adams that it was but a prelude to "a King, Lords and Commons to come." People said that Washington would restrain any excesses of the Cincinnati, but Gerry asked Adams, "Is it certain that he would have a disposition to stop it? He is subject to error . . . and finding himself at the head of a society which are attached by every tye of friendship to his person and for a long time been subject to his nod . . . If he supposes the public interest may be promoted by a change of government, is it not probable he will attempt it. . . . Moreover when a crown is in view who will answer for the patriotism of any man? Who dare be responsible for it? Anyone so unwise as to offer himself a pledge for the self-denial of another to a throne . . . is [so lacking in wisdom as to be] unfit and unqualified for a statesman."

Of course this was all wild surmise on Gerry's part. And presumably he did not know of the excoriation poured by Washington on hapless old Colonel Lewis Nicola in 1782, when in the excitement of celebrating the birth of a Dauphin in France he wrote that a monarchy, with Washington as king, might be a solution of our troubles. Historical research has produced no evidence, beyond Nicola's letter and Gerry's surmise, of a "monarchical party" in the country. Yet many writers have accepted these as evidence.

Gerry's letter went on as follows: "[In] this dangerous tendency . . . [it] is very extraordinary that the military gentlemen should be so vain as to suppose they have all the merits of effecting the Revolution. Very few of them were concerned in the early opposition to the measures of the British Ministry. . . . [Furthermore] have the militia [ineligible for the Cincinnati] no part in the Honor of the Revolution. . . . If the [Continental] Army had been unfortunately cut off can it be supposed *500 000 militia* [author's italics] would have resigned their liberties? Surely not?"

Where even Gerry got such a figure as half a million militia is obscure, but it must have pleased Sam Adams, who regarded a standing army as "the shoeblacks of society."

Gerry then indicated that what would happen was that, since the foreign officers (mainly, of course, French) were part of the monarchical plan, France would land a force here under their command to put Washington on the throne, as an appanage of France. So far as can be determined, this was propaganda circulated in London which frightened no one but timid Tory refugees like Van Schaack. Of all things it was the most unlikely of appeal to Washington with his never changing perception that self-interest had been the sole motive of French assistance. Certain French officers may have been troublesome about it, but who they were is a mystery. Their avid desire to be in the Cincinnati was the normal desire of young men for the honors and ribbons of their service. Long after the Cincinnati ceased to be a political menace, even to men like Gerry, Frenchmen were sending proofs of their American service to Morris, our Minister in Paris, asking for their badges.

Gerry's letter to Adams was written March 24. On May 7, in his grasshopper way, he dismissed the whole business in another letter. Washington had just passed through Annapolis where Congress was in session. "I am confidentially informed that he is opposed to the plan and is determined to recommend the dropping of it altogether."

All this is not to say some worthy men were not worried about the risk of a monarchy, but none but the "wrong-headed" ascribed such an ambition to Washington. Colonel Theodorick Bland, after Washington was President, protested that if a President could by himself "turn out the great officers [the Cabinet] and bring about a change of the Ministry and throw the affairs of the Union into disorder" he could make himself a monarch. But the point lay in constitutional theory, not in doubt of Washington's republicanism.

Gerry's own suspicions of royalism next fell on another great man, of whom he could be sure Sam Adams would be glad to hear the worst. Benjamin Franklin's private morals had long distressed the Adamses. He was then in his eightieth year. "I confess to you," Gerry wrote to Sam Adams, September 30, 1785, "I have a jealous [watchful] eye on the Doctor. He is devoted to the Courts of Versailles and should he come to Congress as a delegate and obtain the chair he may do more mischief than we are apt to imagine but his great age seems an almost insuperable bar to the execution of an extensive plan." He does not specify what the plan was, but we may suppose Gerry feared not only the politics of a royal court but its passionate pleasures as well. But to suspect Washington and Franklin, and no one else, as menaces to republicanism speaks for itself.

It is a wonder that Gerry signed the Declaration and none at all that he refused to sign the Constitution. Anything which men could agree on filled him with suspicion. Sitting in the federal House in the Spring of '89, he was violently against the proposal that there should be one Secretary of the Treasury instead of a Board, as under the Confederation.

"If he is disposed to embezzle the public money, it will be out of the power of the Executive to check or control him in his nefarious practices." A single head would have "abundant opportunities for peculation and unnumbered opportunities for defrauding the revenue." Furthermore, "as the inferior officers who might discover the fraud are to be appointed by the principal will they not consequently be men after his own heart?"

The single secretary plan was of course carried, and the first two Secretaries left office poor men to the amazement of Talleyrand in Hamilton's case. No scandal touched the Treasury (in fact none of the fears of morbid men like Gerry, on any subject, was justified in the event), yet ironically enough there had been several scandals—Robert Morris, Robert Troup, Duer, and others—under the earlier Board of Treasury system which Gerry wished to maintain.

Gerry's career was commonplace enough until President Adams sent him with John Marshall and Charles C. Pinckney as special envoys to France in a final effort to stave off war. This was the mission to deal with Talleyrand, concluding with the XYZ Papers and Gerry's refusal to return with his two colleagues when it was evident that only the payment of a great bribe to Talleyrand would accomplish anything.

It has generally been agreed, even by Gerry's admirers, that his staying on was, to put it mildly, a disservice to his country. Pickering, the Secretary of State, ferociously, but not of course seriously, hoped it would lead to his execution by the French or us.

When in mid-June '98 he was ready himself to leave Paris, he wrote Talleyrand, and sent a copy to Justice McKean in Pennsylvania. It acknowledges a note of Talleyrand's "wherein you inform me that all further explanations respecting the dark intrigue in question will be below the dignity of the French Government. . . . The Government of the United States, pure in its principles, just in its objectives and wise in its council is also superior to all personalities. . . . I complied with your subsequent proposition for remaining here to prevent a rupture. . . . I hoped to have something to take home . . . too late . . ."

When Gerry did return, he found an advocate in a friend, John Wendell, of Portsmouth, New Hampshire, whose letters of 1800–1 "discover," as no one else did, what Gerry's real motives in staying on were. The special human interest of the letters lies, however, in their pathetic resemblance to those of greater men of the time who wrote in the same delusionary words when they wanted to borrow money.

In among them is a note to Gerry by one Turban, a Paris shopkeeper, indicating how changeless is the lure to "buy things" in Paris. It was sent around to Gerry during the Talleyrand talks. It complains that Gerry, having ordered some Valenciennes lace, had not called for it. He had promised, Turban says, that if he did not like it he would take Malines or English instead. Mr. Turban insists on all his "rights," demands that Gerry specify the hour and day he will call, and send him thirty-six louis forthwith. Did the beautiful Mrs. Gerry, then but twenty-seven, capriciously decide she liked none of the three? Lace dealers were more dangerous to trifle with than Gerry may have realized. Was it not the very year that Jane Austen's aunt, Mrs. Leigh Perrot, was sent to prison charged with stealing a piece of lace in a millinery shop in Bath, and Jane and Cassandra tried to join her in a cell?[2]

Wendell's first letter was March 18, 1800. It says the British are busy on the vile principle of dividing to conquer but that "the Vox Pop is ever Vox Dei. Good Republicans are firm that God resigns to let the People rejoice." Wendell then himself apologizes for a certain obscurity in the above, saying, "Excuse my crude ideas which are collected in a sick-chamber amidst the chit-chat of old women."

In a long, more thoughtful letter of April 14 he tells Gerry he is electioneering for him and first makes clear why Gerry stayed in France. "You kept the Enemy at Bay while time was given to your colleagues to get home and prepare their constituents for some eventful consequences . . . you never [displayed] more firmness than at that very time in which you was thought acting a weak Part, instead of flattering M. Talleyrand you boldly set him and his Machiavellian arts at defiance and flatly told him you were fully convinced that your powers were not adequate in your opinion whatever he may think of them.

"And I added [to Mr. Chauncey, who had said, 'Your friend Gerry's conduct as an envoy can't be justified'] that if he had been there he would not have dared to have done with [sic] what Mr. Gerry did."

On May 12 came the next letter, assuring Gerry, of what he had no doubt, that "President Adams is your friend and has the highest confidence in your integrity and even said when you was left behind by your colleagues to arrange with Mr. Talleyrand and was blamed for that, 'I know Mr. Gerry as well as any man on earth and I dare trust the Fate of the Nation to his Integrity' etc. etc." Then, "very creeping for his purpose," Wendell says he wants a loan of $2000. He is prepared, as the needy so often are, to give three notes of

[2]She was triumphantly acquitted at her trial.

$1000 each for it, together with a mortgage "on three estates worth $30,000." If Gerry would endorse for one year, he would be "amply secured."

There was no answer and on July 2 Wendell wrote four long pages on Gerry's greatness and included the Vox Pop-Vox Dei ideas of March, saying then, "Now for a whisper on the loan–I would wish $1,000 in hand and in one month $1,000 more and $1,000 a month later but I will give my own notes payable to you." He says he could easily have had the loan from the new bank Gerry's old congressional colleague, John Langdon, was forming, but the Court had refused Langdon a charter because "the old bank said they were Jacobin disorganizers and anti-Federalists." [A smear campaign?] In any event, "it is better for me to pay 8% interest to a private friend until my own money and effects come into production than have to attend monthly on the caprices of the bank."

The insistence on payments on due dates was then widely regarded as a caprice of the banks. One of the reasons the Assembly of Pennsylvania had proposed to abolish the Bank of North America fifteen years before was "that the punctuality required at the bank throws honest men into the hands of usurers."

Having begun with politics, Wendell evidently thought it wise to go back to them to soften the request for a loan. "Back to politics–I am not to be duped or tampered with and therefore [am] of no party, open to all but influenced by none and no trimmer."

Still no answer as to his necessities from Gerry. So on July 20 he sent a note for $1000 payable in six months, saying, "[Please] endorse. It is most agreeable to me to owe only to one. Politics run so high I am consequently [sic] it is difficult to procure loans."

There is something terribly touching and familiar in the poor man's shifting pleas. The next day he wishes he could get "a loan of $10,000 at three equal payments" thereby clearing up everything, and something of pathetic jocularity in the postscript: "If your friend Talleyrand wanted boncoup de l'Argent, your better friend Wendell wants mais une petite de l'argent. Monsieur T. wanted too much."

By August 8, Gerry had evidently refused help and, not being a rich man, he was clearly justified in doing so. Wendell wrote sadly, "I wished to have had one friend to be indebted to and to turn every payment to that center." There is a quenchless hope in men that the mere consolidation of their debts will pay them. Wendell then says, "Although I should be happy at all times to continue our correspondence yet when it is subject to such dangerous experiments [being read in transit] I will forebear although a regret on my side and wish you and your respectable family every happiness, etc. etc."

Two months' silence followed, then Wendell wrote again, beginning at length as to the chances of Adams against Jefferson for the presidency. He had meantime sent his son to Gerry to ask in person for help, and Gerry had declined to endorse. Grasping at straws, Wendell added, "My son said you would look out for an acquaintance to make a loan and that a sum of money was likely to come into your possession which you would reserve for me—I have threefold security ready."

No answer but in mid-November Wendell wrote he was doing all possible to help Gerry politically. "You are a gentleman of firmness whom Talleyrand himself could not bend and make subservient to his secret purposes." He says he is bitter against Pickering and Hamilton, "who make us hewers of wood and drawers of waters to the British," he repeats Vox Pop-Vox Dei, and then asks, "Will you make the loan?"

On January 12, the next year, 1801, Gerry finally wrote him that he had seven unanswered letters from Wendell to acknowledge. He said he rejoiced in the election of Jefferson though he would have liked to see Adams and him together. As to the loan he said nothing. In passing it is curious to note that he rejoices then in Jefferson's election, although the tie between Burr and him was not broken by the House until

February 17. But Gerry may have been confident Burr could not conceivably win.

In April, Wendell was back at it again—one must wonder what he had lived on for a year if his necessities were so great. This time he started with $10,000, saying his assets were about $65,000. Through April and after he continued to ask. And that was all.

Gerry died in 1814 at the age of seventy while Vice-President. By then his own finances were almost as bad as poor Wendell's. But he had had a great satisfaction. We were at war again with our ancient enemy. In the month in which he had signed the Declaration, thirty-seven years before, he wrote President Madison:

Secret

War is declared, God be praised, our Country is safe.

Sources: With the exception of his letter to Talleyrand, all letters to and from Gerry quoted are in Elbridge Gerry Papers, N.Y.P.L. The letter to Talleyrand is in McKean Papers, Historical Society of Pennsylvania.

CHAPTER XII

The First Civil Servants:

OLIVER WOLCOTT *and* TIMOTHY PICKERING

TWO of the most valuable public servants of their time were Timothy Pickering and Oliver Wolcott, Jr. In Republican eyes they were "jobholders" and "political hacks." In Washington's view they were that rare thing—men of eminent talents, without private fortunes, with a liking and aptitude for permanent public offices of small rewards. Both were Cabinet members under the two Federalist Presidents, Wolcott coming up through the Treasury to succeed Hamilton, Pickering going from Post Office to War to State, not as a first choice for the latter but taking it, without any display of injured feelings, after five other men declined. They were the closest of colleagues, some said of co-conspirators against Edmund Randolph and President Adams. Both were New Englanders but their temperaments were very different. Pickering, however much he was respected, was certainly never loved except by his immediate family. Wolcott, of equal ability and integrity, was plainly a delightful man.

Wolcott, born in 1760 in Litchfield, Connecticut, was the son of a Signer and a governor of his state. He graduated from

Yale in the class of '78, along with Joel Barlow, Uriah Tracy, and Noah Webster. He studied briefly in the famous law office of Tapping Reeve and in '80 first came to Washington's notice while serving as quartermaster of some local forces.

He was one of the Connecticut young literati with Humphreys and Barlow and, like many young men of the time, tried to write "epic poetry." Gibbs, his biographer, said, "Wolcott wrote *The Judgment of Paris* of which it is only necessary to say it would be much worse than Barlow's epic if it were not much shorter." In June of '85 he married the beautiful Elizabeth Stoughton, his townswoman, and until her death in 1805 lived gaily and happily with her and their children.

In the late summer of '89, before Hamilton's appointment to the Cabinet, Jeremiah Wadsworth, a Connecticut congressman, wrote Wolcott that if he would apply for a post in the Treasury the support of the whole state delegation would be his. His qualities were well suited for that department. Hamilton himself later summed them up as "moderation with firmness, liberality with exactness, indefatigable industry with accurate and sound discernment, a thorough knowledge of business and a remarkable spirit of order and arrangement." They might well have been Washington's own prescription for the qualities he wanted in his administrators—moderation with firmness, hard work, a sense of order were what he believed indispensable to success.

Within a month to the day, September 12, Wolcott was confirmed as auditor of the Treasury. It was the third position there in importance, but paid only $1500. He hesitated on the last score but was persuaded, contrary to the fact, that he could live properly in New York or Philadelphia on a thousand a year, particularly with Washington setting the example of avoiding "parade and expense."

Hamilton, only three years his senior, and he worked in the closest accord, and it is one of the glories of our history that through all the immense problems of assumption and funding, the Treasury accounts were never successfully questioned, and no officer of it enriched himself. Their labors were long and arduous, their living and official quarters cramped and unsatisfactory, living costs greatly exceeded their estimates, but Wolcott, a demon for work, viewed the scene with good humor.

In the spring of '90 he wrote his father, "About 100 Frenchmen have arrived with the national cockade in their hats, fully convinced that it is one of their natural rights to go into the woods of America and cut down trees for a living. . . . Joel Barlow has been the principal agent [of their coming]." Nothing could better describe the naïve hopes of the deluded immigrants to whom Barlow, as agent for Manasseh Cutler, had sold what he did not own, or have title to.

It was the month of Washington's illness, which for a time appeared so serious, and so worried his associates as to what would happen if he died. "What is most wanted here is stability and political knowledge," Wolcott wrote his father. There were too many theorists about Republican liberty, and "some few mistake cunning for wisdom."

The use of cunning instead of wisdom applied to Jefferson, the next year, when Everleigh, Wolcott's superior, the Comptroller of the Treasury, died. The Hamilton-Jefferson feud was in its infancy, and immediately on learning of Eveleigh's death, Jefferson, Secretary of State, wrote Washington at Mount Vernon, without word to Hamilton, proposing that Tench Coxe be given the post. It was more than an impropriety. If Hamilton, in like circumstances, had proposed Wolcott as chief clerk of the State Department, Jefferson would doubtless have gone off to Monticello to brood on the Rights of Man. But in addition, as we shall see, Coxe had joined the British forces during the Revolution and been attainted though not prosecuted for treason.

Of course Jefferson was not backing a traitor—Coxe was now "a good American"—but he was plainly trying to disunify the Treasury. Hamilton's proposal that Wolcott be promoted was accepted by Washington without question.

Four months later, when Samuel Osgood resigned as Postmaster General, Jefferson's cunning went to greater lengths. Of all people he proposed Tom Paine, a man who, whatever his services in '76, was by now addicted to drink, lost in debt, and without administrative experience. Fittingly, Timothy Pickering was appointed.

Philip Freneau was then in the State Department as an "interpreter" and from the sanctuary of Jefferson's protection was publishing his violent irresponsible attacks on Washington and his whole Administration. Chauncey Goodrich wrote humorously to Wolcott, "I can easily imagine you have not leisure to write your friends at present, as you find full employment in accounting [to Freneau] for the millions of cash that some of you in the Treasury Department have slily put away in your money vaults."

In spite of his money vaults, Wolcott, after he had succeeded Hamilton as Secretary, wrote his father that "Mrs. Wolcott lives at a farm-house about 6 miles from the city. The place is healthy but inaccessible to company, there being no road near the house. If I were a democrat, I might raise a fund of popularity upon a circumstance of this kind but it is well known that we live as we do because we cannot afford to live better and this destroys all title to merit."

And to Jonathan Dayton (who shortly would be found to have retained $18,000 of government funds for his own use), "Mrs. Wolcott lives in a part of a farm-house in the country with the children. Whatever aristocratical principles she may have contracted by an acquaintance with me, she is obliged to a style of living which will not excite the envy of the most strict democrat."

He was still Comptroller General in the summer of '93 when Genêt arrived as French Minister with funds and orders to force America into the war against England, to separate Kentucky from the Union, arouse the Indians on the frontier, and in general do everything our worst enemies might desire. Genêt was given a tremendous welcome by the Republicans, from nondescripts like Freneau to the eminent Thomas McKean. It is "a strange kind of reasoning," Wolcott wrote his brother, "by which some suppose the liberties of America depend on the right of cutting throats in France." But at the height of the uproar, with the people stirred "to rob and rouse," Wolcott, with Washington's own incapacity for grandiose excitement, wrote, "There is no man in this country, I hope, who does not wish that the French should enjoy a free government. Many justly doubt whether their present measures tend to secure this great blessing, but in my opinion we ought not to discuss this subject too publickly. It is a matter with which we have nothing to do. We should preserve our own peace *and set an example of moderation to the world* [author's italics]." "Moderation" and "magnanimity" were wonderful words in the mouths of the greatest Federalists but even then the fanatics thought they meant appeasement.

It is a small matter, but pleasant to record, that with the "putrid fever" raging in Philadelphia, and Hamilton himself stricken, Wolcott wrote, "The Africans are said not to be affected, and, much to their honour, they have zealously contributed every aid in their power." The word "honour" was not often then applied to men who were or had been slaves.

When Hamilton resigned, Washington appointed Wolcott at once to take his place. Thus as the first career man of record he had come up through the Treasury to the top. It was well for the country that Wolcott was pleased to accept. It was hard to get even clerks to remain at government salaries and, as Washington complained to Hamilton, there were few men in public service "who understand details and endeavor to keep things in order."

It was to Wolcott, as Secretary, that Hammond, the British Minister, brought the fatal intercept of Fauchet's dispatch saying that Randolph, the Secretary of State, had indicated his willingness to accept a French bribe, and Wolcott, as discussed elsewhere, was of course instrumental in Randolph's resignation, plainly sure of his folly or guilt.

As a result of it, and of the ratification of the Jay Treaty, the Republicans, in Bache's paper, the *Aurora*, anonymously accused Washington of having continually overdrawn his salary, with the connivance of Hamilton and Wolcott. The attack, signed by "A Calm Observer," appeared on October 23, 1798. The next day Wolcott replied, pointing out that the method of drawing "had regularly been laid before Congress and printed and disseminated through the United States. It is not credible that the officers of the Treasury having knowingly violated the law [so it was charged] at the same time published the evidence of their guilt."

Hamilton joined in a further reply, saying that "more money has at times been advanced than was due for service but never a dollar for which there was no appropriation. The compensation to both houses of Congress had been paid in advance frequently and the books showed that in Washington's case there had not been in advance one quarter of his salary at any time."

The spirits of both were doubtless raised by the arrival of a cask of peach brandy which Stephen Hopkins had laid down for them "several years ago."

Most letters of the Federalist period are written with the sonorous dignity of the eighteenth century. ("I had supposed that my assertion in writing that these were the facts would have been sufficient satisfaction," Wolcott wrote Charles Lee as to a bill from the executors of Richard Henry Lee's estate.) But there are many as brief and to the point as Charles Thomson's asking Wolcott, "Have you paid the taxes for last year on my account [my house rented to you]?" But there was also often what Thomson called "the graphic faculty of the old Congress" in use of vivid single words. Hamilton writes that though Burr was "by natural disposition the haughtiest of men, he is at the same the most *creeping* to answer his purposes." The flamboyant Mrs. Ricketts, Senator Maclay said in his diary, "made a deep impression on my *milky* character"; General Greene gave a militia general, Cornwell, a note of introduction to Chancellor Livingston saying, ". . . the General has not many of the graces dancing round but is a man of good understanding and guided by the best intentions." A teamster reported that "it rained very *cleverly* and fast." And in a triumph of malice Chauncey Goodrich wrote Wolcott in '96, ". . . it is rumored that Jefferson will not accept the Vice-Presidency; his Virginia partisans say he shall, and will; some suppose it is what he most covets. He can't do otherwise without disobliging his friends and he has too long had a *lurching* for the Presidency to give up his hold on his party."

Some of Wolcott's charming letters to his wife are quoted in Chapter V. They wrote each other constantly. At times one wonders whether the general absence of divorce at the time may not in part have arisen from the high standard of conjugal correspondence.

"I will write to S," Wolcott tells his wife during the army reorganization in '98, "but I cannot with propriety recommend him for a commission in the Army. It would bring me into a sad scrape and it would not in my opinion be proper that he should command who knows nothing of the obligations of obedience."

When he asked the former Continental and friend of Washington, Colonel Fitzgerald, to resign as collector at Alexandria, Fitzgerald admitted his mistakes but was at a loss to account for them. They proceeded from blind credulity and inattention, Wolcott told him.

On May 20, 1800, James McHenry, former Secretary of War, wrote his brother that "At times [President Adams] would speak in such a manner of certain men and things as to persuade one that he was actually insane . . . he said General Washington had saddled him with three secretaries [Wolcott, Pickering, and McHenry]. . . . I had done nothing right. . . . I resigned next morning and Pickering was thrown out a few days later."

Wolcott remained at the Treasury until the following January (1801), when he left office at forty-one with "a small farm in Connecticut and a few hundred dollars in cash." He also had newly acquired LL.D.s from Brown and Princeton and during his eight years as governor (1816–27) his own Alma Mater would so honor him.

No one claimed that he had more than the farm or cash. What some said was that he had only been a tool of Hamilton and hence treacherous with Adams. And there was something else being said—said very carefully, well this side of an actionable accusation.

There is of course no doubt by present-day custom that when Wolcott found he could not be loyal to Adams he should have resigned. But on that basis there is equally no doubt that Jefferson should have resigned from Washington's Cabinet long before he did. Both were men guided fundamentally by moral principles and the political principle never seemed to bother either of them.

Hamilton's conduct during the election of 1800 is distasteful indeed, but much of what he wrote to Wolcott or to Pickering during Adams's four years in office was less conspiratorial than characteristic of the man himself—and may well have been most annoying of all to his alleged fellow plotters. Pickering and Wolcott are described as having a "blind devotion" to him. Both of them were strong-willed, opinionated, and educated men in their own right. Hamilton cast no spell over them. Wolcott can scarcely have been impressed with a letter like this from Hamilton:

". . . to this end a person must be sent in place of Monroe —General Pinckney, John Marshall, Mr. de Saussure of South Carolina, young Washington, the lawyer, McHenry, Judge Peters occur as eligible—all are preferable to Monroe."

Several of the suggestions are absurd. Hamilton then wanders on, "After turning this over and over in my mind, I know of nothing better that you have in your power than to send McHenry.—He is not yet obnoxious to the French and has been understood to have some kindness towards their Revolution. His present office would give a sort of importance to the mission. . . . I believe he would explain very well and do no foolish things."

Wolcott must well have thought Hamilton had taken leave of his senses in proposing to send McHenry—with whom Hamilton constantly found fault in the most contemptuous terms—on a mission where neither Gouverneur Morris nor Monroe, both strong men in their way, could keep their feet "on the glare of ice" in Revolutionary France. If what Hamilton thought of McHenry's incapacity was true he ought not to propose him and if it was not true he should stop saying it.

And the tone of the letter—and of others like them—is pompous and preposterous, with Hamilton writing as though the Almighty were putting the whole problem of America on his shoulders just as he was trying to make a living in private life.

"Sometimes," Hamilton adds, "I think of sending Pinckney who is in England but various uncertainties and possible delays deter me."

"Sometimes *I* think of sending," Wolcott must have said, "I, not the President with the advice and consent of the Senate? On what has this our Alexander fed?"

The other matter had to do with two fires in Washington City within two months of each other, November 1800 and January 1801, the latter the month of Wolcott's resignation.

In November the War Office and all its archives burned, and as Wolcott left the Treasury it was burned with almost all its records. The Federalists were at once charged with setting the fires to conceal their many crimes and peculations. The weakness of the accusation is that no one could say what were the crimes or who received the unlawful enrichments. No Federalists had become unaccountably rich. The government was not "honeycombed with foreign spies."

Thomas McKean, now governor of Pennsylvania, a rabid anti-Federalist, wrote Jefferson, "The burning of the War Office last month and now the Treasury have probably been accidental but as these events were predicted in Philadelphia and a subject of conversation in July, last, suspicions of design will be entertained by many. The circumstance is at any rate unfortunate for the present administration"—presumably in hampering investigation of its predecessor.

It seems clear that McKean himself did not believe it, and though he does not identify the prophets of the fire, he was doubtless referring to allegations by the Republicans' newspaper, *Aurora*. The Federalists said that if the *Aurora* had such foreknowledge, then it must have been of its own plan to set the blaze.

Pickering's head and face were as thin, fierce, and beak-nosed as an eagle's. He was born in 1745, graduated from Harvard in '63, married Rebecca White in April '76, when she was twenty-two. From then until his death in 1829 he was almost continuously in public service. He was of strongly individualistic character and opinion. One of Washington's most trusted officers in the Revolution, rising to be Adjutant and then Quartermaster General, he was at great pains to make clear he was no blind worshiper of the Commander.

His poor eyesight kept him from combat in the war (though he saw action and was reported among the slain at the Brandywine), greatly to the advantage of his country, which got the benefit of his managerial abilities. He seems as gaunt and dour as his face but from Valley Forge he wrote his wife, "I confess I (yes, even *I*) am involuntarily led to respect [beauty in women] whenever I meet it. Be not alarmed, my dearest! The very circumstance contributes to excite and fix my fondness, my unalterable attachment to you, as pretty expressed a thought as a husband has sent to a wife." And so far as is known he was the only man in the army to write home that he had so much meat to eat, he was getting fat. Let us hope it was not improper enrichment at public expense by the Q.M.G.

His grasp of details and his appreciation of their importance was perhaps what first attracted Washington, the great master of detail, to him. Here are examples of Pickering's way of doing things. A Philadelphia merchant named Charles Derby received a bill of exchange of the great Dutch banking house of Hope and Company in payment for goods bought by a John Pigeon. He sent it to Pickering, who replied, "No such man as John Pigeon can be found. [I have sent the bill to protest. Protest fee $150.00.] It was evidently drawn by some Dutchman acquainted with Hope and Co. I suspect the bill is a forgery as their business is done in the most correct and elegant manner whereas the bill you sent is not even spelt right and the signature of Hope and Co. is not like what anyone has seen."

As Secretary of War he wrote to Colonel Return Meigs that three calico and three linen shirts had been received some months ago at the War Office and were believed to be samples of Indian (gift) goods. They were not. "It is important to the public to have the facts authenticated explicitly and on oath. I therefore pray you without delay to make out and swear to a particularly certain description of the shirts." Or as, when becoming Postmaster General in 1791, he wrote all postmasters the necessity of accurate accounting for mail and money: "In detail the business seems to be piddling, all its emoluments arising from trifles, although in the whole it is important."

In '75, Adams had written from Congress to Colonel Henry Knox at Cambridge, "It is of vast importance, My dear Sir, that I should be minutely informed of everything which passes at the Camp while I hold a place in the great Council of America." But twenty years later when he was President "Everything which passes" was of less interest. With the Administration in the greatest need of the attention and leadership of its Chief Executive, he left Philadelphia for a rest. War with France was brewing. His Cabinet was appealing to Washington and Hamilton for guidance—not, it should be said, without a good deal of anti-Adams feeling on their part.

But Adams was superbly indifferent to it. He wrote McHenry, his Secretary of War, "Letters addressed to me in care of Charles Adams, Esq., counsellor at law in New York will soon find me."

In comparison with some of the brilliants of his age group (John Jay, Benjamin Rush, Robert R. Livingston, Charles C. Pinckney, and Anthony Wayne, all born within a year—Gerry a year older, Jefferson and Jeremiah Wadsworth only two years older, and Nathanael Greene three), one is tempted to say Pickering matured slowly. That extraordinary group of younger men born between 1750 and 1760 (Hamilton, Gouverneur Morris, Burr, Rufus King, Madison, Marshall, Monroe, Edmund Randolph, Thomas Pinckney, John Trumbull) long outshone him in various fields. But further consideration suggests less that he matured slowly than that opportunity came or was created by him slowly, and that as it came his stature increased to meet it.

Many of his peers were "great men" in 1785 when Colonel Grayson passed through Philadelphia and told him that the aging gossip Horatio Gates had reported that Pickering had "offered [his] services to Congress, as head of the War office at fourteen hundred dollars a year."

"I know not, sir," Pickering wrote Gates, "who handed you that story but believe me it has not the shadow of truth to support it. Never, sir, did I tender my services to the public at any price whatever. In respect to the War Office I merely signified to two or three of my friends that the post of Secretary would be agreeable to me and stated the grounds . . . and so far was I from tendering my services at $1,400 a year that when, before that idle story was repeated, I had heard that Lincoln [General Benjamin Lincoln, who surrendered Charleston in '79] had offered to serve at $1,500, the overture appeared to me so improper, so degrading that instantly I declared that were I a member of Congress the overture alone, without inquiring for other reasons, would determine me to deny him my vote. The office you will see has since been disposed of [to Henry Knox]. *The Great Man* I believe interested himself in favor of the successful candidate.

". . . Trade in which I meant to engage is unpromising but I have a residue in lands and while God gives me health I can raise bread for myself, my wife and my little ones [eight of the last]."

He went to his residue of lands on the Susquehanna near Wyoming, where the Pennsylvania legislature commissioned him to organize the new county of Luzerne. For twenty years this area had been the scene of deep intersectional feeling and violence, the Yankee emigrants from New England in constant feud with the Pennsylvanians. With Pickering's return, he and his family became the special objects of local outrage. Ironically, young John Armstrong, Jr., was sent to command the militia and "restore order" and his allegedly ruthless treatment of the Yankees drove many out, Pickering and his family among them. Back to Philadelphia he came, unemployed, working for a while as secretary of the Society for Promoting Agriculture. Doubtless he already knew his future colleague, Oliver Wolcott, Jr., but the first letter to him in '89 has to do with Wolcott's establishment of a Connecticut branch of the Society.

Two years later, upon the resignation of Samuel Osgood as Postmaster General, Washington appointed Pickering to the post. When Knox resigned the War Office in '95, Pickering succeeded him and was then of Cabinet rank.

When Randolph resigned, Pickering apparently had no expectation of succeeding him, nor did Washington, who offered the State Department in turn to Thomas Johnson, who twenty years before had nominated him as Commander in Chief, then to Charles C. Pinckney and John Marshall, then again to an older man, Patrick Henry, and finally to Rufus King. All refused, and for several months the efficient Pickering conducted the War and State Departments until in December he was definitely promoted from the first to the second, James McHenry becoming Secretary of War.

The main problem which he faced, under both Federalist Presidents, was our relations with France. Pickering's adversaries held that, like all Federalists, he was anti-French and pro-British, disregarding the fact that as Americans they saw less menace from England than from France.

However, even Hamilton "was not well pleased" with the sharpness of Pickering's manners with the French Minister. He wrote a very wise and valuable letter to Wolcott about it. While the general advice on diplomacy in it is excellent, it seems to have arisen less from the immediate facts than from Hamilton's obsessive belief that to him alone all wise judgment was reserved. In the person of Pickering he found someone of equal conviction.

Hamilton wrote, "I was not well pleased with the Secretary of State's answer to Adet's note communicating the order respecting neutral vessels. There was something of hardness and epigrammatic sharpness in it [a wonderful description of Pickering in general]. . . . [There should be] calm reasoning and serious, shewing steady resolution more than feeling, having force in the idea rather than in the expression . . . the manner should be extremely cautious, smooth, even friendly but yet solemn and dignified."

It must be said that Pickering took practically no notice of the inauguration of President Adams. Holding him and his views in apparent contempt, Pickering "reported" several times a week to Washington at Mount Vernon. He was not wholly to blame because Adams was often at home in Massachusetts and frequently displayed an amazing indifference to the responsibilities of his office.

In his correspondence with Monroe, recalled as Minister to France and arriving home to great Republican acclamation in the summer of '97, Pickering's "something of hardness and epigrammatic sharpness" was at its keenest. He wrote Monroe, who demanded reasons for his recall, "It is not true that removal from office necessarily implies actual misconduct. It may merely imply a want of ability."

Certainly he intrigued constantly against Adams but certainly there was great, though not excusable, provocation. Neither was so much a strong as an unpliable man. Both appear to have provoked the worst in the other. Finally, on May 12, 1800, Adams suggested he would like Pickering's resignation. The latter replied that he had contemplated remaining until the following March 4, "when, if Mr. Jefferson were elected President (an event which, in your conversation with me last week, you considered certain) I expected to go out of course." How a rational man could expect this slap would not arouse even Adams is beyond understanding. Pickering continued that he had not brought his family to Washington, "apprehending Jefferson's election," and had hoped by living alone for eight months with great economy to have something with which to maintain them while he sought a new job. He concluded, "I do not feel it to be my duty to resign."

Within an hour a note came from the new White House:

Sir,

Divers causes and considerations essential to the administration of the government in my judgment requiring a change in the Department of State, you are hereby discharged from any further service as Secretary of State.

John Adams
President of the United States

The dismissal was an outrage to Pickering. He had perhaps forgotten the contemptuous lessons he had read Monroe, one of them that "It is easy to conceive that the President of the United States may be possessed of facts and information which would not only justify but require the recall of a Foreign Minister."

It is also certain that, in rage at the Republicans, he conspired to split off New England from the Union, as Burr did the West. Yet no one doubted that in one case the conspiracy arose from a conviction, though bigoted, of right, and in the other from nothing but personal aggrandizement.

Dismissed from office, he planned to try to resume farming on the Susquehanna lands from which he had been driven fifteen years before. Some Boston capitalists thereupon got together to buy the lands from him at a price which would allow him to live in Massachusetts in modest but decent fashion. Pickering very sensibly accepted the offer.

There were three incidents in the last thirty years of his life most typical of him. About a year after Washington's death it was proposed that Congress appropriate $200,000 to be spent "on a tomb and tombstone [for Washington. This] will be a mischievous topic of popular declamation," Pickering declared. "Washington possessed many virtues but uncommon Prudence was his distinguishing characteristic . . . it was rather an assemblage of virtues than any particular features of greatness which rendered him eminent." (Who has better summed up the personality of Washington?) For a Federalist to take such a stand, and express it so well, in 1801, required both courage and wisdom. It was forty-seven years before Congress set aside Pickering's views and authorized the monument.

In 1825, Pickering, in his eightieth year—he had won a plowing contest five years before—read a copy of the *United States Magazine* of January 1823, in which there was a forty-four-page review of William Johnson's *Sketches of the Life and Correspondence of Nathanael Greene*, in two volumes. The review was by John Armstrong and most of it reads like perceptive criticism. He takes the author to task for being "foppish or affected . . . bombastic . . . extravagant and hyperbolic" and finds the text is "involved and obscure" with a good deal of "vulgar usage."

But what most interested Armstrong and then Pickering was the portion having to do with the Anonymous Addresses at Newburgh in 1783—the apparent incitement of the army to overthrow the civil government.

Shortly after the Addresses were issued Armstrong, then an A.D.C. to General Gates, had confessed to their authorship. It was long ago—since then he had been Minister to France and Secretary of War under a Republican Administration—but he was still proud of it.

William Johnson said the anonymous author was Gouverneur Morris and that "no simple and subordinate officer of the Line would have dared write such letters," adding that "Washington ascribed the Addresses to the pen of one or more of his enemies."

Injured pride of authorship was the main aspect of Armstrong's review. He further wrote that Washington, in addition to reading the Anonymous Addresses to his officers—resulting in their immediate rejection of them—had also read a letter to them from a member of Congress from Virginia, "informing him of a plot [Pickering's words] to overturn our Republican Government and to oust [Washington] from the command of the Army and (what is quite extraordinary) that Robert Morris, Gouverneur Morris and Alexander Hamilton all patriots and decided friends of Washington were the grand conspirators."

Armstrong was puzzled as to why no "chronicler of the times or biographer of General Washington" had mentioned this second letter. He concluded that "the letter must have escaped their research. Was it destroyed by Washington himself under a conviction of its errors and injustices . . . such is our conjecture as Robert Morris became his intimate friend and counsellor, Hamilton his confidential minister; Gouverneur Morris his ambassador to the French Court."

This slander of three dead and famous Federalists—Washington, Hamilton, and Gouverneur Morris—aroused Pickering, who said the reason no chronicler had found the letter was because it had never existed and Washington had not read it. He had himself been a few feet from Washington and "there was no such letter read." Governor Brooks of Massachusetts, then an A.D.C. of Washington's, concurred. He wrote to General Ebenezer Huntington of Connecticut and others for their refutation. None supported Armstrong.

Of Washington's farewell words to his officers which brought tears to so many eyes, Pickering had acerbly remarked that the devotees would declare "the words proceeded from the immediate inspiration of heaven," but let a Republican suggest it and he was up in arms.

Unfortunately the January 1823 issue was the only one of the *United States Magazine* but there was small doubt that from it, after many wanderings, came the story by John Corbin in *Two Frontiers of Freedom*, published in 1940, that Hamilton and the Morrises plotted a "Fascist march" on Philadelphia.

The third example of Pickering's special qualities, in which vigor and non-conformity were so marked, was in a well-reasoned proposal to change the manner of electing the President and Vice-President. He had apparently become aware of the strain on representative government of an Executive whose term was not concurrent with Congress, and who was never assured of a majority in Congress.

His proposal, a long one, may be summarized in this way: the people were directly represented in the House and the sovereign states in the Senate. The two houses should therefore by concurrent vote elect the President and Vice-President from their own members for a term of six years, and they should be ineligible for re-election. An incidental benefit, he observed, was that better candidates would be attracted to both House and Senate.

Sources: Wolcott Correspondence, Oliver Wolcott Papers, Connecticut Historical Society. Pickering to Derby and Gates, Emmet Collection, N.Y.P.L. Pickering letters, Miscellaneous Mss., N.Y.P.L. McKean to Jefferson on fires, Thomas McKean Papers, Historical Society of Pennsylvania.

CHAPTER XIII

A Nondescript of Humanity: AARON BURR

IN the scramble to find a suitable person to succeed Gouverneur Morris as Minister to France in 1794, Washington quickly brushed aside the suggestion that Aaron Burr be named. Yet from the surface record it was then a most reasonable nomination and pressed on Washington by Monroe and Madison.

Burr at thirty-eight was the junior senator from New York. His first wife had died that month of cancer and there were no domestic ties to detain him, though the future Mrs. Madison had just made him sole guardian of her son John Payne Todd.

The Administration felt it essential that the Federalist Morris be succeeded by a member of the Republican opposition. It was even hoped that Jefferson himself might go. Burr had been appointed attorney general of New York by Governor Clinton in '89. Two years later he defeated the Federalist Schuyler for the Senate. He came of a distinguished family. Aaron Burr, his father, and Jonathan Edwards, his grandfather, had been the second and third presidents of

Princeton. At Yale the elder Burr's scholastic record was not matched for a hundred years. Burr himself entered Princeton at thirteen, graduated second only to William Bradford, now shortly to succeed Randolph as Attorney General.

Through his family connections he was well known to all "the solid men" of Connecticut: Wadsworth, the Trumbulls, the Wolcotts and his kinsmen, the Pierreponts and Edwards. Brought up as an orphan in Elizabeth Town, New Jersey, knowing the Boudinots, Lord Stirling, and the Livingston family, few men in the North had such connections or were endowed with greater talents. His record in the Revolution looked splendid. In 1775, at nineteen, he left the famous law office of his brother-in-law, Tapping Reeve, in Litchfield, and rushed to Cambridge to join the army. He was beside General Montgomery in the attack on Quebec when Montgomery was killed. Small and slight, he was seen up to his knees in snow, carrying off his general's body. He was said to have been offered a post on Washington's staff but became an aide to Putnam, fighting at Long Island, Trenton, and Monmouth, leaving the army finally as a lieutenant colonel of infantry. Cheetham, in attacking him twenty years later, said that while he held only "subordinate posts" in the war and was not mentioned in Ramsay's or Gordon's histories, "he had an unsullied though not distinguished reputation."

He had been admitted to the New York bar in '82 and that year married the widow of Colonel Prevost, ten years older than he. Of Burr's wooing, the poet Stedman wrote long afterwards:

> Where's the widow or maid with a mouth to be kissed
> When Burr comes a-wooing that long would resist.

Within a year Mrs. Burr produced the little girl of the tragic fate, Theodosia. A woman friend wrote that staunch and powerful Federalist, Jeremiah Wadsworth, in Hartford, "I know you esteem Burr and his wife, and therefore will be glad to hear that she has made him father of a fine daughter and that he is in much better health than for many years."

In the face of this Washington brushed aside Burr's name to appoint Monroe for lack of a better, as he said.[1]

Washington said that Burr's deficiency was of character. No doubt it did not require great insight to perceive this, though many wise and prominent men did not then perceive it. John Adams dined with him and found him living "in style," though he was actually distressed for money. While he already had a reputation for gallantry with women, it was then little more notorious than that of such trusted colleagues of Washington as Gouverneur Morris or Hamilton himself. Nor was Washington particularly censorious in that regard. If Burr had flirted with Mrs. Arnold, so had Robert R. Livingston, who was pressed to take the French post.

The deficiency went far deeper. One aspect of it is the fact that no man, in anything like similar position at the time, was so utterly indifferent to the form of government his country would adopt. Not only were the letters of brilliant minds like Hamilton's, Madison's, Randolph's, and Jay's full of little else—and not in pride of authorship—but so equally were those of more plodding but still valuable men like Knox, McHenry, and George Cabot, to name but a few.

But far beyond this was the inability, in Royce's striking phrase, in a conflict of loyalties to be loyal to loyalty itself, added to a pettiness, parading as high principle of astounding magnitude. Burr's charm and persuasiveness are famous, so that many were led to believe in the high principle. In fact his biographer, Minnegerode, said admiringly that "to a person of Burr's culture Washington's lack of any considerable education" was sufficient reason for not joining his staff.[2]

[1]It is interesting to note that in '97, when Monroe was back in the United States and it appeared he was going to fight a duel with Hamilton over the Mrs. Reynolds scandal, Burr was to be Monroe's second.

[2]The Washington Papers for the Revolution have many letters from Burr full of complaint and fancied injustices, a number of which are marked for No Answer.

It is impossible to say how severe was Burr's disappointment at not getting the Paris post. He was, of course, a senator, but most of the men of his brilliance had had the larger glory of Cabinet or diplomatic appointment. Jefferson said of him later that whenever an army or diplomatic appointment was in the air he contrived "to show himself . . . always at market."

Whatever the disappointment, it was assuaged two years later when, with Adams, Jefferson, and Thomas Pinckney, he was one of the four nominees for the presidency. There he ran a bad fourth in electoral votes, Adams 71, Jefferson 68, Pinckney 59, and Burr 30. So great, though, had been the split among Federalists and the opposition to Adams that Burr must have felt up to the last he had an excellent chance of the first or second office, and though defeated, high honor had been paid him in being one of four nominees to succeed Washington. His whole way of life must have seemed justified.

Adams's Administration got under way with war against France seemingly inevitable. Adams retained Pickering (State), Wolcott (Treasury), and McHenry (War) from Washington's Cabinet. The first two seemed to have assumed from the start that Adams was unfit to be President and joined with Hamilton, the leader of the anti-Adams Federalists, to dominate if not destroy him politically. They were all three patriots, and their motives must have been better than they appeared, but their disloyalty and their intrigues against the President were outrageous. Very shortly, of course, they destroyed the Federalist Party. Hamilton was already a bitter foe of Burr, but his hatred of the man who was to kill him was less than his contempt for Adams.

By the summer of 1798 war seemed so imminent that a new army, with Washington coming out of retirement to command it, was organized. Almost all the prominent Continental officers either sought important commands or were proposed for them by Adams or Washington. But on neither of those lists did Burr's name appear. Yet Hamilton, of all people, on June 28 wrote to Oliver Wolcott, the Secretary of the Treasury, "Colonel Burr sets out today for Philadelphia. I have some reasons for wishing that the Administration may manifest a cordiality to him. It is not impossible he will be found a useful cooperator. I am aware that there are different sides but the case is worth experiment. He will call upon Mr. McHenry upon going to the City."

With his amazing political arrogance, Hamilton supposed that a word from him was enough to secure what he wanted from a Federalist Administration he wished to destroy. It is a letter which Burr himself might have written. More striking is the fact that it says of Hamilton what, in a later letter to Wolcott, Hamilton so truly said of Burr: "To accomplish his ends [Burr] must lean on unprincipled men . . . he will employ the rogues of all parties."

Pickering replied at once to Wolcott. "Strange ideas are being entertained by the President [Adams] relative to the general and staff officers, yet Colonel Burr will assuredly not be Quarter Master General. He has mentioned to the President the necessity of an immediate appointment of a quarter master general to provide everything belonging to that department *but it is impossible that General Washington should confide in him and therefore, he cannot be appointed* [author's italics]."

Washington appointed Colonel Carrington and in a résumé of possible appointments based on the old Continental regiments mentioned only Jonathan Dayton and Aaron Ogden from New Jersey as possibilities.

Burr's disappointment must again have been very great. He had hoped to be sent to France with Madison but Adams sent the staunchest of Federalists, C. C. Pinckney, John Marshall, and Gerry. Though Burr would in two years be Vice-President under Jefferson, the failure ever to secure a high appointive office plainly accelerated his double-dealing, his wrong-headedness, and his descent to folly.

In September '99 it was alleged that he received a bribe of

$20,000 for proposing a bill allowing aliens to hold lands. He challenged John Church, Hamilton's brother-in-law, to a duel for saying it. Two shots were fired and an apology followed.

But in December the next year Burr must indeed have felt his way of life was justified. Possessed of Hamilton's mental brilliance, of Gouverneur Morris's charm and flair, what did the absence of integrity matter, as the Electoral College gave the austere John Jay one vote, sixty-four to Charles C. Pinckney, qualified by every mental and moral attainment—but a man who would not electioneer—sixty-five to the incumbent, President Adams, and seventy-three each to Burr and Jefferson? And when the tie went to the House for settlement, he knew that almost every Federalist, except Hamilton, preferred him to Jefferson.

One of the most fascinating speculations of American history is the question of what kind of President Burr would have made. Would the weight of the great office have created that humility of which he was perhaps most in need? As it was, thirty-six ballots were necessary before the House voted the presidency to Jefferson, the vice-presidency to him.

Many people have found something both noble and moving in his determination that his daughter Theodosia should be "the most cultured and accomplished young woman of her day." Reading of her letters leads one to feel that she may well have been. Gamaliel Bradford said, ". . . as to Burr's worship of her there can be no doubt whatsoever, and it is the finest and most attractive element in his chequered character and career."

As will be seen, there is every doubt of it, if the words have their ordinary meanings. His "worship" had nothing of decent fatherhood about it. Throughout there is a sort of cerebral incest. Bradford saw in it "extreme subtlety with a child-like naïveité," adding that "it is a singular spiritual phenomenon both for him and for her." Bixby, who possessed the original of Burr's European journal—actually his letters to Theodosia —believed that her "copy must have varied in many respects from the original for it is simply inconceivable that a father who loved and respected a daughter as Burr loved and respected Theodosia could have written for her perusal many of the things contained in his journal." Her copy did not vary. The journal was exhibitionism and intended to be.

Her letters to him gradually became half those of a wise mother, half those of a disillusioned mistress.

As a child in the nineties she was devoted to her stepbrother John Prevost, and wrote him constantly with a schoolgirl's wild sweet ways and words. The letters are signed *Theodosia*, but when the hoyden in her asserted itself they are signed *Burr*, as with the doggerel sent him Christmas week the year of '94:

For fashion's sake I have forsook
What sages call my belly
And fashion has not left a nook
For cheese cakes, tarts or jelly.

In February 1801 she was married to Joseph Alston of Charleston, South Carolina, going with him in March to see her father inaugurated as Vice-President. Except to borrow money from him, even for his inaugural trip, Burr's attitude toward his son-in-law was largely that he did not exist. Theodosia herself seems never to have gone beyond being somewhat dutiful, and from her marriage until her death her father and his troubles filled her life. They were both gifted to a marvelous degree. One needed only character, the other only peace of mind, to have been very great. Aaron Burr Alston was born May 29, 1802. It is ordinarily said that "all the hopes of both were centered on him." Only in a measure was this true. Their hopes were centered on some incredible victory for Burr's dark plans and ambitions.

For years Burr had been distressed for money. His salary of $5000 as Vice-President was said only to equal the interest on his debts. Yet his legal fees had been large, he had not lost in "wild lands," like Robert Morris and many others, nor did he have the heavy expenses for domestic illness of Edmund Randolph, nor the limited means of Timothy Pickering, living on small government pay for so many years. All his emotions were unmanageable and debt a natural consequence.

Yet in 1803, as Vice-President, as the recipient of an LL.D. from Princeton, and as guest of Gouverneur Morris at the Washington birthday dinner, over the protests of Hamilton, he must have felt he had come a long way, and that the future held almost limitless possibilities. Even when a reverse came early the next year—with the Republicans nominating George Clinton of New York to run with Jefferson—it did not look too bad. Burr in turn was nominated to run against Morgan Lewis for governor of New York, from which the way back to the presidency should not be difficult.

Even so, mysterious stories about him were spreading. From London in March 1803 Rufus King had written Robert Livingston in Paris, "A gentleman in New York says the vice-president will visit the west country and the Mississippi territory next Spring and insinuates that it is not impossible that he may thereafter reside there."

The nature and virulence of the attack by Cheetham which followed must therefore have been a surprise to Burr. It was personal, it was vicious, and it rested on the effective political grounds of private immorality. Burr was "an intimate of courtesans." Burr had "naked portraits in his bed-chamber." It followed that he had "defrauded heirs" for whom he had been a trustee. Perhaps all were true. Back of Cheetham, Hamilton was expressing the "despicable opinion" he had of Burr. In the midst of it, Burr must have had a sardonic smile at receiving a letter from that strangest of all the land promoters, the Englishman, Charles Williamson, asking Burr if he could get a divorce in Connecticut or Rhode Island, with or without his wife's agreement, on "the grounds [of] a devil of a temper on her part."

In the campaign Burr carried New York City, but Morgan

Lewis "came down to the Harlem" with enough Federalist votes to give him the election.

June, the month of the challenge to Hamilton, followed. On the fifteenth Burr demanded an explanation of the "despicable opinion" Hamilton had expressed in April. Two days later Hamilton replied in a tangle of logic and legalism, neither avowing nor disclaiming it. Burr replied, asking a direct answer. It was reported that Hamilton would say it was an opinion of him politically, not personally, but this "did not attribute to Colonel Burr any instance of dishonorable conduct nor relate to his private character." Burr sent his challenge on the twenty-seventh.

Great as had been the ceaseless and vindictive attacks on him by Hamilton, Burr's pressing to the limit his "right" to a duel was the supreme instance of his false "high principle." In spite of all the duels that followed for sixty years, the concept of "the field of honor" had been held in contempt by the best men in the country for twenty-five years.

On the night before the duel Burr wrote Theodosia, asking her to burn his correspondence from women, and left instructions with her regarding "a certain lady," while Hamilton wrote the noble, heartbreaking letters now so well known. With incredible malevolence, Burr wrote Biddle a week after the duel, "The last hours of General Hamilton (I might include the day preceding the interview) appear to have been devoted to malevolence and hypocrisy."

Famous as the duel is, it is still hard to realize that Hamilton, the leader of the Federalists, had been killed by a Republican opponent, the Vice-President of the United States. A New York jury, declaring that Burr "did kill and murder against the people of New York," was unable to indict, except for a misdemeanor, since there had been no murder in the state. The grand jury of Bergen County, New Jersey, however, indicted him for murder and, on July 22, Burr fled secretly to Philadelphia and then southward, drawing on various people, mainly Biddle, without "funds [or] friends pledged to him to warrant his drafts." On the way he wrote to Theodosia, "Let me have the idea you are not dissatisfied with me a moment. I cannot just now endure it."

Pierce Butler, at St. Simon's Island off Georgia, gave him asylum, and in October Burr was at the Alstons' in Savannah.

Advising Merry, the British Minister, that he was ready "to assist the United Kingdom in any manner in which they make think fit to employ him . . . particularly to effect a separation of the western part of the United States," this incredible man went on to Washington to preside over the Senate and, in November, at the trial of Justice Chase. Jefferson had him to dinner at the White House and a petition was sent to New Jersey asking that the indictment against him be dismissed. By Jefferson's act Theodosia's brother-in-law was made secretary of the Louisiana Territory and her stepbrother Prevost appointed to the Superior Court in New Orleans.

Among her letters of the month is one of morbid pathos to her husband. She was ill and believed her death was imminent. "I had nearly forgotten to say," she wrote, "that I charge you not to allow me to be stripped and washed, as is usual. I am pure enough thus to return to dust. Why then expose my person? Pray see to this."

More or less with it came one from Burr in Philadelphia informing the Carolinian grandee that "it is high evidence of the barbarism of our Southern States that in an extent of three hundred miles filled with wealthy people and in a hot climate there should not be in any one private family a convenient bathing-room. Perhaps indeed some ruined French refugee may have expended $50 to furnish himself and family this luxury."

In February, "without emotion," Burr presided as the electoral votes were counted, re-electing Jefferson, and displacing Burr with George Clinton as Vice-President.

With the arrival of spring and the second Jefferson Administration, Burr went west, as always almost penniless and unable to practice law in, or return to, New York or New Jersey. On May 5 he reached the Blennerhassetts' island in the Ohio and began his long beguiling of that unhappy pair.

Blennerhassett was a romantic well-to-do Irishman, born in England but educated at Trinity College, Dublin, who had come to America in 1796 with his young wife, who was also his niece, to find a "sylvan retreat." He had found it on an island in the Ohio River near Parkersburg and there built himself a fine house. He was forty, Burr forty-nine, when they met by chance in Marietta, Ohio, and Blennerhassett took him to his house to his own life's undoing.

From the island Burr moved south to Nashville and Natchez, and on to New Orleans, talking war with Spain and the invasion of Mexico and listening also to the same talk from the men of the Western Waters. On his travels he had met, presumably by arrangement, his close friend and fellow townsman of Elizabeth, New Jersey, Jonathan Dayton, the youngest man to sign the Constitution, later Speaker of the House and senator. At Burr's return to Pittsburgh and then Philadelphia in November, rumors followed that he had been hatching revolution, and Dayton and he began their fantastic negotiations first with Merry, the British Minister, and then with Casa Yrujo, the Spanish. Merry was asked for $500,000 to finance a separatist revolution in the West. Merry agreed to propose the matter to London. Dayton saw Casa Yrujo and more modestly asked for $30,000 or $40,000 for the same purpose, assuring him that Mexico was not the objective. He is alleged to have told Yrujo that the plan was to fill Washington with armed men, seize the government, establish the independence of Louisiana and the West, but not molest Spanish interests. Yrujo made a preliminary advance of $1500 and appeared most agreeable to the whole plan and anxious that Merry should not be the lender.

What Yrujo can have been thinking of is hard to say. He had already been Minister here for about ten years and he was happily married to Sally McKean, daughter of the Signer,

Thomas McKean, now governor of Pennsylvania and a strong Republican. Is it conceivable that he would have risked his own career and the vital interests of his country on the word of men like Burr and Dayton without seeking advice from his wife and father-in-law, who knew them so well? Of course, he would have had to say to McKean, "I am proposing to advance money to people who are going to seize the government from your friends in Washington. Do you think it is a sound idea? . . ." But could he actually have thought it so himself? In any event, Dayton came back and told him never mind as the new government in London was agreeable and Burr had decided he did not want Spanish help.

While these intrigues seem "a farrago of nonsense," in one of Washington's best phrases, they are in keeping with the whole scheme. Burr talked to Daniel Morgan about it. Morgan told friends who wrote Madison who wrote Jefferson. Blennerhassett wrote letters to the *Ohio Gazette* on Western separation and Andrew Jackson built boats for the expedition, and Burr prepared to "proceed westward never to return." What he actually did, or planned to do, during 1806 will probably never be fully known, so tangled is the evidence, so dubious the witnesses. It is almost certain that Burr himself did not know. He asserted on the one hand that he "had no design to dissolve or disturb the tranquility of the United States," yet at his trial based his defense less on the utter innocence of treason than on the legal points, wholly justifiable as they were, that no witness had proved an overt act and that "if the overt act be not proved by two witnesses . . . all other testimony must be irrelevant."

In essence, these were the charges out of which his arrest and indictment for treason arose: that Burr plotted the union of the West with Spain; that he plotted an independent trans-Allegheny government; that he raised and led an armed force south for those purposes.

Until his trial, Burr's answers were various: that in March 1806 he had talked with Jefferson himself for two hours and found his schemes of settlement "regarded complacently"; if in time it resulted in overrunning the Spanish dominions in the Southwest and Mexico, no separation was intended; but that, as a matter of fact, "his object [was] agricultural" and his boats "the vehicles of immigration"; his sole purpose was to settle the Washita lands, though if "war broke out with Spain he would lead a force into Texas and Mexico"; as to the "armed force," at whose head he was finally arrested, it consisted of sixty men and nine boats.

The public mind, and doubtless Jefferson's in ordering his arrest, found it absurd and impossible to suppose that the cultured and essentially urban Aaron Burr should at fifty have acquired the pioneer spirit and wanted to live in frontier settlements on the Washita. Certainly there were no "bathing rooms" there. John Adams said he must be "an idiot or a lunatic."

Through the whole business Burr represented himself as acting under "high principles" to achieve modest ends.

His flight to avoid arrest near Natchez, his recognition at Wakefield, Alabama, his arrest and removal to Richmond were as full of suspense and melodrama as the flight to Varennes of the Bourbons and must have pleased him. In the best cavalier spirit his first request was for "decent clothes."

The hearings and trial in Richmond dragged on until September 1807, when the acquittal for treason took place. Burr's defense was greatly helped by Justice Marshall's insistence that Burr was under trial, not inquisition, and had all the rights of an accused, including the presumption of innocence until guilt was proven. It was also helped by Jefferson's declaration that Burr was guilty, to which Edmund Randolph, of Burr's counsel, replied that such a declaration was unconstitutional. "It is not the business of the President to give an opinion concerning the guilt or innocence of any person."

More fascinating than those great issues is the working of Burr's mind. No layman should fasten psychiatric tags on a man, though one must wish Freud could have had Burr's case history. Fantastic as was Burr's behavior in small matters, it is all wholly believable and what was to be expected.

Needing money, he insisted that both Theodosia, though ill with influenza, and her husband come to the 98-degree heat of Richmond to be with him.

In June the hapless Blennerhassett was indicted and lodged in the state prison. His account of it is one long lament to his wife. Very touching is one of her letters to him:

> I hope you have done tormenting yourself about the loss of my picture. I inclosed to you . . . what is of infinitely more value, the profiles of the two darling, lovely boys. . . . Remember that you are adored by
>
> Your
>
> *M. Blennerhassett*

Toward these two whose lives and happiness he had ruined, Burr behaved with airy contempt. They were impoverished by the money they had given him but, typically, he said he had "made financial arrangements in Philadelphia to settle everything after his acquittal."

A man named Luckett held a protested draft of Burr's for $5000, which Blennerhassett had endorsed. On the day that action on it was demanded, Blennerhassett had had trouble paying $2.55 postage on two letters. Burr sent around a note that afternoon saying that Luckett held a draft of him for *$25*, "which it would gratify him if I could discharge." The day before Burr had sent word by Alston that Luckett's account was not "allowed" and not to worry.

On September 13, after their release, Burr dined with Blennerhassett. "He is as gay as usual and as busy on reorganizing his project for action as if he had never suffered the least interruption . . . in six months (he said) our schemes could all be reorganized." As they dined, a musk-scented note came in for Burr from a feminine admirer. Blennerhassett wrote in his diary, ". . . the whole physiognomy of the man now assumed an alteration and vivacity [taking off] fifteen years of his age."

For weeks afterward Blennerhassett was trying to salvage his fortunes and to learn how Burr planned to reimburse him. In October, in a casual by-the-way, Burr "mentioned that he was prepared to go to England, that the time was now auspicious for him." It was said evidently with his usual high principle. Distasteful as the prospect was, he was prepared for the sacrifice.

For once the duller Blennerhassett saw through him and wrote in his *Diary*, "He has no serious purpose of reviving any of his speculations in America and even of returning from Europe if he can get there." There were still legacies to come to Blennerhassett in England and Burr asked for letters to his friends. Blennerhassett decided to give them "and then press him," mistakenly believing that Burr would be grateful and perhaps do something about his debts. With pathetic decency Blennerhassett even confided to his *Diary*, "It is a little painful, I own, to feel oneself obliged to bring even a bad man into the path of his duty by artifice."

Burr was of course superior to all this, and to sordid details of debt. Charles Dickens himself has never "caught" his type more effectively than Blennerhassett did in his entry for November 2. "With his accustomed affectation [Burr] asked what was the amount of my account declaring he had never looked into it since I handed it to him."

The two men separated and Burr went to Biddle's in Philadelphia and told him he feared he might have to commit suicide. A day or so later, however, a better solution suggested itself—for Governor McKean to appoint him chief justice of Pennsylvania. The amazing thing is that on the bench he would no doubt have perfectly fulfilled his duties.

The Signer, Benjamin Rush, wrote John Adams about it, "Burr failed first in obtaining a foreign embassy the first year he took a seat in the senate; second in supplanting Mr. Jefferson; third in obtaining the governorship of New York; fourth, in his western enterprise and now in being Chief Justice of Pennsylvania." Rush went on that he remembered Burr at his commencement at Princeton, thirty-five years before, when he spoke "building castles in the air," and concluded he was "a nondescript in the history of human nature."

Burr seems to have had no idea what he was to do with the rest of his long life. Surely it is one of the major incongruities of human experience that a man should have expected to be chief justice of Pennsylvania when in New Jersey he was still under indictment for murder and unable to go to New York unless to a debtors' prison.

But almost on the fourth anniversary of Hamilton's death Burr fled New York in disguise for Europe. Theodosia was with him, as his "sister," until his departure and his letter to her by the pilot had "a desire to say something at the last moment—a reluctance resembling parting." She was left with his debts, his hopelessly tangled affairs, and his wounded name.

A few weeks after he left her he was dining gaily at Lady Holland's table in London and, like Thomas Paine and Lafayette, making specious claims to a nationality he did not possess but desired the protection of. He, a former Continental officer and Vice-President of the United States, asked for a British passport on the grounds of being "born within the King's allegiance and his parents British subjects," adding that "it was a birthright which I had the right to resume." It brought him face to face with taxation without representation when he had to pay a guinea for a license to wear hair powder.

In Theodosia's first letter to him, written from Philadelphia, one must wonder if there is unintentional confirmation of his imperial ambitions in 1806. "Thank God," she writes, "I am not near my subjects. (Mex)."

In London Burr was received by such figures of society and statecraft as Lady Holland and Lord Castlereagh but on December 2 he went, in his words, to a "rendez-vous at eleven" of a very different sort. All who are fascinated by the chances and coincidences of life must lament there is no full report of what happened, for the "rendez-vous" was "at Mr. Lamb's rooms. He is a writer and lives with a maiden sister, also litteraire, in a fourth story." It would be priceless to know what the gentle, laughing Elia said to and thought of this nondescript of human nature, or Burr of him. Those European travelers and diarists, Gouverneur Morris and Aaron Burr, have much to atone for but their really scarlet sins are that Morris, having oysters on Christmas Eve with James Boswell years before, merely recorded the fact as Burr did the meeting with Charles and Mary Lamb. For that matter on New Year's Day, 1809, we only know that Burr "called on" Sir Walter Scott.

Already, though, familiar troubles were gathering around Burr. In March he was forced to hide from a bookseller from whom he had bought recklessly without means of payment. Like many bibliophiles, he felt that since owning books was "good" the means of acquiring them were unimportant, and since the bulk of these were shipped to Theodosia the debts arose from high principle. Bankrupt and a fugitive, living by his wits, he wrote sternly to Theodosia, "You say that my note by T. was received. . . . Pray were there not three notes and a parcel besides? I thought you had been long since [she was twenty-six] cured of this slovenly way of acknowledging."

On April 4, Lord Liverpool issued a warrant for his arrest. In spite of his protest that he was a British subject and his "rights [as such] indelible," he was released only with the proviso that he would leave at once for Sweden. It did not seem to trouble him greatly. There was an "eighteen year old girl all animation, gayety, ease and badinage" in the coach and at Oxford "a little brunette."

On May 3 he saw the church and lighthouse of Göteborg from the ship's rail and a week later was in Stockholm. Sweden delighted him from the "coffee with cream instead of a dram" in the morning to the House of the Nobles, the Ritter Huset of Gustavus Adolphus, still one of the noblest buildings in all

Europe. There was nothing like it in America, a gentlemen's club, "a billiard room, card tables, a news room with the domestic and foreign gazettes. A library beautifully situated" and from the window he "saw a lady riding *en cavalier* with scarlet waist-jacket and white overalls a la Turc ou Perse very wide—a round hat with feathers. She had a very fine form."

Casually as they seem to be made, there are references in almost every letter to Theodosia to some aspect of sexuality. He writes that he has seen the portrait of "Aurora Camberse de Konigsmere who frightened Charles XII. [She is] wrapped in a silk manteau. The bosom, left foot and right knee (and something more) bare." He saw a Russian medal: "Catherine *lays on the ground naked* [his italics] looking up at an eagle. I will go again." He saw Mademoiselle de Rosin, "one of the loveliest blondes I ever saw. About one inch taller than you. In form much like." He sat a half hour "with Mlle. Ulrich. She is beautiful. Very beautiful about fifteen nearly your size and form." And at Gotha he met "La Princesse Louisa. . . . I demanded a souvenir to which she agreed and would think what it should be. I proposed a garter."

To one of these references, Theodosia replied, "Do tell me, is Miss Gurnson pretty. . . . Has she ever had a lover? I hope she has, such an 'all impassioned, sensitive, brilliant creature' [is there a touch of jealousy there?] should never be without one."

One letter from Sweden, however, tells a story only too familiar today. A Swedish lady was "frightened to death about the Russians [coming to the Coronation]. The Russian soldiers! It is the universal opinion that, if they come, there will be general plundering and other worse enormities."

In August 1809, Burr "reached Elsinore, the castle which has long levied tribute on all Europe." In Copenhagen he was awed and delighted by the King's library of 300,000 books.

Judging by his voracious reading in Sweden, though, he could, given more than the four months he was in Denmark, have read them all. The next month Theodosia asked Dolly Madison to intercede with the President on Burr's behalf, but the answer came back that he "regretted he could not gratify her wishes." She had written that a letter had just come from Burr in which "to my inexpressible relief he says he has in view some means of support . . . yet I fear he may say so merely to alleviate my anxiety for what can he do in Stockholm. . . ." (Her son is spoken of as *Burr.*)

In November he went to Altona, outside Hamburg. It was there Gouverneur Morris had spent the months distraught with desire for Adèle de Flahaut, long his mistress, then a refugee refusing to accept him as a lover. Morris beguiled his time with two young girls of the town, who gave him German lessons.

Perhaps there is something in the air of that bleak, fog-laden town particularly affecting Americans. No one reading the passage in Burr's *Journal* for November 23 without knowing the author could be positive it was not written by Morris, so identic is it with entries in his *Diaries:* "My belle J. came up and took tea with me and then an hour of English lesson. She makes great progress and amuses me . . . dined in my rooms with Mlle J. attending me. . . . Mlle J. has been up and interrupted me very pleasantly for more than an hour. . . ." And it might well be the equally inquisitive Morris as Burr "all day roving at Gotha, having made some acquaintances—some discoveries about these false hips, several little adventures."

On their better side, both men had the same sensitive tenderness for childhood. Either might have written, as Burr did at Kassel, of the "charming, hatless, gloveless child of eleven playing a violin and singing in the snow."

These men, so all but the same in their pursuit of women, were otherwise poles apart. In the midst of dalliance and dissipation, Morris's powerful practical mind was engaged constantly with the great issues of the day and the interests of his country. Burr, Hamilton had said with truth in 1800, was "bankrupt beyond redemption except by the plunder of his country. His public principles have no other spring or aims than his own aggrandisement."

The mental brilliance, the culture, the personal charm of the two men were much akin. There was no quality of Burr's which Morris needed but if by moral transfusion he could have given Burr his sense of public service, patriotism and magnanimity, personal integrity and good sense, Burr's life could well have been a glory to his country and his daughter.

As it was she wrote him to Germany that funds were not available for her to join him, saying, "You should not have tantalized me with this proposed voyage. It is quite out of my reach [Mr. Alston not unreasonably declining to finance it]. . . . You must not show my letters to anyone."

Then in August she wrote in obvious shock and dismay, "Our newspapers say as from authority that you plead your right to remain as a British subject asserting you were born such. Is this so? Answer me at length on this subject."

By the time the letter reached him he was trying to leave Germany for Paris. In spite of the efforts of John Armstrong, the American Minister, former A.D.C. of Gates and friend of Burr's, to prevent it, he entered Paris in February 1810. He was now fifty-four and he lived the life of a later "lost generation" thirty years younger. Like them, he went "around town" to the Café of the Blind where the performers were blind, the Café of the Thousand Columns, and the Varieties, "so crowded we could not get in."

Talleyrand, at a banquet in whose honor in Philadelphia Burr had presided, would not receive him, though Fouché did and listened to a plan for a French invasion of Mexico under Burr's leadership. He saw the Emperor Napoleon come in during the third act at the opera and had "a good view of him."

In the next box, however, he "made a very pleasant acquaintance. She invited me to supper which I declined. How wonderfully discreet. But then I engaged to call on her tomorrow. How wonderfully silly."

Yet such was the silly way this man of magnificent potentialities went. For three hours before visiting her he read Jeremy Bentham's *Notes on the Judiciary*. Then twice a day for a time he visited Madame Paschaud, with her "very black hair and eyes and a fine clear fair brunette." She was the wife of a bookseller then in Geneva, and reminded him of Dolly Madison. The combination was made to order for Burr—books, brunette, and an absent husband—and as he wrote Theodosia, "I rather think she must be the cause that I have not written."

He told the brunette, so he wrote Theodosia, that he wanted to be in "a little room looking into the garden" with her, though even "a bed at an inn" where he would do "anything but sleep with [her]" was alluring. As it was, he went to the painter Vanderlyn's studio to watch him painting his *enceinte* model; or to another friend's to find him in bed "and by his side a lady. Her back towards me. She did not turn nor look." But on nearer view he found it was a German beauty he had already met. She engrossed him and he her, for that matter, as she asked him when her lover was out of the room to breakfast with her the next day.

Most of the time he was almost literally penniless, borrowing four francs of his landlady to get his shoes repaired and then later "forty sous from Julie the maid, all she had."

When he was successful in borrowing larger sums from the more affluent—Edward Griswold let him have $300 on his request for "$600/1000 to be repaid on arrival in United States"—he spent it like a madman either on books and trinkets for Theodosia or on toys or souvenirs for her child.

He would write her of his woes and his women, and then pay twenty-two guineas for a watch, telling her, ". . . now don't scold me for I can sell it for the same money as soon as I shall have no other means of getting bread." Two days later he pawned *her* watch and rings for $200 and bought more books, but in two weeks the bookseller was at his bedside for twenty-seven livres, overdue, which Burr paid him, leaving himself with three sous.

This forced him to break into "a little treasure of coins" he had made for his grandson. It amounted to only one Danish and two Swedish thalers but with it Burr's "first resolution was to go and amuse myself with some folly" as he had been three days without sugar "and more than ten without coffee." He managed to touch Griswold for an additional 150 francs and a Mrs. Robertson gave him supper by her fire, with the room temperature at fifty-one degrees.

Very shortly he had to go "to hunt a gold chain five feet long" for a woman and pledged the twenty-two-louis watch and a ring for five livres to do it. He got the chain "and supped on stewed prunes."

With all this and more he excoriated Theodosia, then more than ever in torment as Blennerhassett demanded payment from Alston of $35,500 under threat of publishing letters incriminating him. Yet she wrote Burr May 10, 1811, "Go to New York. Make your stand there. If you are attacked you will be in the midst of the Tenth Legion. . . . If the worst comes, I will leave everything to suffer with you." He wrote back from Osnabrück that he would go to Amsterdam, Paris, Bordeaux, and "thence to thee." In mid-June he wrote he could have sailed from Amsterdam but must go back to Paris "for a thousand nothings of which the most important are to buy [her child] some beautiful marbles and you some silk stockings." Written to a daughter by a busy man of large affairs, how charming this would be. Coming from him, Theodosia must have said to herself, "How can he possibly write such things?" Unconsciously he pictured himself in a line to her two days later. He said through Picardy the roadside beggars threw roses in the coach, "a pretty way of calling our attention."

That same day, coming into Paris, he saw 250,000 people caught in the rain at St. Cloud and wrote Theodosia the women tucked up their gowns "so you could see through wet, transparent chemises."

July 4 in Paris he went out to the Boulevard "to buy Bayle's works and Dictionary, eight volumes elegantly bound," adding guiltily, "You will see ruin in such a purchase."

Eight months later, stranded again in London, he tried to sell the Bayle to Lord Lansdowne only to find, of course, it was already in the great library at Bowood. Then he found there would be a hundred per cent duty on it if he sold it. He tried to sell his watch but "London was full of all sorts of bijous and watches in the hands of distressed emigrés from France and Germany." But he could and did sell "your eight pairs of beautiful stockings."

Finally he set sail from Amsterdam. The ship captain who heretofore "had been so proud to have [me] and would not hear me talk of money previously" abruptly demanded 450 guilders for the passage. Burr sold his grandson's watch to raise it.

He had forgotten the British blockading cruisers, "four of them in full sight, not two leagues off," and his ship was brought into Gravesend. All the fall of 1811 and winter of 1812 he waited. On New Year's Eve "about twelve o'clock [he] took up a French novel, Adèle de Sénanges, and read till three." It was by Adèle de Flahaut, Morris's former mistress, and had been written partly at Altona. Apparently Burr knew nothing of the long affair, as indeed few people did in America, and Morris was now married to Anne Randolph.

In January Russell, the American chargé in London, gave him a passport for any place but New Orleans. Burr was reduced to living on rice, toast, and water by then but a girl whom he picked up in London he sent home in a hackney coach.

On the very day before his final sailing on the *Aurora*, March 25, for Newburyport, a letter came to him from a woman in London:

Will you have your profile taken and leave it with me? It is done in less than five minutes; the expense a mere trifle. You must have had a solitary wet walk last night.

Toujours la même

May 4 he was in Boston Harbor. Unbelievably, it was snowing hard and he remained on board alone, disguised by a wig and a beard, though his baggage was on the dock and Aaron Burr on the flyleaves of his books. The Collector of the Port was Henry Dearborn, the Continental veteran who had fought beside him at Quebec thirty-seven years before, and his son recognized Burr. He secured a room incognito. "The door never opens but I expect to hear the comer exclaim out 'Colonel Burr,' " he wrote to Theodosia. He sent a messenger to Harvard College with some of his books and raised forty dollars.

Finally he wrote to Jonathan Mason, who had been a senator from Massachusetts while Burr was Vice-President. They had been born the same year and were classmates at Princeton. He asked Mason to come to see him. There was no reply and Burr wrote again asking the wealthy Mason either to buy his books for "$6/800" or to make him an advance of $300 on them. Of Mason's silence Burr wrote Theodosia, ". . . when a man takes time to consider whether he will do a good or a civil action, be assured he will never do it." He was quite right. Mason replied after ten days in the conventional way of refusing such requests then and now. He said he had wholly withdrawn from commerce and it was not convenient to make advances.

It reached Burr May 24. On the nineteenth he had written Theodosia in South Carolina that his New York creditors were inexorable but "I have a project of entering in the holy state of matrimony. The charming object is already designated and love, almighty love! The fair object is a worthy lady some few years older than myself" (he was 56), and she had, he believed, both a fortune and the good nature to share it with him. Two days later, perhaps for once abashed, he wrote that it was better to marry than go to jail. In any event nothing came of it and on May 30 he sailed as Mr. de Gamelli on the sloop *Rose* for New York. They reached New York on June 7 and the next day he was landed by skiff at 66 Water Street and for the rest of the month was in hiding.

There early in July came the letter from Theodosia: "I have lost my boy," Aaron Burr Alston, the son of the governor of South Carolina. Now it did not matter that Burr had sold the watch and the coins he was bringing him.

What Burr really felt, what he wrote to Theodosia, we do not know. On August 12 she wrote him, "I am not insensible to your affection nor quite unworthy of it tho' I can offer nothing in return but the love of a broken, deadened heart, still desirous of promoting your happiness, if possible."

On December 30 she started north on the ship *Patriot*. It was lost in a great storm and nothing ever heard of it. Most of Burr's papers were aboard.

Burr lived until September 14, 1836. Almost the last of his papers in the New York Historical Society is a check to himself or bearer on the Bank of Manhattan for $8.44.

The record of his life speaks for itself. Not the least of it is that it brought discredit on such rare qualities as personal charm, lightheartedness, and love of books and learning. It was practically without a redeeming quality since it is evident that love of Theodosia—alleged by many to have been that quality—was not love at all but a mixture of tyranny and mental cruelty. At its best it seems to presume her love was to be had by gifts. At its worst it is almost the taunting of a devoted and faithful woman by the boasts of his own vices and infidelities.

In none of his correspondence with men is there a breath of public spirit, or of the public good, or of public duty. He was in no way the victim of malign fate but wholly, to a degree few men have been, of his own unmanageable desires.

Sources: For a life of Burr, readers may best make their own choice of many biographies. His and Theodosia's letters quoted herein are from their Papers, N.Y.H.S., except hers to Dolly

Madison from Box B3, Various Accessions, Library of Congress. King's letter to R. R. Livingston about Burr is in Livingston Collection, N.Y.H.S. See also Charles Biddle's *Autobiography* (Philadelphia, 1883); *The Blennerhassett Papers* (Cincinnati, 1864). For *The Private Journal of Aaron Burr*, see the full Bixby Edition, 2 vols. (Rochester, N.Y., 1903), Rare Book Room, N.Y.P.L. Compare M. L. Davis's somewhat Bowdlerized edition of 1838.

CHAPTER XIV

Two South Carolina Grandees: THE PINCKNEY BROTHERS

IN retrospect the astonishing miracle of the Revolution is the fact that thirteen colonies, characterized by the widest differences of outlook and interest, of British pressure and interference, of climate and culture, adhered to it. Twelve of these colonies, without regard to equally great differences in area and population, each produced a small but remarkable group of men who trusted and respected each other, worked confidently together, and were, in large measure, interchangeable in their competence and devotion to independence.

In many matters, public and private, there were bitter differences of opinion among them—the conservatives hated the levelers—but within the councils there was an amazing respect for another man's opinions, a willingness to discuss them, to reach a workable compromise, and above all to accept each other as equals in spite of differences in education, manners, or worldly goods. In the Declaration's own quiet phrase, these men individually possessed a decent respect for the opinion of mankind.

Nowhere was this more marked than among the grandees of

South Carolina, and nowhere might it more easily have been expected to be absent by those who suppose wealth, culture, and breeding are destructive of a sense of obligation, service, and the common weal.

This sense of the whole was greater than the parts of their lives. It transcended the society of Charleston, with its grace and elegance, or the outdoor life on the great plantations where "in perfect health we have passed the Equinox *without a hurricane* [Thomas Pinckney's italics]"; it was more than their wealth sea-borne in many cargoes to London; more than their law practices.

They lived like the great noblemen abroad but, it would seem, almost all without their vices and profligacy. In a sense they combined the robust vigor of Squire Western with the erudition and charm of the young Charles James Fox, adding to it the practical business experience of a banker of the City of London. Cavalier and capitalist, at home in countinghouse, law court, or country sports, aristocrats yet careerists, these men exemplified the wonderful variety of which the patriot leaders were made. Proud and jealous of South Carolina, worlds away from the dour zealots of New England, they rose without hesitation to stand by Massachusetts and risk their lives and all they possessed in her defense.

A marvel of the Revolution is that, of all the men who opposed it, none came to any later greatness. It is a marvel indeed to think that the grandee families, men and women, at once perceived that America was their "country," and that it was sweet and fitting, as the Romans had said, to suffer and die for it. In none of them was brother against brother.

Only a trained genealogist could do justice to the fascination of the intermarriages of the Rutledges, Pinckneys, Middletons, Moultries, and Laurenses in South Carolina.

Charles Pinckney, royal chief justice of South Carolina, and his marvelous wife, Elizabeth Lucas, founder of the indigo industry, had two sons, Charles Cotesworth, born 1746, and Thomas, born 1750. Both went to the Westminster School in

London, Christ Church College, Oxford, and the Middle Temple, both were Continentals, both envoys extraordinary, both nominees for Vice-President of the United States and Charles for President also. The elder first married Sarah, sister of Arthur Middleton, a Signer of the Declaration, whose sister was married to Edward Rutledge, himself a Middle Templar, a member of the Continental Congress, an officer in the Florida campaign when he was captured at St. Augustine, and later governor of the state. John Rutledge, wartime governor of the state, a first justice of the United States Supreme Court and nominated for Chief Justice, was his brother.

Thomas Pinckney was married first to Elizabeth Motte, one of whose sisters, Hannah, was married to Thomas Lynch, the father of the Signer. After his death she became the second wife of General Moultrie. After the death of Elizabeth Motte, Thomas Pinckney married another of her sisters, Frances, widow of young John Middleton.

Their second cousin, Charles Pinckney, captured when Savannah fell to the British, a delegate like his cousin Charles C. to the Constitutional Convention, a later governor and Minister to Spain, married Mary Laurens, a daughter of Henry Laurens, president of the Continental Congress, and a sister of the brilliant Colonel John Laurens, killed in action at the end of the Revolution.

Arthur Middleton, a graduate of St. John's College, Cambridge, a Signer, married Mary Izard and an Izard married Emma Middleton.

So "the connection" ran.

The careers of Charles Cotesworth and his brother Thomas Pinckney are wonderful examples of how the best men of the time looked on their public duty. If the duty meant risking their lives in battle or if the very greatest interests of their country were involved, they responded at once. If it was anything less, like a Cabinet post, they preferred to be left to the busy indolence of their private lives.

There is not a great store of their private letters and papers but in those that are extant there is a special quality—as it were, an amateur attitude toward life in the best sense of the word. They make it clear that the patriot leaders were human beings of whose lives not every waking moment was devoted to statecraft and great issues of the future. Above all, though, is the light they throw on a happy family life of the time, intimate, affectionate, high-spirited, and decorous.

In the spring and summer of 1777, Thomas Pinckney, unmarried at twenty-seven, a Continental officer on duty in the defenses of Charleston, wrote his sister, "I should be very glad to have a good squad of linen sent down to me at once as it is both inconvenient and expensive to send a boy to town every two days which I must do when I have no more than two shirts sent to me at one time. Remember me to my Mother, Sally [Mrs. C. C. Pinckney] and the brats."

The "squad" of linen adds a fine military touch to one of the main preoccupations—canards about the dirtiness of the period notwithstanding—of the officers of the time.

He sent Toby, with his next letter, "for some clean linen, my *couteau de chasse* from Oliphant's, and my gun and scabbard from Crawford . . . please purchase a washing tub for me . . . [and in a P.S.] some ink." The hunting knife was in French, perhaps out of compliment to the imminent arrival of "the French nobility," Lafayette among them.

A few days later, having been home, he wrote in some alarm in spite of his martial valor, "I know I have to expect a severe lecture from my Mother and you, my dear Harriott, for carrying away the closet key. . . . [Pray] give vent to your anger in the epistolary way for I can better bear it at a distance as I shall then only hear the growling of the thunder without any danger of the lightning." No nonsense, no momism with spoiled sons, in that house.

Four days later he asked for his pavillion, mosquito boots, *couteau de chasse*, and silver shoe buckles to be delivered to Toby. "We expect all the French nobility together with our Generals to dine here today." Before long he wanted "as much scarlet broadcloth as will make a facing for the blue coat which Mr. Dent has sent home . . . the yellow cloth for waistcoat and whatyecallums with the buttons from the blue velvet must be conveyed to the same place . . . to have the whole executed in the most elegant taste." He was describing the uniform of the South Carolina Line, the Continentals. Then, reasserting an older brother's superiority, he added he must see her "solutions of quadrilateral equations and her progress in analytical science." Before long he was recommending she "read over the last two volumes of Rousseau's *Eloisa* which I think you have." The two references are part of an enormous refutation of the myth that women, even of well-to-do families, were largely uneducated at the time.

On the day after the Battle of the Brandywine, of which he did not of course know but in which his brother Charles Cotesworth was engaged, he wrote, "I am informed E. Rutledge has a letter from General Washington. Pump the news out of him and tell him that he is a shabby fellow for not coming yesterday to the Island to partake of our turkey, ham, roast mutton, boiled mutton, beef stakes, etc. etc."[1]

Two days later he wrote, though with eighteenth-century expansiveness, the familiar letter of a young officer then and now: "This line will prove not entirely disagreeable to you when you are informed it comes to invite you to a party of pleasure, of which pleasures a very fine turtle, presented to us by Captain Biddle is according to the opinion of some to form no inconsiderable part. . . . Saturday next . . . I hope you will bring some young ladies with you. . . . Boats at Exchange Wharf at 9 o'clock."

These young, lighthearted letters, saying so much between the lines of happy normal family life, are quite different from those written to "Honored Madam," their remarkable mother,

[1]A marketing list on a postwar June week end for the Pinckney town house read: "Veal cutlets, turnips, eggs, steaks, pees, grits, plums, turtle steaks, ice, knuckle veal, corn, melon, carrots, okra, goose, shrimps, leg mutton, soup today and Sunday."

by her warrior sons. Theirs, filial reverent, dutiful, yet human, give one pause in a day when parents themselves appear to feel any respect for the Fifth Commandment may blight their children's lives and require the services of an analyst. Mrs. Pinckney's breathe with love, pride, and faith in these extroverted men of action.

It was not only in South Carolina that young men delighted to honor their fathers and their mothers. J. P. Wyllis, Yale, 1773, a Connecticut Continental, writing "Honoured Sir," his father, of the impending battle of the Brandywine, closed:

> ... Time will admit no more but that I am with greatest respect,
> Your dutiful son
>
> P.S. I dare not ask the favour of a reply from my Father.

and from Yorktown: "I sincerely congratulate you on such an important event–Charleston is our next objective. If [this] is legible and pleases my Father, 'tis satisfaction sufficient to his dutiful son." And how charming is Abigail Adams's letter to her second boy, Thomas: "When you address me again, let it be by the endearing epithet of Mother, instead of the formal one, Madame."

Writing her son Thomas in the afternoon of the morning he had left for the East Florida campaign, Mrs. Pinckney begins, "You see my dear child you are no sooner out of sight but I begin to scribble." She tells him she already misses "the racket and the little hurry of the mornings."

The closest either son comes to disrespect is in a letter from Thomas, campaigning in Georgia, which says, "My mother must have strange notions of the duty of a soldier when she imagines we could leave camp to attend the House of Assembly when nothing but the River Savanna parts us from the enemy. We could not in that case with any modesty blame the conduct of the militia."

In May '79 their financial losses from Prevost's sudden

siege of Charleston had already been severe. Thomas, coming back with Lincoln's column to raise the siege, was to be married in July to Elizabeth Motte, and his brother immediately offered to divide "what remains to him" with his mother and brother. Mrs. Pinckney heard of it through Thomas and wrote him, "You say I must be sensible [aware] that you cannot agree . . . nor can I take a penny from his young and helpless family [though how worthy of him is this truly generous offer]."

Prevost's forces fell back to Georgia. The summer in Charleston was relatively quiet, though the most stouthearted were apprehensive of the future. In October the French fleet appeared off Savannah, which Prevost had fortified, and Lincoln moved quickly to join D'Estaing in any attack on that city. It was made on October 9 and beaten back with heavy American losses. D'Estaing sailed for France and Lincoln fell back to Charleston to await the attack they knew was coming from the British, under Sir Henry Clinton, who was bringing 8000 troops south in Arbuthnot's fleet.

It was believed Charleston could hold out. The works were strong and Lincoln had 2000 Continentals and 3000 militia. But Clinton landed to attack from the land side and, on April 8, Arbuthnot's ships ran past Fort Moultrie.

Lincoln could have gotten away with his whole force but Charleston was the chief city of the South, and commercially and politically of enormous importance to the cause.

Fort Moultrie fell on May 7, 1780, and Lincoln surrendered with all his forces on the twelfth. It was a great prize for the British, not least in the capture of Generals Lincoln and Moultrie, John Laurens and Charles C. Pinckney, and three Signers of the Declaration of Independence.

Just before the surrender Thomas Pinckney escaped through the road left open for evacuation, carrying with him a letter to Washington from his brother, already a British prisoner of war. His brother, Charles wrote, had "avoided the captivity and is now resolved to quit his country, his fortune and his family in conformity to those principles he has ever held virtuous."

How it was smuggled out of the lines we do not know, but with it was a characteristic letter to

Dear Tom,

Here is a note to General Washington and a letter to Mrs. Rutledge who has some gold of mine lodged there by my Mother and Sally. As I am sure you will be in want of money, divide, use and apply for it, my dear Tom, without hesitation and may it be of service to you.

Mrs. Pinckney saw her "dear and greatly beloved son whose society alleviated every pain" as he rode north to join Washington. En route he encountered elements of the New Jersey, Maryland, and Delaware Lines sent south under De Kalb. On July 25, General Gates arrived to take command. Thomas Pinckney joined the force. Behind him he left his wife, awaiting her lying-in at her mother's.

His mother wrote her:

Use no ceremony with me, beg Mrs. Motte or any of the ladies with you to write. Be assured, I am, Dear Betsy,

Your most affectionate Mother.

On August 16, in the disaster and rout at Camden, Thomas Pinckney's leg was smashed and he lay in bed for twenty-five days, a prisoner, his leg suppurating and in the medical situation of the time likely to cause his death. He had been carried off the field in a wagon to the home of Mrs. Clay, a friend of his mother. To him there she wrote the poignant letter, "My dear, my greatly beloved Child, 'tis saying little at my age to tell you how readily I would part with life could that save your limb. But how little I can do for you. . . . I have no doubt you will do all in your power to preserve a life so truly valuable to all your relations and friends." Yet in the heat and the flies, the pain and anxiety, the wounded warrior on September 10 says, "I wrote to my honoured Mother three days ago but so favorable an opportunity" has arisen that he writes cheerily again, signing it, "I am, my Dearest Mother's most Dutiful and Affectionate Son." The same day she was writing to his wife, "I congratulate you and Mr. and Mrs. Motte [her parents] on the birth of a son in which Harriott and all the family sincerely join. May he be a blessing to his parents and all his connections. We long to see him. Who is he like. . . . Inexpressible was my grief upon the first news of my dear child's misfortune [but word has come that he improves]. . . . Sally has a fine boy, another Charles Cotesworth."

Thus, with their fathers in enemy hands, the sons and heirs of the Pinckneys came in the world.

The eldest son, in Charleston, was offered an opportunity by the British to live in his own house, no doubt with the idea that it would draw him to join the Loyalists, fawning on Clinton. He replied, "Candour obliges me to inform you of my political sentiments. I entered into this cause after much reflection and through principle. My heart is altogether American and neither severity nor favour nor poverty nor affluence can ever induce me to swerve from it."

Then with a proud but very pleasing superiority to ordinary men he informed his mother that he did not wish his wife to write to him for the British censor to read, "as letters between husband and wife are too apt to be turned into ridicule by persons of no delicacy of feeling."

In November, however, Sally and his children came through the lines to visit him along with Miss Moultrie and Miss Lynch, sister of the young Signer who had been lost at sea. It was a drear November. On the twenty-third all his estates were sequestered, his young son "appeared dead" but survived, and Betsy Pinckney was near death.

"Thanks, many thanks, my dearest boy to you for writing by every opportunity," Mrs. Pinckney wrote Thomas. "You never expressed greater truth, my dear child, than when you said you know I love you.

"Misconduct in you and misfortunes happening to you may

grieve and afflict me and embitter the little of life that remains but I can never cease to love you."

There is a letter in the Pinckney papers for June 1781 from Thomas which it is hard to believe was not a telegram. It was sent, after his exchange, from Billingsworth on the Delaware as he went south with the reinforcements going to Lafayette in Virginia. Its *nine* words are: "All well after a pleasant passage inform all concerned."

Except for the Northwest Posts, the British held out longest at Charleston and not until December 14, 1782, did Greene's forces enter the liberated city amidst great festivities.

The hard business of reconstruction lay ahead. The state had been ravaged by the British. Trade was at a standstill and rents in Charleston were *down* one third from prewar.

The two Pinckneys, more fortunate than most, had both their plantations and legal practices to go back to.

The original document of one of Charles's first postwar cases—March 1783—is in the New York Public Library. Small though it is, it is one of those wonderful examples of how the patriot leaders thought, not in terms of revenge but of due process of law. Almost as Pinckney, pupil of Blackstone, wrote his opinion, Hamilton in New York was defending the Tory, Waddington. Pinckney wrote:

Hypothesis: a man notoriously attached to the British Interest accompanied a party of the enemy to the house of an American Citizen and while there did not appear to be under any constraint or to accompany the enemy through fear. [The house was looted.] Can the American citizen obtain any satisfaction from this man for the depredations committed by the Party whom he accompanied.

Answer: I am of opinion that this man's voluntarily accompanying a British party to distress a fellow citizen . . . makes him at best a trespasser. It is not necessary that all the party should do actual mischief. . . . "If several come and the one does the trespass and the others do nothing but come in aid, yet all are principal trespassers and shall render damage . . . and the party injured has his election to bring his action against them all, or against any more or one of them, but he cannot bring a second act against any others of them."

Then amidst the reconstruction and the reunions, one of the vague, dreadful fevers of the time struck his household and Sally Middleton, his beloved wife, sickened and died on May 8, 1784. Some twenty-five months later Charles Cotesworth Pinckney married Mary Stead. Death was always so close then, life so uncertain, that few men or women of the time remained long without remarrying.

After the wedding the Thomas Pinckneys went north to New York and Newport and, like most Southerners, were "absolutely melting with heat in New York." Pinckney himself was apparently not very well, weighing only a hundred thirty-two pounds. Newport, however, revived them though they "stayed to themselves." There were other Carolinians there and St. George Tucker said those "gentlewomen talk like negroes."

The last is a minor but fascinating question. Had these educated and traveled aristocrats, the writers of their beautifully styled and polished letters, acquired "a Southern accent" by then? By the Civil War, the evidence of fictional dialogue would seem to indicate they had. Seventy more years of close association with slaves may well have done it. The backwoodsmen doubtless spoke that way during or even before the Revolution, but it is hard to believe the influence of Oxford and the Middle Temple was so completely lost among the South Carolinians.

It would be hard, for example, to read the letter of February 22, 1787, from Charles Cotesworth Pinckney to his mother except sonorously.

Honoured Madame,

I have the pleasure to acquaint you that my Brother was elected with the greatest éclat to the office of Governor. There were one hundred seventy votes out of which he had one hundred sixty three. The others were votes of a whimsical nature.

Pray ask Harriott for some cayenne pepper seeds and large common pepper seeds. I have several clients in the next room who are impatient. . . .

Late in April 1791, Thomas Pinckney received a note from John Rutledge, saying that President Washington "arrived here [Clifton, near the North Carolina border] this morning" and that "General Moultrie requests that you will have your boats at Santee to assist in carrying over the President's horses."

The occasion was the President's first Southern tour, in which he found so much pleasure. A few days later he was at the coast and was "visited at two o'clock by a great number of the most respectable ladies of Charleston—the first honor of the kind I had ever experienced and it was as flattering as it was singular." The next day there were two hundred and fifty-six "elegantly-dressed and handsome ladies" at his reception and four hundred more the next day. With the large families and intermarriages of the time, they may well all have been Pinckney-Rutledge-Moultrie-Motte-Middleton-Izard-Lynch-Laurens "connections."

The men of these families largely exemplified Washington's concepts of what a man should be. Most of them were Continentals, of either the army or Congress. Well to do and well educated, they felt and responded to the obligation of public service but, as with the master of Mount Vernon, their lands and their crops were their most vital interest. "Everybody on this river will I believe begin their harvest this week. Some have already cut rice," Thomas Pinckney wrote his sister.

Altogether it was most natural that the following November he should have accepted the legation in London. The letter which his brother Charles Cotesworth wrote him on hearing it is a wonderful illustration of how those widely educated, public-spirited men regarded public office and of the reliance they put on knowledge for its own sake. The long letter says nothing of the benefits his brother will personally derive, but deals only with how he can best fit himself to carry out his duty.

Dear Tom,

I congratulate you on your appointment and though you may be assured I feel every fraternal pang at the absence which will be occasioned by it I am exceedingly glad and entirely approve of your resolution to accept this office. I am glad to find you have determined not to hastily appoint a private secretary and indeed I own I would rather that you should be your own than have one whose political principles would thwart your negotiations and whose moral principles were such as you could not totally depend upon.

With regard to books in the diplomatic series you will find in my study Vattell's on *The Law of Nations;* the *Treatise* of Wequefort on *Ambassadors* (which is the book of the greatest authority relating to the rights of public ministers) I have for sometime missed. Vattell has however given an abridgement of him in one of his last chapters. You will also find in my study the *Questiones Publici Juris* by Grotius and all Lord Chesterfield's works. The second volume of his *Letters to his Son* contain very good advice for a Minister. You have Sir William Temple's works, his letters are excellent. The papers published by Lord Hendrickson are in Ned Rutledge's study. He begs you will take them.

Memoirs you should also get. I believe my sister has Sully's *Memoirs*. His negotiation with Elizabeth is a masterpiece. Chesterfield recommends several French works in this line which are excellent. Jenkinson and not Eden is the author of the Treatise I carried to Georgia. I forget of whom I borrowed it. I have desired Mrs. Pinckney to lend you the *Droit d'Europe*, a very excellent little work.

The perusal of these works will employ you till I see you and I have endorsed the bill you enclosed. Russell has accepted it and I now enclose his receipt to you. I am happy to hear my Mother is so well and that my sister Betsey is recovering. Give my duty and love where due in Tradd Street and be assured I am

Your truly affectionate brother
Charles Cotesworth Pinckney

Thomas did not sail until the following June and meantime Charles had an eye to his plantation. "We shall find some difficulty in supplying you with corn though we will make a point to do it. Pray let us know the corn you have consumed this year. . . . Your negroes have in general behaved well but they all wish to be removed from Philander's gang to Moses and on this subject plagued Fraser a great deal, but they are now easy. . . ." He reports that Mr. Jefferson has sent them "forty olive plants" and hopes that his brother's dispatches to the Secretary of State will be "very frequent and regular." He will himself send the newspapers and gazettes regularly and has told his small daughter Elizabeth to collect them every morning for her uncle.

As soon as Thomas had sailed his brother sent him a charmingly sentimental request.

I send the enclosed lock of Mrs. Pinckney's hair which I will beg the favour of you to have put in elegant taste into a fashionable gold ring for my little finger. You may judge of the size of it from your own but I think mine is rather slenderer.

P.S. On the inside of the ring let M.P. be engraved in cypher.

It was July, the height of the hot Charleston summer, but sentiment and love seem to have been in the air. The postscript continues, "Henry Izard has declared himself the lover of Emma Middleton," and then reports that E. Rutledge is well. Rutledge and Charles C. Pinckney had each married a Middleton, sisters of the Signer, Arthur Middleton, and in April Mrs. Rutledge had died. "It is reported," Pinckney writes, "(but he has not made me a confidant yet) that he visits Mrs. Everleigh constantly once but more frequently twice a day." In the October following they were married.

There is only one more bit of romantic gossip in his letters and that the following spring, when "the only private news relates to Miss Laurens who took it into her head to fall in love with one Courtney a player and without even having spoken to him wrote him a letter offering him her hand and fortune. Dr. Ramsay discovered it and he and Mr. Rutledge for the present keep her confined but she declares she is resolved to have him, at least so says the town."

What seems the familiar infatuation of a stage-struck girl had tragic overtones. Frances Eleanor Laurens was then an orphan of fifteen, her mother having died the year before her father was killed in almost the last and wholly useless action of the Revolution. All the talents and graces were present in his person and a career of enormous value to his country lay before him. He had been on Washington's staff in all the battles and had also been selected, even above Hamilton, for the vital financial mission to France in 1780 where he had had complete success. In character, intellect, and person he was perhaps the brightest "ornament of the Revolution."

With the arrival of Thomas Pinckney at the Court of St. James's, there were two American envoys in Europe who for education and practical ability have seldom been equaled. Personally, they were the greatest possible contrasts.

In Holland was William Short, the youngest of them, then but thirty-three, a graduate of William and Mary, a founder of the Phi Beta Kappa, a "son" and disciple of Jefferson, whose secretary and chargé he had been in Paris. When Jefferson came back to be Secretary of State, Short expected the Paris post. Had the choice lain with Jefferson alone it would probably have gone to him, but the choices of Gouverneur Morris for Paris and Pinckney for London were Washington's own.

In devotion to duty, grasp of American finance, and understanding of Europe, Short was pre-eminent. It is hard to account for all the disappointments of his long life. He lived until 1849 with no rewards but personal wealth. At this time he had been in Europe since 1784. This was against him. He was a bachelor, though so was Morris. It seems likely that what weighed most against him was the absence of something burly and successful in his nature. Or perhaps it was "stature." As a second, an adviser, he was outstanding, but was never quite equal to the place of a principal. Yet if for thirty years—or indeed his whole life after 1785—he had not been inwardly torn to pieces by unhappy love, he might, with his great qualities, have risen to any position.

When Morris got Paris, Short was sent as Minister to Holland. The problems there were not political but financial. Holland was the banking center of Europe. The American bonds were heavily held and the maintenance of our credit there was essential to our economy. Short did his work well.

In Paris was Gouverneur Morris, one-legged but strikingly handsome, reckless at times in public affairs and private amours, yet wonderfully clearheaded and devoted to duty; a graduate of Columbia, a member of the Continental Congress, the *redacteur* of the Constitution, and by birth and breeding much like the Pinckneys. As Minister, facing the constantly changing "governments" of the French Revolution, he stood, as he said, on a glare of ice, trying to stop the invasions of our neutrality in the Anglo-French war, the seizure of our ships and the jailing of their crews.

Representing us in Madrid was a man very different from the other three, William Carmichael, who like Short had not been home since 1779. He had been born in Maryland, the year unknown, and at the start of the Revolution gone to Europe, serving first with Silas Deane, later with Franklin, and, after a brief term in the Continental Congress where in general he was in the Adams-Lovell-Lee coterie opposed to Washington, going late in 1779 to Madrid with John Jay. Little is known of this unfortunate yet pathetic man, and what is, does him little credit. He had married twice, leaving a daughter by his second wife, but by 1792 he was all but lost in debt and drink, a disgrace to his country.

Yet to him was left too long the negotiations with Spain as to opening the Mississippi throughout its length to the Americans of the Western Waters.

This was the oldest of American diplomatic problems and the issue that divided not only Federalists from Republicans but Northern Federalists from Southern.

It is an irony of our early history that independence was wrested from England with the help of the French and Spanish Bourbons who typified all that we opposed; that at the end of the Revolution our former ally, Spain, kept the Mississippi closed to us, while France treated us as a satellite rather than an ally, and that in turn the mere fact of our independence was the greatest menace to their holding their possessions in the New World. They had both come to our aid to break the British power and not because either believed in liberty or democracy. Fortunately the patriot leaders all understood this, though at Valley Forge in the late spring of '78 and at Yorktown there was between individuals a natural brotherhood-in-arms transcending politics. And there was also a not unadmirable feeling of special gratitude to the French King personally on the part of Washington and the Continentals. Pinckney summed it up, writing his sister from London early in '93: "You will undoubtedly condole with all feeling minds in the miserable fate of Louis the unfortunate; we particularly who have been used to consider him in some measure as our benefactor cannot help being deeply affected with this sanguinary procedure." And of course the special charm and genius of the French race played its part. There was none of this in the feeling toward Spain and His Most Catholic Majesty.

When by the Treaty of Paris in 1783 Britain yielded all her territories south of the Canadian border to us (though delaying the evacuation of the Northwest Posts), Spain claimed that her conquest of the Floridas (to present-day Vicksburg) placed, in Professor Bemis's words, "a bar of inviolable Spanish territory across the lower Mississippi." Although Britain had had navigation rights on it, and had ceded them to us, such a cession was without legal right since she had already been dispossessed of the Territory.

To this in effect John Jay, as the last Secretary of Foreign Affairs before the federal government was formed, agreed, and a roar of protest went up from the men of the Western Waters, speaking particularly through Monroe and Madison, the latter urging the Continental Congress in April '87 to send Jefferson to Madrid from Paris to negotiate. Jay persuaded Congress to refuse which, with the Constitutional Convention a month off, they readily agreed to do. Jay's position was that this was not a permanent assent on his part but rather a postponement for twenty-five years of a question which could not be solved for the moment.

Washington himself was not in disagreement and it was hoped, shortsightedly, that the trans-Allegheny trade which might have gone down the Mississippi could be brought to the Atlantic seaboard by opening and canalizing the headwaters of the Potomac.

In an international court of justice the Spanish position would have been legally unassailable. In addition, as Jay somewhat acidly pointed out to his opponents, any change in it from without rested "on the extent of the powers" of the United States, then feebler than at the outset of the Revolution.

Against this "paper closure of the river," the Westerners asserted the Great Law of Nature. In less than ten years its fiat had gone forth. The form it took was an expanding torrent of settlers, tens of thousands of restless, vigorous men and women pouring over the mountains into Kentucky and Tennessee. There were no levees on the Mississippi which could contain the floods of water or of human beings.

Utterly unable to understand the fierce, almost limitless self-reliance and "independence" of such people, the Spanish government believed they would seek her protection, and that by bribery of such men as James Wilkinson they could insure the allegiance of the masses. Ignorant also of the basic nature of the Protestant faiths these people brought with them, they offered the "privilege" of private but not public freedom of worship.

In London Thomas Pinckney's objectives were the evacuation of British troops from the Northwest Posts; the settlement of private claims from the Revolution—reimbursement by the British for slaves carried off; settlement of private American debts with British merchants; stoppage of the impressment of American seamen—but above all "the freedom of the seas," the right to trade in American bottoms in any port in the world on a most-favored-nation basis. It was already evident that the new Republic was as "mercantile" as Britain.

Mr. and Mrs. Pinckney and their children arrived and were cordially received. Many of the rulers of England had known him at the Westminster School, at Christ Church, Oxford, or at the Middle Temple before the Revolution. Their colored nursemaid was a sensation in "cap and dress, shoes, stockings and stays," and they were wealthy enough to live well at a personal cost of $2500 a year beyond Pinckney's salary and allowances. But in the settlement of disputes there was no progress, the war with France consuming all the attention of the British government, or so they claimed. Presumably they felt if America was willing to wait twenty-five years to open the Mississippi she could wait a little longer for the Posts and the claims.

Pinckney's failure was not a personal one. As Gouverneur Morris had said of his own failure, as special agent in London the year before, "I trust [my critics] will never avow to the British nation a disposition to make sacrifice of their interests to please a pleasant fellow . . . it will not do to say to a House of Commons the American Minister was such a charming fellow that we could not resist him."

In April '93, Genêt, the new French Minister, had reached Charleston and clandestinely begun his plan to finance a separatist revolt in Kentucky, to incite the Indians on our frontiers, to arm French privateersmen in American ports, and in short to do all possible to bring the "French party" in America to power. Charles C. Pinckney had him to dinner and wrote his brother that Genêt "appeared to be a very sensible and intelligent man about twenty-three years of age." He was all that, indeed, and all first impressions of him were favorable. Confronted and apparently surprised by the general horror at Louis XVI's execution, he contrived, C. C. Pinckney wrote, to make it impossible to "judge from this distance whether the measure was positively wrong, or excuseable or justifiable."

The letter concludes with the ominous news that Mrs. Pinckney, Sr., had gone to Philadelphia as her symptoms of cancer deepened. In July he sent word of "the irreparable loss we have sustained by the death of our beloved mother."

On April 16, 1794, after long consideration of various alternatives, and against strong opposition, John Jay was confirmed as envoy extraordinary to London for the purpose of securing the settlement which Pinckney had been unable to achieve.

The blow to Pinckney's pride must have been stunning. He was being superseded in the main objective of his mission as the wretched Carmichael in Madrid had recently been by the temporary transfer of William Short from Holland. Gouverneur Morris had been recalled from Paris at the request of the Franch government and, while Washington considered shifting Pinckney there, the fact that Jay could not remain as Minister in London, as well as the fact that it was felt essential for Morris's successor to be a Republican, prevented that.

All this meant that for the duration of Jay's mission Pinckney must remain as a fifth wheel. But he and the Churches, Hamilton's in-laws, went down to meet the Jays, and Pinckney, like the patriot and great gentleman that he was, ably seconded Jay in all he did. "We have received from him numberless civilities which we had no right to expect," Jay's son wrote to his mother.

During this time Pinckney labored under a greater burden,

of the sort history takes so small account of. His beloved wife, the charming, vivacious Elizabeth Motte, was sickening and before the year was over had died in London, leaving two young children.

Meantime in Madrid all Short's and Carmichael's efforts to settle the navigation of the Mississippi, the Florida boundary, or the right to deposit American goods in New Orleans were fruitless. In alliance with England against France, Spain's worries over the French seizing New Orleans were lessened. She was building new forts in Mississippi and Alabama and inciting the Indians against the American settlements, hoping thereby to induce the latter to accept her "protection." Additionally, she had in Philadelphia two nonentities, Jaudenes and Viar, without rank or credentials, empowered, so Short and Carmichael were told, to make a treaty. Their main activities were trying to spread the Whiskey Rebellion in Pennsylvania and inciting Kentucky to separation. Short and Carmichael, though snubbed and ridiculed, were given to understand that if the United States would agree to an alliance the river would be opened, the boundary equitably settled. The alliance, however, would involve the United States in guaranteeing the Spanish possessions in the New World against the revolution which our example had so greatly stimulated.

The extent of the British naval victory at Toulon in February '94 had alarmed the Spanish, and Godoy, the Spanish Prime Minister, felt that a separate peace with France was desirable. When Short learned of this he at once proposed that Spain recognize the American claims as to the Florida boundary and the Mississippi navigation and that he return to Holland through Paris to act as an intermediary for peace "on his own."

Back of the offer lay his consuming desire to see again his beloved Rosalie, the Duchesse de la Rochefoucauld. The death of her old husband in the massacres of September '92 had removed the one bar to their marriage, so he felt, if he could only find her. Communication with her through Gouverneur Morris had been difficult and sporadic and at any time the dread hand of the Revolution might take her from hiding to the guillotine.

No one can say what achievements might have been possible for this brilliant and devoted servant of his country, had he been able to marry Rosalie. But at the very moment of her widowhood—and mortal danger—he had been sent from Paris to the Hague and from there across France, without seeing her, to Madrid. Beside the terrible anxiety for her safety was the all but equal one that, though she loved him, he could not be sure she wished to marry him. In a period of license she had not been willing to be his mistress, though perhaps had yielded once to him. Her letters to him were of exquisite tenderness but even as a widow she was confined by the traditions of French marriage, and the Duc, her husband, had been also her uncle, and her mother-in-law was her own matriarchal grandmother.

In everything Short did there was the tragic effort to combine his country's interests with his own. He wished to resign and be free to pursue and protect her, but dared not risk it since the greatest protection he could give her was an American envoy. If he could bring her to the altar, Robespierre himself would not dare lay hands on the wife of a foreign minister.

To his offer of mediation with France, Godoy made no definite answer all the summer. In September he declined it, telling Short he had sent proposals direct to Philadelphia. He did not tell Short that he had heard from there of Jay's mission, nor did Short know of another blow to his pride and his peace of mind that had been delivered in Philadelphia.

In outrageous explanation of the disrespect and inattention shown Short and Carmichael, Godoy let it be known that "unless the Ministers whom the United States should nominate were to be considered by His Majesty in every circumstance as possessing that character, splendor and carriage which corresponds with residence near the royal prison . . ." their efforts would also be futile.

Edmund Randolph, our Secretary of State, said that a new envoy was sent because of this inadequacy in Short and Carmichael. Godoy insisted later that he had spoken only of Carmichael, and if so he was well within his rights. It is incredible that the American government should so long, in view of all their reports on him, have left such great interests to such a man.

Realizing at last that "character, splendor and carriage" were requisites for success at Madrid, the post of envoy extraordinary was offered first to Jefferson and then to Patrick Henry. Character they both had, but not outward splendor or carriage; yet both were great ornaments of the Revolution and could not have been treated as the other two had been.

Both declined, and on August 28, 1794, the Senate confirmed the nomination of a man possessing all the outward and inward qualities required, Thomas Pinckney.

At first sight it might be supposed that the appointment was a *douceur* to Pinckney's feelings about Jay's presence in London. The stakes were too great for that. The selection was the best that could be made, not only because of Pinckney's character and presence but because, though in second place, he had participated in all the negotiations with Britain and could negotiate in Madrid with a knowledge no one else possessed. And though a Federalist, he had from the beginning been on the side of the Westerners about the Mississippi.

Whatever the satisfaction the appointment may have brought, or the approval it showed of his character and conduct, the fact that his beloved wife had not lived to see it must have deeply oppressed Pinckney.

His brother wrote Ralph Izard, ". . . it is impossible for me to say whether the nomination of my brother to Madrid will be acceptable to him. Perhaps such a great diversity of scene and new business may be a relief to his afflicted mind."

For five months Short knew nothing of the fact that he was

to be superseded by Pinckney as the latter had been by Jay. Nor from Randolph, Pinckney, Jay, or John Trumbull, Jay's secretary, did any word reach him of Jay's progress. Under the circumstances of naval blockade, the sealed Pyrenean frontier, and the vast delays in all mail, this was not surprising —though one would think a courier might have been sent. But it was characteristic of the whole ill luck of Short's life. All those months he was begging Monroe, now Minister in Paris, to get him some word of Rosalie.

Word of Jay's progress was, however, reaching the Spanish government, who felt that an Anglo-American alliance was in the offing. Late in December Gardoqui, the Spanish Foreign Minister, suggested to Short that they discuss a general partnership between Spain, France, and the United States. Whatever Short's private heartaches and public disappointments, he was never confused about the interests of his country. He told Gardoqui that a settlement of all American rights must precede any discussion. Thereupon Gardoqui, through his own Ambassador in Paris, without word of course to Short, asked Monroe to act as a general promoter of such a partnership without any prior settlement. Monroe declined and of course informed Short.

When one considers the efforts of veteran European diplomacy at the time to achieve their anti-American ends by naïve intrigue and double-dealing, and by bribery and corruption, it is difficult to avoid becoming chauvinistic. It apparently never occurred to them that men could be unpurchasable or that representatives of a small, new country were their equals in experience of men and affairs and their superiors in judging them.

Word that a treaty had been signed in London was known in Madrid at the very end of '94. Pinckney, however, was still in London and not until January 13, 1795, did Short know he was coming out. He at once offered his resignation, as custom required, but stayed on even after Pinckney's arrival, aiding him loyally and effectively.

On February 9 poor Carmichael died but Pinckney did not leave for Madrid until mid-May following. Professor Bemis says that had he "understood the international situation as thoroughly as Short he would have lost not one moment in setting out for Madrid immediately he was notified of his appointment." He arrived in Spain on June 28 and Professor Bemis concedes that it was the psychological, the perfect, moment for success.

It seems most unlikely that Pinckney sat aimlessly in London from October 1794 to May 1795 and far more likely that, aware as he was of the Republican opposition there would be at home to the Jay Treaty, he wished to be sure the whole negotiation would not be repudiated, and he be told in Madrid, "You see, it is quite useless for us to talk to an American envoy." When he left London the treaty was within a month of ratification, though it had been "burned" in his native state.

Pinckney went through Paris in mid-June and there left "my poor little ones to [Monroe's] protection and the good offices of Mrs. Monroe." In the famous school run by Madame Campan, Genêt's sister, they became fellow pupils of the Monroe children and those of Josephine de Beauharnais. A fascinating story could be written of the daughters of the famous who were there and at the school in Bethlehem, Pennsylvania.

Ahead of Pinckney as he traveled south, the French armies were crossing the Pyrenees and on July 22 Spain signed a separate peace with France at Basle. The treaty reached Madrid August 3, was ratified at once, and Godoy was named the Prince of Peace by his sovereign. At his first meeting with him, Pinckney told him the United States would not make an alliance, would not guarantee any Spanish possession in the Americas, and demanded navigation, deposit, and the Florida boundary as a matter of right. Godoy was "much mortified" by what they would not do, erroneously supposing the Jay Treaty contained the equivalent of an Anglo-American alliance against the Spanish interests in the Western Hemisphere.

For a time it looked as though Pinckney was to be no more successful than Short and Carmichael, though the negotiations continued, while the Spanish Council continued to believe that through people like Wilkinson and the Kentucky separatists they could maintain the status quo and in the end buy the allegiance of the trans-Allegheny emigrants.

Talks and bargaining with Pinckney went on but, on October 24, Godoy told him Spain would never grant the right of deposit in New Orleans. Pinckney at once demanded his passports. It was a bold step in the credit for which Short has a share. Three days later, in an amazing Spanish volte-face, Pinckney and Godoy signed the Treaty of San Lorenzo, Spain yielding without condition everything that America wanted. Symbolic of the whole republican triumph over absolute monarchy is the preamble citing eighteen titles and two et ceteras of Godoy's as against "Thomas Pinckney, a citizen of the United States."

Almost on the day of the signing Charles C. Pinckney declined the offer to succeed Edmund Randolph as Secretary of State, as in turn did Thomas Johnson, Rufus King, and Patrick Henry. In Pinckney's case one cannot but feel he refused out of a special sense of what was fitting with his brother in Madrid and what the opposition could say whether he won or lost. The reluctance to public service, except in the greatest emergency, also entered in, since in the following January he declined the War Department left vacant by Pickering's promotion to the State Department.

The treaty reached Philadelphia on Washington's birthday. Four days were required for copying and "presentation." The Senate received it on the twenty-sixth and as Washington wrote Pinckney in his own hand March 5, "On the 3rd instant the ratification of it was advised and consented to by an unanimous vote of [the Senate]. Hence you may form an opinion of the general approbation of your negotiations." For the first time in our history the Father of Waters rolled indeed unvexed to the sea!

Pinckney started for London, Paris, and home in triumph, leaving young Charles Rutledge in charge of the legation until David Humphreys was transferred from Algiers. John Rutledge, the father of Charles, his mind, it was said, affected by his wife's death, had been nominated to be Chief Justice by Washington, the Senate, however, rejecting him. Spain sent the Marquis de Casa Yrujo out as minister to replace the wretched Jaudenes and Viar, who had, Pickering said, been making $50,000 a year personally out of the sale of export licenses for flour for New Orleans and the Spanish West Indies. Yrujo would shortly beg his royal master's permission to marry the daughter of Thomas McKean, the Signer, "the old wretch," who would lead the anti-Federalists in the coming presidential campaign. Short left Madrid for France and in July wrote Monroe from Rosalie's house at Roche-Guyon that he could not come up to Paris for the July 4 celebration at the legation. Lovely as it was to be in her company, he was still unable to win her assent to marriage. The reason will never be known. Her letters have every tenderness except desire. But if in return for all his self-sacrificing and invaluable services to his country he could succeed Monroe, who had been recalled, as Minister to France he would still be in position to press his suit. He had wanted the Paris post desperately since Jefferson had left it seven years before, and it had seemed repeatedly in his grasp. Had he had the triumph of the San Lorenzo Treaty, the lady might have been swept away. But Thomas Pinckney had come out to receive the roses, leaving Short, as he himself said, with the thorns, and while he was still at Roche-Guyon he heard that Charles Cotesworth Pinckney was coming out as Monroe's successor.

Back home, John Adams and Thomas Pinckney were nominated by the Federalists against Jefferson and Burr to succeed Washington. Under the electoral system of the time, any of the four men could become President, and so great was the anti-Adams feeling that there were sound reasons for believing Pinckney would win. Hamilton was committed to him.

As Robert Goodloe Harper wrote Izard, "Thomas Pinckney is our sheet anchor. It is not Pinckney or Adams with us but Pinckney or Jefferson. The great point is to prevail on Pinckney to stand. Every effort will be used by his pretended friends and by Ned Rutledge among the rest to persuade him not to let his name be run (Ned Rutledge will say he will never consent to serve as vice-president). He may be assured . . . the intention of bringing him forward was to make him president."

Washington of course had never made a political speech nor sought a vote in his life. While there is something very fine about not "seeking office," it was not a practice which other men could successfully follow in the turbulent years following his retirement. But Thomas Pinckney, like his brother in the same situation four years later, refused to make any efforts toward his own election. In large measure the refusal was patrician in the best sense of the word. A Continental officer, wounded at Camden, governor of South Carolina, Minister to Great Britain, envoy extraordinary to Spain, a Federalist, but the opener of the Mississippi, his private and family life an open book, what more did people need to know?

It is strange to consider that the most powerful work against him was done by his cousin Charles Pinckney, a Signer of the Constitution but known later in South Carolina as "Blackguard Charlie," and a man whose private life was a disgrace. His work on behalf of Jefferson and Burr resulted in his own election to governor and lost the state's electoral votes to his cousin. The results, in doubt to the end, were Adams 71, Jefferson 68, Pinckney 59, and Burr 30.

John Armstrong wrote Gates that he was astounded by Jefferson's edging out Pinckney. In all the storm against Gates, after the Camden debacle, Pinckney, who was wounded there, had defended him.

By coincidence, as the election was settled, the French Directory in the person of De La Croix, the Foreign Minister, refused to recognize Charles C. Pinckney as Minister. In February he asked for his passports and went to Holland. When he returned it would be to face Talleyrand, to whom, when a refugee in London four years before, Thomas Pinckney had given letters of introduction to his American friends, his brother among them.

To Charles C. Pinckney the spotlight now shifts except for one event in Thomas's life. On October 19, 1797, a date of later interest, he married his deceased wife's sister, Frances Motte, the widow of John Middleton.

By the end of the previous May, our former French allies had seized and brought into French ports 316 American vessels. In spite of this there was still a strong "French party" in the United States in opposition to those Federalists, particularly of the Cabinet, who saw no means of redress except by going to war. The Napoleonic victories on land and the likelihood of British bankruptcy led the "French party" to feel that the Anglo-French peace was near and that the United States had best await that event, even if it meant an embargo on all our foreign commerce.

In the face of these passions, President Adams courageously decided to have one more try at accommodation with France and nominated three men—Charles Cotesworth Pinckney, John Marshall, and Elbridge Gerry—as envoys extraordinary. The Senate at once confirmed them.

On October 8 they presented their credentials to Talleyrand, now Minister for Foreign Affairs in the Directory. He received them politely but unofficially, and ten days later Hottinguer, the *X* of the XYZ trio, asked to see Pinckney alone and opened those incredible discussions. The Directory, he said, was angry about a speech of President Adams's and it was essential to find means of pacifying them. The following steps had suggested themselves: a private payment of 50,000 francs to Talleyrand for Directory and himself; an American loan to France and assumption by America of amounts owed by France to American suppliers and claimants for damages.

Why Talleyrand selected Pinckney to hear it first is an interesting question. He had met Gerry during his own American exile and perhaps was shrewd enough to see how little there was to this Signer of the Declaration. Thomas Pinckney, as Minister in London, had befriended him with letters to friends as Talleyrand went to that exile. Perhaps he mistakenly supposed there was something easygoing in his brother.

That the man who thought of this incredible scheme, and evidently believed it would work, should, eighteen years later, have dominated the Congress of Vienna by his wisdom and foresight indicates it is never too late to learn. It is safe, however, to say there is no record of any representatives of the young American Republic so completely misjudging the practical possibilities of a situation or the opposites with whom they were dealing as did this "shrewd" master of Europe's "formidable politique."

Pinckney, outwardly unmoved, told *X* he would have to talk to his colleagues. Alone with them, Marshall and he were furious but Gerry urged them not to break off the negotiation. They decided wisely to ask for the proposal in writing.

On his brother's wedding day Pinckney asked for and received the written proposal, somewhat evasively stated, and was also told that Hottinguer, *X*, came not from Talleyrand but from his agent Bellamy, *Y*. *X* and *Y* called the next day and saw all three Americans. After some palaver *Y* said there was another condition—the disavowal in writing of everything President Adams had said to Congress which the Directory objected to. That done and reparations for the insult paid, plus the bribe, there was no reason why a treaty might not be made.

On October 20, *X* and *Y* came to breakfast at Gerry's invitation and again raised the stakes with a proposal that America also buy from France 32,000,000 Dutch florins at twice their market value. Told that the American answer was in the negative, *X* begged them as practical men to change their minds before the now all-victorious Bonaparte turned his attention to North America. It was during this discussion that Pinckney shouted the answer, "No, not a sixpence," later transmuted by someone else at a banquet into "Millions for defense; not one cent for tribute."

"The third murderer," Hauteval, Z, now appeared and urged them to go to see Talleyrand privately about it. Marshall and Pinckney refused but on the twenty-third Gerry went, though Talleyrand would not see him for five days, while the demands and threats continued.

On November 11 all three Americans signed a note demanding official reception. Talleyrand made no answer but by blatant social attentions tried to draw Gerry away from the other two, and in December "a beautiful female agent" was sent to beguile Pinckney, perhaps choosing him as the handsomest member of the delegation. Had Gouverneur Morris been the object of her attentions he doubtless would have accepted the lady's favors and transformed her into an American agent. Pinckney simply said no, and in January, securing Gerry's signature only with difficulty, a joint note was sent Talleyrand that he must either negotiate or they would leave.

He did not reply until March, when he said the Directory would not talk to Pinckney or Marshall but would with Gerry. Even Gerry then joined in refusing, but said, "To prevent war I will stay." Pinckney and Marshall left him without a farewell on April 24. In July Gerry followed them.

This, one may say, was indeed the failure of a mission. It is, after all, not very much to stand by the interests of your country without succumbing to blackmail. Jay and Thomas Pinckney at least brought back treaties which the Senate ratified. These snubbed men came home with nothing to show. But if they did nothing in particular, Pinckney and Marshall did it very well. During the whole period they were without guidance or communication with America except as Rufus King, our Minister in London, advised them. Their own dispatches reached Pickering, the Secretary of State, in one batch, March 4, 1798.

It required enormous balance of mind—that greatest quality of the best of the patriot leaders—to stand what they did, not yielding, yet never saying or doing the ultimate thing which would have provoked war; seeing through absurdities and studied insults, yet never supposing their own dignity and peace of mind mattered except as their country's interests were affected.

Had Pinckney or Marshall been different men—Aaron Burr or Roger Sherman at the extremes—who knows what the wavering Gerry might not have persuaded them to? He was senior of the three, then fifty-three, Pinckney fifty-one, and Marshall forty-two, and closest politically to President Adams, and Jefferson as Vice-President had written him that he was the one of the three on whom peace depended. He was in a position to regard or make himself the *chef de mission*, if he had had the force to do so. While it is no explanation to point out that the other two had been Continentals and in the range of the guns at Trenton, Germantown, or Charleston—and Marshall at Valley Forge, Pinckney then a prisoner—yet few would deny that the most valuable servants of the young Republic were the men who had been in battle to create it.

There were Americans in Paris at the time, as there always have been, who pointed out that the gratuities Talleyrand wanted would have been much cheaper than a war.

Senator Watson of New York wrote Joel Barlow, "This at best is but a renegade arithmetic, something worse than is used when a man sets a price upon his integrity or a virgin upon her chastity. . . . It has often been said that gudgeons would bite at naked hooks, but perhaps it was never before expected that they should furnish the hooks."

When Pinckney came back to America and war seemed inevitable, Washington, called out of retirement to command the new army, chose him along with Hamilton and Knox as one of his three chief subordinates. And between the last two there broke out that disgraceful row as to who should be first.

It was of it that Charles C. Pinckney made his most felicitous comment:

"Let us first dispose of our enemies. We shall then have time to settle the question of precedence."

As the century ended Freneau and Tom Paine brought forward charges that Thomas Pinckney, while Minister in London, had engaged in "improper intrigues," that "improper influence" had been used to secure the post, and that, having been educated in England, he was in effect seduced by them as Minister.

One of Washington's last letters, November 17, 1799, was to McHenry about it. ". . . Could he who had fought against that country and bled in defense of his own in the conflict, a man of acknowledged abilities and irreproachable character be suspected of undue influence . . . the whole is a mystery to me. . . ." The charge, it turned out, was based on a letter of John Adams to Tench Coxe alleged to read, ". . . suspecting as I do much British influence in the appointment . . . I should keep a vigilant eye on [Thomas Pinckney]."

The letter is very characteristic of John Adams, the petty gossip of Continental Congress days, but when now Pinckney wrote him about it he replied in words which may well be studied today. He admitted that such a letter might exist, or that he might have said something of the sort, though he disclaimed knowledge of or agreement with it, and then he wrote, "I can conclude with observing here how fallen on evil times, on evil times indeed are we fallen, if every conversation is turned to be betrayed and misrepresented in newspapers and if every frivolous and confidential letter is to be dragged by the hand of treachery from its oblivion of eight years and published by malice and revenge for the purpose of making mischief."

Sources: The Pinckney Family Papers are in the Library of Congress and permission to quote from them has most graciously been given me by their owners, Miss Josephine Pinckney of Charleston, S.C., and Mrs. Charles Cotesworth Pinckney of Richmond, Va. C. C. Pinckney's legal opinion quoted is in Misc. Mss., N.Y.P.L. Harper to Izard on Thomas Pinckney, *American Historical Review*, 1909. See, of course, *Pinckney's Treaty* by S. F. Bemis.

Index